An Ideal Crime

To pay his way through Law school, Jim Thorpe takes a job as a night watchman in security vaults. Life might have seemed all solid slog had it not been for his employer's daughter, who frequently pointed out that all work and no play made for a very dull life indeed.

Then there is a robbery at the vaults, and the guard who has changed shifts with Thorpe is killed. Soon Thorpe himself is under suspicion, and he must fight a long and bitter battle, which takes him to France and Spain, in order to clear his name and salvage his idealism...

A Question of Principle

Eltham is a rich, successful barrister, about to take Silk, Rickmore a poorly paid PRO with a local firm; they have nothing in common other than the fact that their wives are sisters.

When Eltham unavoidably runs a man down in his car, he does not stop, but drives on, hoping to escape detection and save his career. But when Rickmore learns enough to identify Eltham as the hit-and-run driver, he is faced with the agonizing question of where his loyalties lie – with truth and justice, regardless of the nature of the victim, or towards the brother-in-law he does not like?

By the same author

JEFFREY ASHFORD

An Ideal Crime

A Question of Principle

Diamond Books
An Imprint of HarperCollins*Publishers*
77–85 Fulham Palace Road
Hammersmith, London W6 8JB

This Diamond Crime Two-In-One edition
published 1994

ISBN 0261 66259 7

Cover photography by Monique Le Luhandre

Printed in Great Britain

An Ideal Crime

CHAPTER 1

Mrs Harbuckle put the two boiled eggs, one in an egg-cup, one in the saucer, on the table. 'There was a talk on the wireless the other day and the doctor said more than three eggs a week are dangerous.'

'According to the pessimists in the medical profession, everything's potentially dangerous, even mothers' milk,' Thorpe replied.

She was not to be sidetracked so easily. 'You eat a lot more than three each week.'

'I'll tell you when I start getting the shakes.'

'You can laugh all right now; it's when you get to my age —if you ever do—that you begin to think.' She checked that everything was on the table; wholemeal loaf, butter, homemade blackberry and apple jam (blackberries picked well away from any road for fear of lead poisoning), tomatoes and well-washed lettuce, and low calorie salad cream. 'As I always said to Ron, you've got to do your thinking today for tomorrow.'

Her husband, Thorpe thought, had not taken her advice to heart if local gossip was accurate; when he'd died suddenly, he'd left little but debts.

She folded her arms across her ample bosom. 'And another thing. It's not right them making you always do nights.'

'The job is for a night guard.'

'Doesn't make it any righter.' Her views were always sharply determined and immune to logic. 'It's not natural and what's not natural is wrong.'

He topped the first egg and helped himself to a slice of bread which he buttered, too generously for her approval.

'Nights are meant for sleeping, that's what.' In an absent-minded manner, she pulled out one of the chairs from under the oval dining-table and sat. 'If you don't sleep when you should, things go wrong.'

'But working nights when there's really nothing for me to do means I'm getting paid while I study.'

'Studying should be done during the day, when the brain's in the right rhythm.' She was a great believer in rhythms. She leaned forward slightly and said pugnaciously: 'Why don't you get a grant like everyone else and then you could study during the day?'

He'd told her several times before, but he still answered patiently. 'It's not all that simple when you're my age.'

'Other people get 'em easy enough. You know what you need to do? Go and see 'em and tell 'em you've got to have one. And don't take no for an answer. That's the only way these days with those kinds of people. Tell 'em, not ask 'em.'

He made no comment. If he'd explained, she wouldn't have understood. When he'd applied for a mature student's grant, he'd been interviewed by a woman only slighter older than himself, attractive, very aware of the fact, and ever ready to fend off advances long before any was made. Her tone of superiority had become one of open antagonism when he'd mentioned the name of the minor public school to which he'd gone. She'd informed him that he couldn't expect to go through the rest of his life privileged. He hadn't bothered to argue the merits or demerits of private education, but had explained that after leaving school he'd decided to take a break before working for a degree and had joined a charitable organization which sent volunteers out to some of the poorer parts of the world to help with community projects—he'd been sent to East Africa to help improve water supplies in far-flung villages . . . She'd lectured him on the presumption of people who worked among the disadvantaged solely in order to bolster their own egos. He'd cut the interview short and had left. He had not bothered to ask for a second interview with someone else.

Why not? He wasn't certain. Pride, stupidity . . .

'The telly went all funny again last night.'

Mrs Harbuckle's words jerked his mind back to the present. He finished the first egg.

'The picture kept jumping about, just like it did when I called 'em in to repair it last time. They swore it was all right. But it's not. They're all the same these days. Won't do their jobs properly.'

Her character was frequently contradictory, he thought. Always complaining, yet she had a good sense of humour and could laugh at herself; bitter about some things, yet generous about others; a sharp businesswoman who demanded her money be paid exactly when due each week and counted it very carefully before accepting it, yet she often gave him delicacies with his meals for which she didn't charge.

'As I always used to say to Ron, things don't get better by talking.' She slid back the sleeve of her frock to look at the digital wristwatch of which she was very proud, having won it in a competition concerning the pleasures of eating baked beans. 'Time keeps moving, so I'd better be off. I told Marge I'd drop in and see her this evening, if my feet weren't too bad.'

'How is she now?'

'She says she's better, but I don't know. Her Tony's worried and he's every right to be. When you're her colour . . .' She shook her head in an expression of dire foreboding. She buried her friends with profligate frequency. 'You'll remember to lock up, won't you?'

'Yes, of course.'

'There was a break-in two roads away the other day. The wife came home to find all her clothes chucked anywhere and because she and the husband aren't the people to leave much lying about, the thieves poured paraffin over the food and used a spray-can of paint to write filth on the living-room walls . . . Hanging's too good for the likes of them . . . I've put the stuff ready for you in the kitchen.'

After she'd gone, he finished his supper and then carried everything through to the kitchen where he washed up. He then made himself sandwiches and coffee, which he poured into the vacuum flask. He went up to his bedroom. Which subject did he study tonight? Roman law, criminal law, contract, tort, real property . . . He went over to the small, battered desk—it had been Mrs Harbuckle's husband's and she had insisted on his using it as soon as she learned he was a student—and picked up the folder on torts, crossed to the small bookcase and chose the text book and questions-and-answers paperback on the same subject; he put everything on the foot of the bed.

Wondering what kind of a night it would turn out to be, he crossed to the window and looked out. It was not yet dark and he could see the chubby clouds drifting in front of a gentle easterly wind. Perhaps the forecast was going to prove right for once and the weather was settled at fine. One of the clouds moved on to reveal an early star. It reminded him of the stars on those tangy, imagination-provoking, African nights when they'd often seemed so close one could all but reach up and touch them. From the village would come the sounds of an old man hawking, a couple suddenly having a blazing row, a woman shouting to her children, from beyond the village the sounds of insects and animals, hunted and hunters. In the middle of such ancient vastness, man could only feel insignificant. He knew a sharp nostalgia, knowing even then that he was remembering the good and forgetting the bad . . . One night, in the bar of a ramshackle, tin-roofed building which had called itself Hotel Ngavasho, a drunken Greek had said to him that every man arrived in Africa as an idealist, every man left it as a realist. His upbringing had made certain he had been an idealist. Was he now a realist?

He changed into a thick shirt and polo-neck sweater since the vaults were cold whatever the temperature outside and Fifield made certain that the available heating was inadequate as heating cost money, and the pair of soft leather boots which a pock-marked Arab had made for him in Nairobi. (The Arab had quoted a price which he'd been ready to pay. But he'd been with an old African hand who'd called the Arab a swindling rogue and had claimed they were worth only a fraction of their quoted price. In the end, after considerable haggling, a reasonable price had been fixed and the Arab had called for three cups of over-sweet coffee with which to cement the transaction. Once outside, his companion had told him he'd been a fool to be prepared to pay what had first been asked. His reply that the original sum had been less than he'd have paid for them back home had been met with quizzical amusement.)

He went downstairs and set the video, which he rented, to begin recording at six the next morning when there would be one hour of law lectures delivered on behalf of the Open University, then left the house after locking up. He walked down Ponds End Road, past a dozen houses which differed from the one he'd just left only in minor details, turned right, and right again. This brought him to Ealing Broadway station where a Central Line train was standing at the platform, ready to start its run. He sat, briefcase on his lap, and as the doors slid shut and the train started, he stared at the advertisement immediately above a peroxide blonde. The advertisement for Sunlast Holidays said that travel broadened the mind. A graffiti writer had added the comment that Sunlast holidays minded the broads who travelled. He wondered when he'd have the chance to travel again. Certainly not until he'd obtained a degree and passed the bar exams. By then, he'd be thirty-three or -four. Years ago, an elderly friend had said that it was ridiculous to think of doing voluntary work in Africa immediately after finishing school since this would delay his obtaining professional qualifications. His parents had quietly replied that to serve others was the highest qualification any man could wish to strive towards. A comment which had made their friend swear with all the fluency of a man who'd been at sea for several years . . .

At Oxford Circus, the blonde left after looking at him with a quick dislike which gave him the impression that she had been expecting him to sound her out. He must look more affluent than he was, he thought with brief amusement. The doors shut, the train started, and they pounded their way through the tunnel to Tottenham Court Road.

"Evening, mate,' said the ticket-collector, not bothering to look down at his monthly season ticket. 'So how d'you fancy Real Joy in the three o'clock at Folkestone tomorrow?'

'I'm afraid I don't know the horse,' he answered.

'You don't? You don't know Real Joy?'

'Sorry. But if I dream about it I'll let you know.' He passed through the barrier. Maybe that would convince the ticket-collector that he wasn't after all a punter's patron saint—a status he'd accidentally acquired when he'd agreed that Merry Widow was bound to walk the two-fifteen at somewhere or other and Merry Widow had come home first at twelve to one and the ticket collector had had a fiver on it because of his commendation . . .

It was a ten-minute walk through streets that had begun to quieten and just before reaching the beginning of Devreux Road he came to a stop in front of a large, tall building under construction. He wasn't certain, but it seemed as if another floor had been added since he'd last taken a close interest in the place. Fifield claimed that the building was going up so quickly the workmanship must be completely slipshod and it would collapse within the first couple of years, but that was wishful thinking. Ever since he'd heard that there were to be new vaults opened there, he'd been hoping for some dire catastrophe up to, and including, a highly localized earthquake.

Thorpe continued on into Devreux Road. It was a road of nondescript buildings which housed offices and a few businesses, mainly dealing with clothing in the wholesale markets; it was a road of monotony and stifled ambition.

Half way along on the left-hand side a square sign flush with the wall directed customers of Fifield Vaults down a flight of eight steps into a basement area. Originally, Fifield had asked for permission to hang the sign at right-angles to the wall so that it was far more obvious, but the local council had refused his application on some specious ground. He now claimed that his bad luck had started from that moment, as if the new vaults would never have been built had that sign been at right-angles.

Thorpe went down the steps to the door on which were painted the words, 'Please Ring'; an arrow indicated the bell-push. He rang. The television camera focused on him and he thought of giving the old two-finger salute, but remembered that for some time now Fifield had been lacking a sense of humour. After a moment, the door slid sideways and he entered. The door slid shut behind him.

The reception area was nine feet square. Overhead was a pod in which were three two-hundred-watt bulbs which gave a light bright enough to distress some people; but the brighter the light, the greater the detail recorded by the video camera to the right of the lights and set in a slight recess in the ceiling. The inner walls were of reinforced concrete with trembler alarms set in them and there were three steel doors, one in each of the walls. In an effort to make the scene slightly less stark and cell-like, Fifield had hung some of his paintings on the wall; those clients who were knowledgeable in art, Thorpe sometimes thought, would probably have preferred bare walls.

A voice, pitch raised and thinned, said through a speaker: 'Is everything all right?'

'Everything's smooth,' Thorpe answered, using words that showed he was not under any sort of a threat.

The door on his left slid open, to the accompaniment of several low grunts of sound. He stepped into the office. It was a small room, made smaller by the amount of equipment which had been shoehorned into it; two desks, one larger than the other, three metal filing cabinets, a free-standing safe, a battered wooden cupboard, a working surface on which was a kettle and toaster, neither of which worked very often, a sink, and a very small refrigerator. To the right of the sink was a door which gave access to a lavatory. On the wall opposite the larger desk were three TV screens; these showed the street, the reception area, and the actual vault which housed the strong-boxes. The only touch of levity was more paintings.

Fifield, seated behind the larger desk, was brooding over a mass of papers and a desk-top calculator. He nodded a good-evening as he reached out to the control panel and pushed the button to shut the steel door.

'You look busy,' said Thorpe.

'Bloody figures . . . I pay an accountant a fortune and then have to do half his work for him.'

'Halve his fees.'

'And listen to him screaming?'

'Then console yourself with the thought that the only time you're really content is when you have no worldly goods.'

'When you're skint, you're in the shit.'

'Less philosophical, but probably more accurate . . . Can I do anything to help? Maths was never my strong subject, but I can just about work a calculator.'

'I'll have another go at 'em tomorrow.'

Thorpe had not expected his offer to be accepted. Fifield was obsessively secretive about the finances of the business; Trudy Johansen had once been quite hurt by the fact that he wouldn't trust her with certain details, on the grounds of general security.

Fifield gathered the papers together. 'Brought some work with you, then?' he said as he looked across briefly. 'What's it tonight?'

'It ought to be real property again to see if I can begin to grasp the subject, but I decided to relax, so it's torts.'

'As I remember them, they're wrongs which don't add up to crimes. I'll tell you something you won't find in any of your text books. When you're poor, there aren't many torts, but there are one hell of a lot of crimes; when you're rich, there aren't many crimes, but there are one hell of a lot of torts.'

Thorpe chuckled.

'You think I'm joking? Come back five years after you've started practising and see if you can still claim there isn't one law for the rich and one for the poor.' Fifield put the papers into a folder and closed it.

'Being a policeman's given you a biased judgement. One great thing about our law is that it's the same for everyone. Be a man ever so high, the law stands higher.'

'And be you ever so low, the law sinks lower.'

'Come off it, Paul . . .'

'You're like some starry-eyed youngster discovering love. Don't you have any idea what life's really like out there? D'you really think there's equality in anything?'

'There is in British law.'

'God help your clients!' He pulled open the top right-hand drawer of the desk and put the folder into this, shut the drawer and locked it. 'I spent nearly thirty years seeing guilty men escaping justice because of their social or financial positions, guilty men going free because they could afford a smart-arsed lawyer who turned up some technical point of law and the judge in his infinite wisdom decided that that was more important than the crime.'

'You're always going to have trouble with technicalities in any system of law. You must have definitions, but the moment you've got them you've trouble in interpreting them . . .'

'I'll tell you one thing. You're already talking like a lawyer.'

Thorpe framed a further comment, but did not deliver it.

There was some subjects on which Fifield refused to reason logically.

Fifield pushed back his chair, stood, yawned. When he spoke, his voice had lost all its previous belligerence. 'What's the weather like outside?'

'Fine and quite warm. The forecast on the six o'clock news was for the good weather to continue.'

'Maybe. I could take the English weather if only it would make up its mind and then bloody stick to it for more than a couple of hours.'

'Has your asthma been bad?'

'No worse than usual, for what that's worth . . . All right, then, I'm on my way home so see me out as soon as I've got my mac.'

As Fifield moved away from his desk, Thorpe crossed to it and sat. He brought the control panel—on the end of a long lead—nearer to himself. Automatically, he checked the TV screens; vault and reception were empty, in the road there were no suspiciously parked vehicles and the few pedestrians were clearly concerned only with hurrying home.

Fifield was ready. Thorpe pressed one of the red buttons and the steel door slid open. Fifield went through. Thorpe pressed a green button and the door slid shut.

'Jim,' came the call through the speaker beneath the screens.

He leaned towards the microphone. 'Yes?'

'I clean forgot. Susan's coming down on Saturday; will you come and have grub with us in the evening?'

'I'd love to. Thanks.'

'Six-thirty, then. That'll give us time to sink a couple of jars before we eat.'

He opened the outside door. On the screen, he watched Fifield climb the steps. The first two he took normally, then he began to slow and when he reached the pavement he held on to the railings as he regained his breath.

CHAPTER 2

Thorpe turned away from the screen, reached across for the log-book, and signed himself in. At the beginning, he'd been amused by Fifield's insistence on a fixed and never varying routine, but before long he'd understood the wisdom of it. The job was, especially at night, monotonous and boring and one's concentration and sense of anticipation were continually in danger of being dulled. To have to do certain things at certain times forced one to pay attention to what was going on and if the doing of them was irritating, so much the better.

He picked up the telephone receiver, dialled the local station, and spoke to the duty PC. 'Fifield Vaults. Is it OK to test the alarms?'

'That's OK, mate; there's no panic on just at the moment.'

There were three alarm points in the office. One button was under the lip of the desk, by his right knee. He pressed it twice. He went over to the door. To the right, was a second button. He pressed that twice. The last button was in the far corner, low down and concealed behind a fake electric plug. Fifield's reasoning for placing it there had been that if villains ever managed to force their way into the office and overcome the guard on duty, they would dump him wherever they thought he could cause them the least trouble; in other words, in that corner. Thorpe gave the signal for the third time.

He returned to the desk and picked up the telephone receiver. 'How were the three?'

'Loud and clear and they woke the skipper up . . .' There was a chuckle. 'The skipper swears he wasn't asleep, he was just resting his eyelids and doing heavy breathing exercises.'

He said goodbye and replaced the receiver. He logged the

fact that the three direct emergency alarms had been tested and been found to be correct. He looked up at the TV screens. On the pavement, a couple were approaching the camera from the left, arms wrapped around each other, bodies pressed tightly together. They made him think of Susan. He went over to the smaller desk, opened his briefcase and brought out the folder and books, carried them back, sat, and began to read.

Tort was the branch of law which dealt with the relationship between private citizens, a relationship which arose without any of the parties having to undertake any act. Every citizen was entitled to have his person, his reputation, and his property, held inviolable at the hands of any other private citizen. A tort was the violation of this right in circumstances where the injured party was entitled to appeal to the civil law for damages. The word tort was ultimately derived from the latin word tortus, which meant twisted or distorted . . .

He looked up. It was no good. Instead of assimilating the differences between torts and crimes and noting with the pleasure of a dedicated aficionado the Jesuitical finesse with which one was distinguished from the other in that grey area where a casual person would have found no difference at all, his mind was filled with images of Susan. Naturally curly black hair, brown eyes which could be sharp but could soften like a doe's, high cheekbones which spoiled the symmetry of her face but added character, a retroussé nose, a mouth which could laugh or sulk with equal intensity, and a figure which suited modern tastes right down to the ground . . .

He'd learned about Fifield's family soon after starting work at the vaults. Trudy had said: 'Very sadly, Mr Fifield and his wife didn't get on well together and so they separated. His daughter went with her mother.' Vinay had been far less circumspect. 'I've never met the ex-missus, but I gather she was a real eyeful and as lively as they come, so God knows why she came to marry someone as stick-in-the-mud as him. Then, a few years back, she met a man with a lot more money and life than Paul and that was that. Took off so quickly she burned her shoes as well as her boats. Their daughter went as well. I've met her. Not exactly beautiful, but a classy looker. But snooty, like money always is.'

He'd had a chance to judge Susan after he'd been at the vaults just over a month. Turning up to relieve Fifield, he'd found her there. Beauty lay in the eye of the beholder; in his eyes she was truly beautiful. She'd been in a temper about something and had barely acknowledged the introduction. But then Fifield had said something and she'd corrected him, incorrectly. He—Thorpe—had corrected her and she'd voiced her resentment of this in no uncertain terms, but instead of taking offence, he'd laughed, then given her chapter and verse for his correction. Abruptly, in a way that he later discovered was characteristic, she'd snapped out of her bad mood and had become lively and amusing . . .

A fortnight later, Fifield had, with obvious pleasure, said that she was coming to stay with him for the weekend again; he'd expressed his surprise because there normally were several months between her visits. His pleasure and surprise had revealed a lonely man, deserted by his wife, who longed to see more of his daughter than he did. He'd gone on to invite Thorpe to supper on the Saturday. Susan had been good company from the beginning, with no sign of petulant bad temper. Just before he'd left, she'd remarked that she'd probably be down again soon. Three weeks later, she'd rung him up and suggested a night out, Dutch. By the end of that evening, he'd begun to walk on air.

He was certain his parents would have liked her, even though they'd undoubtedly have found her belligerent feminism, her acceptance of modern moral values, and her abrupt changes of moods, difficult to understand. In their eyes, a lady had always to be virtuous and self-effacing.

They'd been quiet, gentle people, undemonstrative in private as well as in public. They had loved their neighbours and had never judged or lost their faith in them; if wronged, they'd turned the other cheek . . . Their code of living had, despite a temporary teenage rebellion on his part, largely become his . . .

He'd tried to explain all this to Susan when, on a night that Fifield had been out at some meeting, he'd drawn back from pursuing their love-making to its logical conclusion. He'd represented his act as a compliment to her. She'd accepted it as a quixotic stupidity and had called him— among other things—a useless prig. She hadn't come down from Oxford since then. But she was coming this weekend . . .

He turned back to his work. Tort was a branch of law which dealt with the relationship between private citizens . . .

Fifield had bought his house in Acton many years previously, before prices had really begun to climb. Now, he chuckled about the bargain he had obtained, but Thorpe, reading between the lines, was certain that at the time it had been an extravagance into which he'd been driven by Mary, his wife. It was impossible to judge now what had caused her indifference to financial considerations, but it was obvious that she had always been demanding a bigger car, better clothes, more parties, leaving Fifield only one small jump ahead of the bank, the building society, and the credit firms.

The house was semi-detached, but it had been built in the early Thirties to standards which were now only a memory. There were three main bedrooms and a fourth, or maid's room; in reality, this last was a box-room, but when the house had been built there had been a lot of hungry salesmen around who had known something about up-market images.

There was a small front garden and a much larger back one and both were meticulously maintained by Fifield who was a keen if unimaginative gardener. Thorpe opened the wooden front gate and walked up the crazy-paving path past a bed of roses, geometrically planted, which were just beginning to flower. He stepped under the small porch and rang the front doorbell; two-tone chimes sounded inside.

Fifield opened the door. Even at home, he still dressed with a certain degree of formality. A man of many aphorisms, one of his favourites was the observation that people put more trust in a man with short back and sides. 'Dead on time, then, since it's not work.'

He might have intended to speak with amused irony, but it didn't sound that way. However, Thorpe replied lightly; 'I've always managed to get my priorities right.'

'Like the rest of the modern generation.'

He wondered if father and daughter had been rowing?

'All right, then, let's have your coat . . . I told you, Sue's down for the weekend?'

'Yes, you did.'

'Never gave me any proper warning to get things ready. Had to get a load of extra food in.'

Did he ever acknowledge to himself just how much her visits meant to him; and were all his complaints a way of hiding the answer from himself as well as from others?

Fifield turned. 'Jim's here,' he shouted.

Susan came down the short passage from the kitchen into the hall, accompanied by Tilly, a Yorkshire terrier. Tilly, finally realizing there was a visitor, began to bark as she came forward and sniffed Thorpe's trousers. Her tail suddenly wagged more quickly and she pawed him. He bent down and picked her up and with a gesture of affection she reached out with her tongue and tried to lick his cheek.

'Don't let her be a nuisance,' said Susan.

'It's nice to be made a fuss of.'

'Poor man; doesn't it happen very often?' Susan spoke with ironic concern. 'I wonder why?'

'Maybe I look too well fed.'

'Or could it be, too piously self-satisfied?'

'Probably.' She was in one of her bitchy moods. He hoped the evening would prove to be one of those when her mood changed with mercurial rapidity.

'Let's stop standing around here, blathering,' said Fifield irritably. 'Come on in and start drinking.'

'You'll have to start without me,' she said. 'But I don't suppose you'll raise any objections to that.'

'What's that supposed to mean?'

'It doesn't mean anything other than what it says. Why should it?'

'Sometimes, you're just like your mother.'

'Now isn't that a strange coincidence?'

'No. Just my bloody bad luck.' Fifield marched past Thorpe to enter the sitting-room.

'Poor Father,' said Susan, more loudly than was necessary. 'He's in a bit of a state. I suppose it's because I told him Brian's just bought a new Daimler. He can be so childish about things like that.'

Since she'd told him some time ago that any reference to his ex-wife's husband's finances infuriated him, the remark could only have been made deliberately. On the face of things, a mean and spiteful act. But, decided Thorpe, her father had probably upset things initially, perhaps by complaining because it was so long since she'd last been down. Nothing annoyed her more quickly than any attempt to dictate to her her way of life . . .

From inside the sitting-room Fifield shouted: 'Are you coming in, or d'you reckon to spend the rest of the night in the hall?'

'You'd better go along,' she said.

'Like a good little boy?'

For the first time, she smiled. She turned and went

back down the passage to the kitchen. Tilly began to struggle and he put her down and she scampered after Susan.

The sitting-room still bore the imprint of Mary's tastes; expensive furniture, wall-to-wall carpeting in a colour that contrasted sharply with the brightly patterned curtains, an elaborate stacked audio entertainment unit on which she'd played Duke Ellington's records by the hour, and several porcelain elephants of different sizes on the mantelpiece. Thorpe was surprised that over the years Fifield had not altered or replaced things so that Mary's influence vanished. Perhaps the reason was a masochistic one.

'There's beer or sherry,' said Fifield.

'I'd like a sherry, please.'

'You never drink beer, do you?'

'I don't really like it.' He imagined, with a sense of amusement, that in Fifield's eyes that was an admission of weakness. Fifield was an enthusiastic beer-drinker, as was evidenced by the growing sag of his stomach.

'You might as well sit; there's no charge.'

Thorpe crossed to the nearer armchair. It looked as if it were going to remain a difficult evening, with his being used as a buffer between father and daughter. Oh well, it wouldn't be the first time and he'd quite broad shoulders . . .

Fifield passed him a glass of sherry, then settled in the second armchair, a pewter tankard in his right hand. He drank. 'I had a word with the foreman at the new building this morning—he says the vaults may be open before the rest of the building is finished; could even be in six months' time.'

Fifield's bad temper was explained. 'I thought it was going to be at least a year.'

'There's some sort of bonus scheme been introduced and everyone's working like crazy. Stupid bastards.'

Normally, Fifield castigated the ordinary British workman for his laziness.

'Six months and then we're finished.'

'D'you think it really is that serious? I wouldn't have thought the new place would have such an immediate and dire effect on us . . .'

'Then you're not thinking straight. It's a big company which opened vaults in Manchester a couple of months back and in Glasgow at the end of last year. They'll advertise like hell and spend a fortune on all those things like carpets which don't add to security, but make the punters feel they're getting much more for their money.'

'Surely in our job people aren't going to be concerned about the décor?'

'People are soft. They buy for looks and don't care what's inside the packaging, whether it's a box of chocolates or a bloody strong-box in a vault.'

'I reckon you could be wrong in this case.'

'You do, do you?' Fifield drank, then wiped his mouth with the back of his hand. 'Well, it doesn't matter whether you're right or wrong, because like as not we're not going to have the chance to find out. I had a letter from the landlords. The rent's going up just under twenty per cent when the present lease expires in November.'

Thorpe whistled. 'Can they do that?'

'They've bloody done it, haven't they?'

'But can't you appeal?'

'You're the lawyer; you ought to know there's no rent restriction on commercial property . . . What's more, the other leaseholders in the road won't get together and hammer out a common rent policy; two of 'em have already agreed to pay extra.' He finished the beer, leaned back, and stared into space. 'When I was coming out of the Force, I looked round and saw the way things were going and decided that the theft of property was going to be a growth industry and so I commuted my pension, borrowed from the bank, and started the vaults, working all hours. And I'd made it. Until those bastards decided to build new vaults up the road . . . You know how they'll start off, don't you? Like big business always starts when it's got a little bloke in its sights. Undercut until the little bloke's run out of business and then charge the customer a bomb.'

The bitterness was understandable, thought Thorpe, but not the sense of defeat. Big business never had all the guns . . .

Susan entered, closely followed by Tilly. When she sat, Tilly jumped up on to her lap. 'Things seem to be under control in the kitchen, but even if they aren't, I still need a drink. And for people's information, the meal's an experiment over which I've laboured hard and long, so no criticism.'

She'd recovered her good humour. Thorpe cheered up. 'Who'd ever dare criticize?'

'Either or both of you, since you've no idea how hard work cooking is . . . It's an extravagant and unusual meal.' Her tone became provocative. 'You don't like the unusual, do you, Jim?'

'What makes you say that?'

'You're so conventional.'

'It's become conventional to like the unusual.'

'Then it's no longer the unusual.'

'Quite. So the unusual has become the usual, leaving the usual the unusual. But the unusual has to be liked so that also becomes unusual . . .'

'For God's sake, talk some bloody sense,' interrupted Fifield angrily.

'Don't you appreciate our double act?' she asked sweetly. 'Then let's switch to drinking. Can I have a Rossi, please?'

'There's only beer or sherry. I suppose there's plenty of Rossi up in Oxford?'

'That's right. Paid for by me. And when I brought a bottle here, you said you weren't so poor your own daughter had to bring the drink . . . I'll have a sherry. And for heaven's sake cheer up or Jim'll think he's come to a funeral.'

Fifield stood. 'Funeral? That just about describes what's happening to the business.'

'Oh God, not that again! Can't you forget it, at least for tonight?'

'When everything I've got is tied up in it?'

'Worrying about it won't alter anything.'

'It's easy for you to be so carefree. If I go bust, you'll not suffer, but'll go on living up there in luxury.'

'That's a filthy thing to say—to suggest that because I won't be directly affected I don't care what happens.'

Fifield walked across to the mantelpiece and lifted the lid of a small silver cigarette box. He swore.

'You told me you were giving up smoking,' she said sharply.

'And now I'm starting again . . . Give me a fag, Jim.'

'I don't smoke,' Thorpe replied.

'No, you don't do you?' His tone was contemptuous. 'Then I'll just have to go round to the pub and get some.' He walked over to the door.

She spoke angrily. 'Don't be so stupid. You know what the specialist said about your asthma and smoking.'

'He's an old woman.' He went out and slammed the door behind him.

'Unless he has a couple of quick pints at the pub, tonight's not going to be very amusing for anyone,' she said calmly. 'He was in a temper when I arrived and things are getting worse.'

'It's understandable.'

'Is it? And do you always try to find excuses for other people?'

'That's better than deliberately exacerbating their grievances.'

'My God! The man almost snapped at me!'

'You've been quite rough on him.'

'And he was very rough about Mother before you arrived. And in case you're interested, I'm rapidly becoming bored with you sitting there and me sitting here and nothing happening to shock my maiden aunt.'

He went over and kissed her.

'Again.'

'First tell me, do you have a maiden aunt?'

'Good God, no! My only aunt is mother's sister and my imagination's not good enough to believe she could still be a maiden . . . Now, again, and this time don't come up for air until you're on the point of suffocating.'

The three of them went out into the front garden. Thorpe stared up at the sky. 'Not a cloud around now . . . I had a card from a friend who's holidaying in Melos. The temperature's in the late eighties or early nineties every day, the sea's like a warm bath, and the local wine's so cheap you can swim in it when you get tired of the sea.'

'I've always wanted to sail around the Greek islands,' said Susan, 'tracing out Odysseus's voyage to Ithaca across the wine-dark sea.'

'When you go, beware of Scylla and Charybdis.'

'But not to bother about Circe. I'd be immune to her wiles. Or at least I hope I would.'

'What the hell are you talking about?' demanded Fifield.

'Surely you know?' she said tactlessly.

'If I did, I wouldn't ask.'

'Scylla was a six-headed monster and Charybdis a whirlpool, on either side of the Strait of Messina; if you avoided one, you ran the risk of being scooped up by the other. Rather like trying to escape income tax and getting clobbered by capital gains tax. And Circe was a lady, to use the term loosely, who amused herself by turning men into pigs because that was how they behaved. She founded women's lib.'

'Bloody nonsense.' Fifield coughed heavily.

'I said you shouldn't smoke.'

'I'll smoke if I want to.'

'Then don't expect any sympathy.'

'If I did, I'd be disappointed.'

'Oh, God, you men!'

Thorpe said: 'I'll be on my way, then.'

'I'll run you back, Jim.'

'There's no need . . .'

'Don't be so stupid. Dad, all right if I borrow the car?'

Fifield went to answer, but coughed again and had difficulty in drawing breath.

'For heaven's sake, get back indoors and use the Ventolin. And then go up to bed and light the lamp.'

Fifield, hardly waiting while Thorpe hurriedly thanked him, went indoors and shut the front door, cutting off the light which had been spilling out.

Thorpe waited by the gates as she backed out the green Maestro, then went round to the passenger seat. As he clipped on the seat-belt, she continued backing out on to the road and then round, to face north.

'Not much of an evening for you,' she said, as she engaged first gear.

'It was all right except when the two of you really started slanging each other.'

'You probably won't believe it, but I really do try hard not to go for him when he's like he was tonight. But the trouble is, he's never begun to forgive Mother and he positively hates the thought of Brian. I imagine he sees me as some sort of a traitor because I went to live with her, but when Mother left him I was still young enough for it to be natural for me to stay with her . . . It's all so complicated. Why do families twist their emotions into knots?'

'Not all do.'

'All right, yours didn't. But look what they've done for you!'

'What have they?'

She smiled as she drew to a stop for traffic lights.

'Well?'

'Maybe I'll tell you later.'

The lights changed. She turned left into Uxbridge Road and then at the Broadway turned right past the tube station. Four minutes later, she braked to a halt in front of his house. She switched off the engine, leaned over, and kissed him. After a while, she said: 'Are you asking me upstairs?'

'Mrs Harbuckle . . .'

'Is fast asleep by now and you told me she's getting deaf . . . There's your answer.'

'To what?'

'To the question you asked me earlier.'

CHAPTER 3

In the name of economy, Fifield Vaults were run with the minimum number of staff; Fifield took the daytime watch, Thorpe the night-time one, and Trudy Johansen, who worked a short-hour day, was the secretary, personal assistant, and office boy. Then, because of the need for reliefs at weekends and holidays, two other men were employed on a casual basis; both Nithsdale and Vinay were retired policemen, in their early fifties, conscientious, dependable, but lacking much initiative which was why neither had risen above the rank of PC.

Mike Nithsdale was tall and square and fit enough to look younger than he was. His face was chunky and unbalanced, described by one friend as rough-hewn and never finished. He was a cheerful man, often laughing, who had remained an optimist even after the death of his wife after a long illness a couple of years before. He said, as Thorpe stepped into the office and the steel door slid shut behind him: 'So how's the budding barrister?'

Thorpe put down his briefcase. 'No sign of flowering yet.' He hung his mackintosh on the stand, sat on the edge of the

larger desk. 'In fact, I've reached the stage where I'm
beginning to wonder who's crazy, me or the law? Some
of the cases leave me totally bewitched, bothered, and
bewildered. And a few more B's as well. I mean, two sides
go to court to sort out an argument in which the facts are
perfectly straightforward, but by the end of the case the
whole thing's become so complicated there aren't any facts
and the judge decides it on an obscure, arcane point of law
of which only he can see the relevance.'

'You're beginning to sound like Paul.'

He laughed. 'As cynical as that?'

Nithsdale picked up a pack of cigarettes and tapped out
one: he struck a match and lit it. 'But not as sour . . . Have
you noticed how sour he's become?'

'He's got problems.'

'Who hasn't?'

'Not his size. He reckons that when the new vaults open
they'll take most of our trade.'

'Why grow ulcers before it happens? It'll be all the same
in a hundred years.'

'Sure. People will still be worrying themselves sick.'

Nithsdale pushed back the chair and stood. 'My eldest
daughter's down from Morpeth with her two kids. Proper
little demons,' he said proudly. 'Turn the house upside
down. The cat's taken to hiding in the cupboard in my
bedroom to keep out of their way.'

'An intelligent cat.'

'You wouldn't say that if you knew it. When they were
handing out brains, Star was in the queue for balls . . . I'll
be on my way, then, and leave you to your work. You will
defend me when I get hauled up in court, won't you?'

'That's a promise.'

'Free of charge, of course.'

'I imagine that would be a breach of legal etiquette.'

'According to what some of the brief markings are at, I'm
not surprised. I was involved in a case once when counsel

for the prisoner had his brief marked five hundred guineas.
And every day after the first one he got a . . . What d'you
call it?'

'A refresher.'

'I know one thing, I'd feel refreshed if I was getting
hundreds of guineas every day.' He crossed to the stand and
took from it the rolled umbrella which he preferred to a
raincoat. He crossed to the door. 'OK, Jim, chocks away
. . . I wonder which part of the house I'll find in ruins
tonight?'

Thorpe sat down behind the desk and pressed the appropriate button; the steel door slid back. Nithsdale stepped
out and Thorpe was about to close the door when Nithsdale
stepped back to straddle the doorway, in contravention of
the rule that no door must ever be left open for one second
longer than was necessary. 'Just remembered. Ten minutes
before you arrived, Susan Fifield, the old man's daughter,
rang and said would you get on to her in Oxford.'

'Thanks.'

'Dick's met her, but I haven't. What's she like?'

'Quite pleasant,' replied Thorpe, carefully showing little
enthusiasm.

'If she's anything like him, she's a bit starchy.'

'I don't think you could call her that,' he said, remembering her passionate demands.

'Then maybe she takes after her mum. Met the ex-Mrs
Fifield, have you?'

'Not yet.'

'To listen to him, you'd think she was a real bitch. But I
reckon that living with him was never easy. And her new
husband's rolling in the necessary, isn't he?'

'I gather he's quite well off.'

'She obviously knows what's important in life . . . Well,
I'm off. See you again soon if one of us doesn't die in bed.'

Thorpe worked the doors, watched Nithsdale stride
briskly along the pavement. *Obviously knows what's important*

in life. How similar in character was Susan? It would be years before he made enough at the bar to support her in any generous lifestyle. His father had once told him that although a marriage to be successful had to be between equals, the man always had to earn the bread in order to keep his self-respect . . .

He dialled Susan's home number. Her mother answered and asked him to hold on. Susan had never suggested that he went up to meet her mother. There were several possible explanations for this, some of which he carefully did not pursue.

When Susan came on the line, he told her that her father had been ill and off work.

'Yes, I know. The asthma always gets him badly when he's worried, but he's so stubborn he just won't allow that it can be triggered as much by mental as physical stress . . . And the stupid man's gone back to smoking. I told him what I thought of that.'

'Tactfully, I hope?'

'You know me.'

'That's why I'm asking.'

'I was very tactful and I suggested he took a week off and went out to his flat in Mallorca, because he's always better out there. If he talks to you about it, be enthusiastic, will you?'

'He doesn't consult me over his intentions.'

'Could that be because he can't really understand you?'

'A family failing?'

She laughed. 'I understand you right enough. What defeats me is why you stick so close to your archaic principles.'

'Perhaps because the temptation to break them has never been sufficiently strong.'

'You bastard!' she said, more in anger than amusement.

'For those few kind words, I thank you.'

'I suppose you think you were being funny?'

'I've already realized my mistake. Just put it down to my

gaucherie and forget it . . . Tell me, what can I do for you?'

'I've a damn good mind to say nothing.'

'Remember, to err is human . . . I'm human, but you're divine. So forgive.'

She relaxed. 'You're a fool.'

'That's better.'

'You know, Jim, you can be exceedingly annoying. It's almost impossible to stay angry with you. Look, I want you to come to dinner on the twentieth; you will, won't you?'

'Like a shot.'

'Mother and Brian are flying out to somewhere exotic so I thought I'd come down for the night.'

'It sounds to me as if there could be some special significance to the date—is it your birthday?'

'Weren't you brought up not to be inquisitive?'

'Will you be twenty-two or twenty-three?'

'To flatter, one has to be subtle.'

'I'll try and remember that.'

'You're far too much of an open book to be subtle . . . So it's the twentieth at six—that's a Wednesday.'

'Hell! . . . I'm terribly sorry, but I won't be able to make it.'

'Why not?' Her voice was once more sharp.

'I'll have to be here, working.'

'For heaven's sake, I told you.'

'You told me what?'

'That Father says you're to get one of the others to do that night.'

'You didn't tell me.'

'I damn well did.'

'Let's not argue the point. Are you sure he said that?'

'Of course I am. What's the matter? Would you rather not come?'

'That's being ridiculous. The thing is, your father's such a stickler for maintaining routine and the routine is that I'm on duty every night from Monday through to Friday.'

'Then for once he's thrown aside his principles. And I can think of someone who might accept that as an example.'

'Who?'

'I know—you can't imagine who! You will come, then?'

'Mr James Angus Thorpe accepts with pleasure the very kind invitation of Miss Susan Fifield to dinner at six o'clock on Wednesday, the twentieth of June, at number thirty-two, Melthorpe Avenue.'

'Good. By the way, do you like garlic?'

'Despite being brought up by respectable parents, I love it.'

'Then I'll experiment with a garlic chicken.'

'It sounds delicious, but how will that go down with your father?'

'Very well, provided no one tells him what he's eating. Promise me you won't split?'

'Even the Inquisition will never force the information past my lips.'

'I doubt things will get to that pitch.'

A couple of minutes later, he rang off. He leaned back in the chair. He must buy her a birthday present. What?

With a start, he realized that he had not yet carried out the routine checks. He telephoned the police station and warned them that he'd be sounding the alarms.

In a house in south Brixton, three men stood around a table on which were laid out a large-scale map of London, north of the Thames, and a plan of Fifield Vaults in which each of the security devices was marked.

The tallest of the three, using a pencil as a pointer, traced out a route on the map. 'The pub's half way along this road . . .'

He was interrupted. 'I still don't like it, Titch.'

'I wasn't asking.'

'But I'm telling. There's something wrong.'

'What?'

'I don't know, do I?'

'Then belt up.'

'Why ain't the grasser ever come face-to-face?'

'Ask him, not me. Now bloody belt up.' His voice was loud and harsh. He didn't want to be reminded of the questions which he'd asked himself so many times and to which he'd never got any satisfactory answers.

CHAPTER 4

Mrs Harbuckle was in one of her more pugnacious moods, explained by the fact that there was a strike of TV cameramen and her favourite programme had been blacked out. 'I suppose you'll be back late?'

'Not very,' Thorpe answered.

'When you do get here, don't make a noise.'

'I'll be as quiet as a mouse.'

'I've been woken up by mice before now . . . Not that there's any in this house and what's more, never has been.'

'Good heavens, of course not.'

'Those were two special lamb chops I bought for supper and now you won't be eating.'

'I did mention a couple of days ago that I was going out tonight.'

'I don't recall you saying anything.'

'Won't the chops keep until tomorrow night?'

'Only if I put 'em in the fridge and then they'll dry out.'

'If you wrap them up in film?'

'Don't believe in using that stuff.'

He gave up. 'I'd better be off if I'm to get there by six. I do hope the TV comes back on.'

'Shouldn't think so.' Her voice rose. 'I'd give 'em strike, I would. When they're already getting ten times what my Ron did. Greedy. Don't matter about anyone else . . .'

After a while there was a pause and he hurriedly wished her goodnight and then ducked out of the room before she had time to complain further. When he reached the end of the road, an empty taxi came into sight and he hailed it. An extravagance, but this was a birthday night.

He knocked on the front door and from inside came the shrill sounds of Tilly's yapping. Susan opened the door. He stepped inside and handed her a small package, carefully wrapped in soft paper. 'Happy birthday.' Tilly muzzled his legs for attention.

She unwrapped a small box inside which was a silver bracelet charm, in the shape of an elephant. 'I've been searching for one of these for ages! . . . How on earth did you know I wanted one so much?'

'Read the tea-leaves.'

'You're a liar, because you don't like tea.'

'That doesn't stop me reading someone else's.'

'Stop drivelling and kiss me.'

Instinctively, he looked towards the sitting-room door.

'No cause for panic, Father's out at the moment. And for your future information, in the world in which the rest of us live, a kiss is not considered particularly incriminating.'

'What a pity,' he said, before he kissed her.

After a while she drew apart. 'I'm sorry, but we've got to stop there. I must go through to the kitchen and check the cooking.'

'I'll come and help.'

'And have me so distracted I put garlic in the chocolate mousse?'

'It would be different.'

'Too different for Father . . . So carry on into the sitting-room.'

'To hear is to obey.'

'But give me another kiss just before you do obey.'

When she moved away from him, she said: 'There are

times when I begin to think you have the right ideas after all!'

He went into the sitting-room. There was a newspaper on the arm of the sofa, but he'd already seen the *Daily Mail*. He looked around for something to gaze at while he waited and he noticed that the painting over the mantelpiece had been changed. He studied the one that was now there. Like all Fifield's paintings, it was a landscape, but unlike any of the others that he'd seen, this one possessed some special quality. He was still looking at it when he heard the front door open.

Fifield came into the sitting-room. 'Sorry not to be here when you arrived, Jim. Went to have a word with old Partridge and he insisted on me tasting his new dandelion wine.'

Fifield's manner was very cheerful, far different from what it had been on Thorpe's last visit. If this was the effect that dandelion wine had on him, then grow more dandelions.

'Name your poison, then. I know you don't like beer, but there's sherry, gin, or some of that stuff Sue likes.'

'Rossi? That would be lovely.'

'As far as I'm concerned, you can keep all these foreign lash-ups.' He crossed to the drinks tray.

'I like your new painting,' Thorpe said.

'Do you?'

'There's something about it . . .' About to say it possessed an extra quality, he realized that to do so would, by inference, be to suggest that Fifield's previous works had lacked this. '. . . really attractive. It's in the south of France, surely?'

'That's right.'

'Whereabouts, exactly?'

'Nowhere, except in my mind. My dream cottage in the sun, overlooking my own vineyard, paid for by the football pools.'

'But that hill—surely that exists somewhere?'

'Just drew a shape that's always intrigued me and then added a bit on the top: a fun hat.'

Perhaps that extra quality which he'd been unable to define had been imagination, tinged with a sense of humour.

Fifield came across and passed him a glass. 'Let's drink to dreams,' he said.

They sat in the Granada which Wicklam had stolen the night before in Bracknell; it was parked under the shadow of the walnut tree which gave the pub its name. Wicklam was behind the wheel, Lauermann in the front passenger seat, Orr in the back. Mostly, they were silent. Even with all their experience, they still suffered tension when they waited.

A number of people left the pub through two of the doorways, marking the fact that it was closing time. Tension sharpened. Orr whistled tunelessly, Wicklam fidgeted the wheel, Lauermann rubbed the side of his nose. People crossed to their cars and drove out of the car park, none of them bothering to glance at the Granada. Then all movement came to an end.

'He ain't coming,' said Wicklam suddenly. 'It's a bloody blagger.'

Each of them knew a growing sense of anger as if, indeed, the job had already proved to be a non-starter. Then they saw the man step out of a third doorway, a carrier bag in one hand. His hair was red. Only one member of the staff had red hair. He walked down to the pavement, turned left.

Wicklam started the engine and drove out. Their timing proved to be good. As the man turned into the street on his right, they were fifty yards behind him. The road he'd entered was poorly lit because two of the street lights had been vandalized.

Wicklam accelerated gently, then let the car roll forward under its own momentum. In the back, Orr picked up a small leather cosh that was filled with lead. The car passed the man, came to a stop. Orr opened his window. 'Hey, Red,' he shouted.

The man came to a halt, his round, puffy face showing surprise.

'Bert says he wants you back at the pub right away. We'll run you there.' Orr opened the door.

'Go back for what?'

'How would I know, mate? Come on, get a move on or Bert'll be blowing his top.'

The landlord was noted for his quick temper. Without bothering to ask any more questions, the man climbed into the back. The cosh hit him on the back of the neck and he collapsed. Orr struck again, not because it appeared to him to be necessary, just making certain. Wicklam drove on.

The carrier bag had dropped to the floor and Orr pushed a leg aside in order to pick it up. He looked inside. 'It's there, all right.' He put the bag on the seat, used wide surgical tape to gag the man's mouth, thin cord to secure his arms and legs.

They went down three roads which brought them to Devreux Road. Orr picked up the cosh from the seat and slipped it into the right-hand pocket of his coat. He nodded to show he was ready. His forehead beaded with sweat.

The car stopped. Carrier bag in his right hand, Orr stepped out on to the pavement, shut the door and—for the benefit of the camera—waved his thanks for the lift. The car drove off.

He crossed the pavement, went down the steps, rang the bell.

'What d'you want?' asked a voice through the grille to his right.

'I've got your beer. Red said to bring it to you.'

'Where's he?'

'Had a bit of an accident half an hour ago.'

'Why didn't he phone?'

'How do I know? I'm only the messenger boy. And if you

don't want the beer, I'll be on my way home and get my grub.' He turned to face the steps.

'All right, mate. Just checking.'

The door slid back. He stepped into the reception area, feeling naked under the powerful overhead lights.

'What kind of accident did he have?'

'Jesus, chum, you've got more questions than my old woman's got complaints . . . Someone spilled a drink and he slipped on a slice of lemon and landed on his arse with a thump. Last I saw of him, he was going around on all fours, like a bloody chimp.' It had been Lauermann's idea to introduce a note of farce; when something was presented unseriously, it was treated unseriously. 'So he didn't feel up to crawling this far in case he was had up for importuning and he said for me to bring you the booze.'

The office door slid open. Vinay crossed to the doorway. 'I hope Red's not too badly hurt?'

'I'd say it's more bruising than anything.'

'You never know. A pal of mine sat down, not knowing someone had left a piece of metal tubing on the seat, and he cracked his coccyx. Never been the same since.'

Orr held out the carrier bag and Vinay took it in his right hand. Then Orr moved with bewildering speed. He brought the cosh out of his coat pocket and slammed it down on Vinay's head before Vinay had done more than drop the carrier bag to leave his hand free. He staggered back, his exploding mind trying to concentrate on the absolute need to reach the nearest panic button . . . A second blow blasted him into unconsciousness. A third was unnecessary.

Orr dragged Vinay into the office and bound and gagged him. He pressed the button to open the outside door, then went through and stood at the bottom of the steps and took from his left-hand coat pocket a very compact, Japanese-made walkie-talkie. He extended the aerial to its maximum height and held the instrument so that the aerial projected just above the level of the pavement—the one thing they'd not been able to discover was whether transmission would be effective if made below street level. He said four words which signified that everything had gone according to plan.

He returned to the office. Vinay hadn't moved and his breathing was laboured, his complexion a dusty colour. Satisfied he'd cause no trouble, Orr went over to the larger desk and turned to look at the TV screens. He saw the other two as they walked towards the camera.

They'd had several drinks before the meal and a couple of bottles of Banda Azul with it. Fifield's good humour became broader and more uninhibited. He had a fund of stories from his time in the police force and he told them with the skill of a born raconteur; even Susan, whose manner made it clear she'd heard them several times before, frequently laughed aloud.

After clearing the table, Susan stayed in the kitchen to make coffee and Thorpe and Fifield returned to the sitting-room. 'You'll have a brandy, Jim?' Fifield asked.

'Thanks.'

'Spanish, not French, but unless you're one of them drink snobs, there's nothing wrong with that.' He went over to the tray of drinks and picked up an oval bottle. 'Bought this last time I was in Mallorca; just under two quid for the litre. In this country it's something like ten quid for a normal-sized bottle. Say what you like about the Spaniards, they know what's important in life.' He half filled two medium-sized glasses. 'Ever been to the island?'

'No, I haven't.'

'Forget the fools who tell you it's one vast concrete jungle. They just don't know. Most of it is still beautiful. Sit on the front on a moonlit night and stare out at the bay and you start holding your breath in case it vanishes.' He suddenly slapped his thigh. 'Now, there's a thought!' He picked up the glasses and carried them across, gave one to Thorpe

'Why don't you have a holiday in my place? It's empty all
the time I'm over here. And for someone your age, Puerto
Fortaix is paradise.' He leered at Thorpe. 'Hundreds of
birds on the beach, most of 'em topless, just waiting to be
pulled.' He turned and went over to an armchair, sat more
heavily than he'd intended so that brandy spilled over the
rim of his glass. He lifted his hand and licked it. 'You
remember SuperMac? You've never had it so good. I'm
telling you, you've never had it so easy. When I was a
youngster, a man had to work bloody hard to get what he
was after, but these days all he has to do is sit around and
choose. It's good to be young, eh?'

'Some of the time.'

'Only some? You're too goddamn serious. Life's for lov-
ing, not living.'

Susan, accompanied by Tilly, came into the room with a
tray on which was coffee, cream, and sugar.

'I've just had a brilliant idea,' said Fifield loudly.

'By whose standards?' she asked.

There was an edge to her voice, Thorpe thought. He
reckoned to know why. Fifield had drunk enough not to
worry about what he said or how he said it and it had
become obvious that his background was the local pub and
not a club in St James's Street. She had been living in a
different setting sufficiently long to prefer to forget that fact.

'By my standards, of course. I've been telling him about
all those lovelies with bare titties on the sands at Puerto
Fortaix: I've told him, go out and stay in my flat and feast
your eyes on what's on offer.'

She caried the tray over to Thorpe. 'No doubt the idea
appeals to you?'

He helped himself to cream and sugar. 'Passionately.'

Fifield laughed coarsely. 'That's the spirit! Make hay
while the sun shines because if you're fool enough to hang
around the clouds'll come back and it'll rain like the second
Flood's just started . . . Have a cigar, Jim? I brought some

real good ones back last trip and I've been keeping 'em for special occasions.'

'No, thanks.'

'Don't use 'em? And you don't like cigarettes or beer. So what the hell d'you do to keep amused?'

'Take regular showers.'

Fifield laughed again. Susan held the tray in front of him, but he waved it away. 'I'll get a cigar first, love.' He stood and had slight difficulty in catching his balance. 'Keep 'em in the dining-room . . . Are you sure you won't change your mind, Jim?'

'Quite certain, thanks.'

'Put lead in your pencil.'

'I always use a ballpoint.'

Fifield left the room, his gait a shade unsteady.

Susan put the tray down, picked up the remaining cup without adding either sugar or cream, and went over to the settee. As she settled, Tilly jumped up by her side. 'So the thought of a lot of half-naked women on the beach appeals to you passionately?'

'How else?' Thorpe replied.

'In that case, I'll take my holiday at the same time. I don't like the idea of your getting into bad habits.'

Orr, after drilling two holes to the side of the lock of the first strong-box, inserted two hardened, hooked steel rods and manœuvred these around. In under half a minute the lock clicked open. 'They're going to be a doddle,' he said with satisfaction. He opened the door and slid out the inner section which was in the form of an open-top box made from fine wire mesh.

'What's in it?' Lauermann demanded impatiently.

He brought out a small cardboard box, dropped the container, opened the box and lifted out a strip of foam packing and then a miniature, exquisitely painted on ivory and framed in delicately carved rosewood; there were others underneath. He thought he'd seldom seen anything so beautiful.

'Let's have it, then.'

He passed the miniature across.

'That's no bloody good.' Lauermann threw the miniature down on the floor and the frame split and a flake of ivory stripped off, destroying the corner. 'Come on, get moving on the next one.'

CHAPTER 5

Thorpe was in his bedroom, studying the intricacies of various consumer protection acts, when he heard the telephone ring. A moment later Mrs Harbuckle shouted up—in tones of irritation since her morning viewing was being interrupted—that the call was for him. He went downstairs, his mind occupied by the interesting and arcane knowledge that 'bacon flavour' meant the product had to be flavoured with bacon, but 'bacon flavoured' merely meant it had to taste of bacon . . .

The caller was Fifield. 'Jim, get along right away.'

'What's up?'

'Where the hell d'you live? Haven't you heard the news? The vaults were broken into last night. Dick was badly worked over and he's in hospital. They say his condition's critical.'

'My God! . . . I'll be with you as soon as I can be.'

As he replaced the receiver, he visualized Vinay. Round, pleasant face, fronted by a Roman nose which had earned him the nickname of Schnozzle; a small, over-trimmed moustache of which he was proud; crooked teeth. His wife was dumpy, homely, and inclined to fuss, but there was no mistaking their warm affection for each other. Thorpe had never met their only daughter, but apparently she was a rebel and careless of the hurt she caused them by her behaviour and her expressed contempt for their standards . . .

He returned upstairs, changed his shirt, and left after briefly telling Mrs Harbuckle what had happened—she showed little interest; on the small screen, there had just been a moment of great drama—and explaining that he didn't know when he'd be back so that there was no point in waiting lunch for him. Three-quarters of an hour later, he turned into Devreux Road.

A couple of police cars were parked by the vaults and a PC was standing at the head of the steps. Surrounding the PC was an ever-changing circle of onlookers who stood and stared.

'Sorry, but you can't go down for a bit,' said the PC.

'My name's Thorpe and I work here.'

'I see. Hang on a moment.' The PC went down the stairs, put his head inside, and spoke to someone. When he returned, he said: 'That's all right, Mr Thorpe. Go on down.'

He went down and into the reception area. Men in uniform and civvies were moving around continuously and, to his untrained eye, haphazardly. He carried on through the open doorway into the office.

Fifield was slumped in the chair behind his desk, his face slack from strain: the telephone in front of him was ringing, but he was ignoring it. At the smaller desk, Trudy, fiftyish, plump, neat, was talking to someone over the telephone and obviously having trouble. She sighed as she replaced the receiver. ''Morning, Jim. If there's anything good about it.'

'Have you had any word on Dick?'

'I telephoned the hospital half an hour ago. He's still critical and they can't give any sort of a prognosis.'

'What happened?'

'The beasts hit him on the head with a cosh and it seems he has a weak skull and his brain's been damaged.' There was a catch in her voice. She was fond of the Vinays and occasionally spent a day with them. 'I tried to have a word with Vera, but she . . . Well, she just wasn't in a fit state to talk to me.'

'How did anyone get near enough to him to cosh him?'

'I just don't know.' She fiddled with the keys of her typewriter. 'They wounded someone else as well.'

'Who?'

Fifield answered. 'An assistant bartender from the Walnut Tree.'

'Where did he come into it?'

'He was bringing the beer . . . I must get to Vera and see if there's anything I can do . . .' He became silent.

Fifield had once told him that the most taxing job a policeman was called upon to do was to break bad news to relatives or friends; it didn't matter how well one had been counselled by psychologists on the way in which to deal with those newly bereaved, how often one had done it before, every time was a mind-wrenching occasion.

The telephone on Trudy's desk rang. The caller was another despositor, demanding to know whether her strong-box had been looted.

A PC stepped into the office. 'Any of you Mr Thorpe?'

'I am.'

'CID says will you have a word with them now. They're in the room on the other side.'

Thorpe left and crossed the reception area to the small room normally used by clients when they wanted to examine the contents of their strong-boxes in complete privacy. The table was now in use as a desk and a telephone and a portable electric typewriter had been set up on it. Seated in one of the two chairs was a man slightly younger than Thorpe whose square-shaped head was crowned with a shock of unruly chestnut-coloured hair and sided by batwing ears; he wore a sports jacket with leather-patch elbows. He came to his feet. 'Mr Thorpe? I'm Detective-Sergeant

Fuller.' He leaned across and shook hands. 'Just a few questions, if you've time?' He indicated the second chair, in front of the table; sat. He opened a notebook and flicked through the pages. 'Been working here long?'

'Just over six months.'

'And you do nights? Sooner you than me, that's for sure.' He reached the right page, picked up a pen. 'Let's have your full name and address.'

Thorpe gave them.

'You weren't on duty last night, although it was a week-day. How was that?'

'Mr Fifield had invited me to his place for the evening and had said to get either Dick or Mike to spell me.'

'You sound as if you're friendly with the boss?'

'Reasonably so, yes.'

'I want you to have a good think before you answer the next question. When you've been on duty during the past fortnight, have you noticed anything at all suspicious? For instance, someone in the street who's been hanging around with nothing to do?'

'No. There's been no one like that.'

'If there had been such a person, d'you think you'd have noticed him?'

'Yes. One of the things we're always on the lookout for is someone hanging around for no particular reason. Using the outside video camera, we can see pretty well to the end of the road in either direction.'

'There's no offence intended with the next question, but in any set-up like this, the security's only as good as the blokes who are using the equipment. So unless you kept a good watch on the screen, you might not have noticed someone who was around for only a relatively short time, might you?'

'Is that a tactful way of asking if I'm in the habit of falling asleep at three in the morning.'

Fuller smiled.

'If I begin to feel sleepy, I get up and pace the floor. It's a dodge Mr Fifield put me on to. Then if you do fall asleep, you wake up pretty smartly when you crash into something.'

'Fair enough. So we can say quite definitely that there's been no one hanging around outside at night time?'

'Yes.'

Fuller wrote briefly. 'D'you know what happened last night?'

'No. I didn't even know there'd been a robbery until Mr Fifield telephoned me earlier on at my digs.'

'As far as we can judge at the moment, it went like this. Soon after closing time, Jack Adams, one of the assistant barmen at the Walnut Tree, left there with a couple of bottles of beer for Vinay. On the way he was stopped, bundled into a car, and coshed. One of the men in the car then took his place and delivered the beer. He was let in and he coshed Vinay. From then on, it was a straightforward robbery . . . Now, I've got to ask you this. Did you know Vinay was in the habit of having beer brought to him when he was doing a relief night duty?'

'I . . . Well, not exactly.'

'What does that mean?'

Thorpe replied uncomfortably: 'It was just something Dick once said to me.'

'What did he say?'

'That the night moved on much quicker with a couple of beers under the belt.'

'That surely could've meant that he brought the drink in with him?'

'I told him that if Paul ever caught him bringing beer into the place he'd never get another hour's work and he said he didn't carry it in, it arrived after the boss was gone and miles away.'

'Did you report this to Mr Fifield?'

'No.'

'Why not?'

He remained silent.

'Wasn't that being less than loyal to the boss?'

'I suppose you can say that.'

'You couldn't decide who to give your loyalty to?'

'Yes.'

'It's a pity you chose how you did.'

'I couldn't know what was going to happen.'

'That's what people always say.'

It was so easy to know now what he should have done then, thought Thorpe.

A PC looked into the room. 'The DI's shouting for you, Sarge.'

'Tell him I'll be along in a jiffy.' The PC left. 'Mr Thorpe, has anyone ever tried to get you to give details of the security set-up of these vaults?'

'No.'

'You've not been offered any form of a bribe?'

'If I had have been, I'd have reported it.'

'Because it would obviously pose a threat to the vaults?'

'Yes.'

'But the fact that Vinay was having beer brought in when he was on duty at night surely posed a potential threat?'

'That was different.'

'Was it? . . . Well, that's about the lot.'

Would the detective-sergeant have betrayed a companion quite so readily? wondered Thorpe, as he made his way back to the office. Moral problems were the more easily solved the further distanced one was from them.

Fifield was speaking over the telephone, Trudy was typing. Seconds after Thorpe had entered, Fifield put down the receiver. He looked up. 'Have they finished with you?'

'For the moment, at least.'

'Then take over from me. Tell anyone who phones that until the police give us the go-ahead, we can't say how many or which strong-boxes have been looted, but that as soon as we're allowed to check we'll notify all clients who've had stuff nicked. And if they start on about compensation, tell 'em we're in touch with our insurers.' He stood. 'I'll be at the hospital.' He walked round his desk and across to the doorway.

'Mr Fifield,' Trudy called out, 'don't you want your mackintosh in case it comes on to rain?'

He left without answering.

'He's so upset,' she said despondently.

'He's bound to be. He was pretty friendly with Dick.'

'It's bad enough reading about his sort of thing, but when it happens to you . . .'

She sounded scared. 'Lightning never strikes twice,' he said, trying to comfort her.

'I read about an American who's been struck seven times.'

'Americans tend to be over-enthusiastic.'

'I hope that's right . . . Poor Mr Fifield! And it's not just Dick who's upsetting him so. He asked me to telephone the insurance brokers earlier; they said things might be difficult because it looked as if one of the staff had been at fault and there's a clause in the contract exonerating the insurance company from any responsibility in the event of employee's negligence.'

'That's all it needs, isn't it? Who was it said that no one kicks you harder when you're down than life?'

CHAPTER 6

Detective-Inspector Cartwright came into the office at a quarter to six that evening. Of medium height, he moved with the jerky quickness of someone who was always striving to do more than was possible. He might have been handsome, with dark, easy, regular features, touched with a hint of the Mediterranean, but his mouth expressed too much weary cynicism. The lesson he'd learned from life was that while man's capacity for good was limited, his capacity for evil was infinite. 'We're packing up now,' he said, snapping each word short.

'Does that mean we can start checking out the boxes?' Thorpe asked.

'Yes. And I'll want a list of names and addresses of renters who've lost stuff.'

'I don't know about that.'

'Why?'

'The information regarding depositors is confidential.'

'It stopped being confidential the moment one of you let the mob in.'

The remark was made with careless disregard for any ruffled feelings.

A sergeant looked in, saw the detective-inspector and stepped inside and spoke in a low voice. Cartwright checked his wristwatch, nodded, dismissed the sergeant with a quick nod of his head. He turned back. 'I'll have that list by midday, please.'

Perhaps, thought Thorpe, nettled by the other's manner.

The police left the vaults, carrying their equipment with them. As the last PC climbed the steps up to the street, Thorpe closed the doors. He looked at Trudy. 'That is known as shutting the stable door . . . Did Paul say when he was likely to be back?'

'No, he didn't. I suppose everything will depend on how Dick is and if there's anything he can do to help Vera.'

'How can you help someone in her tragic position?'

'Just being there so she's not on her own. Surely that must make it a little easier for her?'

'Perhaps.' Grief was like pain, peculiar to each mind and therefore really unshareable.

She was silent for a moment, then she said hesitatingly: 'I'm sorry to fuss, but I've got a class tonight and the time is getting on.'

Soon after her husband had left her for a Glaswegian tart,

she'd started evening ballet lessons. No one had been cruel enough to point out to her the absurdity of a woman of her age and build learning jetés and fouettés ... 'Sure. You move on. I can handle things here now.'

She tidied her already tidy desk-top, opened a drawer and brought out her handbag. She collected her collapsible umbrella from the hatstand. 'But what are you going to do now?'

'How d'you mean?'

'You've been here all day and it's been so tiring—I've quite a headache—so you shouldn't do the night shift as well. Heaven knows when Mr Fifield will be back to ask, so why don't you get on to Mike and see if he can relieve you?'

'It's an idea,' he answered, suddenly made conscious by her words of just how tired he did feel.

'He rang earlier to find out how Dick was and said he'd do anything he could to help—I'm sure he'll come in if he can.'

'I'll get on to him right away.'

'It's been ... a terrible day.' Her strongly featured, almost masculine face worked and he thought she might start crying. But she managed a brief, forlorn smile before crossing to the door.

On the television camera he watched her climb up to street level. This robbery must surely prove to be the death blow to the business. In that case, she, together with the rest of them, would be out of a job; she would probably find it impossible to get another. He hadn't realized before how a crime wasn't specific to the people it directly affected, but that it sent out ripples of suffering which washed over bystanders.

Nithsdale had said that he'd be at the vaults by eight, after hurrying his evening meal. It was twenty to when Fifield returned.

His colour was poor, he was breathing through half opened mouth, and he was having considerable trouble in clearing his lungs before drawing in fresh air; his asthmatic cough, a quick, dry bark, was almost continuous. He crossed to his chair and slumped down in it, brought a Ventolin dispenser from his pocket, inserted the mouthpiece in his mouth, and briefly pressed the release button.

'Is there anything I can do?' Thorpe asked.

He shook his head. After a while, he said breathlessly: 'I'll be better in a moment.'

'You look as if you ought to be in bed.'

'It was seeing Dick through the window of the intensive care unit . . . And trying to console Vera . . .'

'How is he?'

'A doctor told me on the QT that it's touch and go . . . Know something? Vera phoned her daughter and asked her to come and help. She said she was too busy.'

'The world can get very bloody.'

'With her father lying there, nearly dead, and she's too busy to help her mother . . . Christ, if I could get my hands on her . . .'

Thorpe had always imagined that Fifield had seen so much tragedy in his working life that he had become inured to it—had had to, in order to be able to continue the work. But it was obvious that he'd been very deeply affected by this tragedy. The reason had to be the obvious one, that a personal relationship made everything so much sharper and more brutal.

Fifield sat more upright and when he next spoke his voice was stronger. 'What's been happening here?'

'The police have finished and moved out. They say we can check the boxes now. The detective-inspector told me he wants a list by midday tomorrow of the names and addresses of renters who've lost stuff. I told him you'd have to OK that.'

'We'll have to give it to them.'

'There'll need to be at least two of us here, won't there, if someone's to keep watch in the office while we check boxes?'

'Yes . . . Maybe we ought to start now.'

'With you in your state and me ready for a marathon sleep? Forget it until tomorrow . . . And incidentally, I've been on to Mike and he's coming to do tonight.'

Fifield didn't comment. He reached down to his coat pocket and brought out a pack of cigarettes. When he saw Thorpe's expression, he said: 'There's one goddamn difference between knowing what one shouldn't do and not doing it.' He lit a cigarette. 'The business is finished, you know?'

Arguing against his own convictions, Thorpe said: 'Maybe people won't panic as much as you expect.'

'Inside a week we won't know what a client looks like.' He looked round the office. 'Three years back I sat here and told myself everything was running smoothly, my gamble had paid off, and I was going to make real money. Makes me one of the world's bum tipsters . . . Why the hell did he do it?' he demanded, with sudden violence. 'Two bottles of beer. That's all it goddamn took to ruin me; two lousy half-pint bottles of beer.' He looked at Thorpe. 'Did you know he had beer brought in?'

Thorpe cleared his throat. 'I . . . Well, he did once say something . . .'

'It's all right, I'm not blaming you for not passing on the news. God knows how many times I stayed dumb because I'd be letting my pals down if I spoke up.'

Thorpe looked at the electric clock, hoping against hope that Nithsdale would be early. He longed to escape from the man to whose coming financial ruin he had, however inadvertently, contributed.

The area housing the strong-boxes was rectangular, much longer than it was wide; it held an air of mustiness despite the fact that it was completely dry. The strong-boxes, three rows high, were set in reinforced concrete; inside each was a fine-mesh container. Normally, the vault was a scene of careful order, but following the robbery it was in a state of considerable disorder. The villains had had time to force roughly two-thirds of the boxes and wherever the contents had turned out to be neither cash nor something readily convertible into cash, or too distinctive to take the risk of handling, these had been dumped on the floor together with all the containers. It was a sight to sadden anyone who loved beautiful things because the ivory miniatures from the first box had not been the only antiques contemptuously discarded.

A table had been set up at the near end of the vault and on this were placed all the items it was, for the moment, impossible to identify by box number. Thorpe had just placed a leather-bound diary on the table—written up in a personal shorthand; another Pepys, committing his indiscretions to paper?—when a message came through the speaker in the ceiling. 'Jim, will you come to the office, please.'

He left the table and approached the door and this slid back to let him into the reception area. The door of the office opened and he was about to go forward when two men came out. Detective-Sergeant Fuller said in his breezy manner: "Morning, Mr Thorpe. If you don't mind, there are a few more questions. This is Detective-Superintendent Bell.'

Bell was in early middle age. He had a heavy face, touched with humour, and the hint of a double chin. 'How d'you do?' He shook hands with a dry, firm grip. He had light blue eyes which had a disconcerting habit of frequently appearing unfocused, then suddenly focusing. His hair was thinning and, from the frequency with which he smoothed down what was left, he was very conscious of the fact. He led the way into the room opposite the office and they sat.

He opened a folder which Fuller handed him, but instead of looking down at it, spoke to Thorpe. 'I'm afraid I have some very sad news. We've heard from the hospital that Mr Vinay died earlier this morning.'

'Poor Vera,' Thorpe murmured.

'So this has become a murder case and I'm taking charge of the investigations . . . Sergeant Fuller had a word with you yesterday, didn't he?' Bell brought out a spectacle case from his coat pocket, settled a pair of half-moon spectacles on his nose. He read the top sheet of paper in the folder. 'You normally do the night turn, but on Wednesday evening you went to Mr Fifield's house and Richard Vinay spelled you. Who made the arrangement with Vinay?'

'I did.'

'Any particular reason for asking him and not Mr Nithsdale?'

'Mike had done the last relief and it's office policy to offer them equal opportunities.'

'That was your only consideration?'

'What other could there have been?'

'I don't know. That's why I'm asking. I understand you knew Vinay was in the habit of having beer delivered here when he was on night duty?'

Thorpe chose his words carefully. 'I surmised something of the sort happened. I didn't know the details.'

'You didn't tell Mr Fifield what you'd surmised?'

'No.'

'Then in so far as you can tell, he wasn't aware of what was going on?'

'I'm certain he wasn't.'

'You do realize that if you'd reported the matter the robbery might never have taken place?'

'Of course I do now,' he replied bitterly.

'Did you suggest to Vinay that his actions were rather stupid?'

'No.'

'But you must have realized that they were?'

'Yes.'

'You didn't foresee that as a result of them there might be a robbery?'

'No. One doesn't . . .' He became silent.

'One doesn't think it will ever happen close to home.' Bell sighed. 'Did you mention anything about this to Nithsdale or Mrs Johansen?'

'No.'

'Do you imagine they knew what was going on?'

'I've never had any reason to think they did.'

'So in so far as you're aware, you were the only person to suspect that when on night turn Vinay was in the habit of having some beer brought from the Walnut Tree?'

'Yes.'

Bell fiddled with the edge of the folder, rubbing it between finger and thumb. 'Did either Mrs Johansen or Nithsdale know you were swapping Wednesday's duty with Vinay?'

'I just don't know.'

'Have you often swapped duties?'

'Normally, Paul is dead against anything like that. But it was his daughter's birthday.'

'Has there previously been a time when you've swapped duty nights, for whatever reason?'

'Soon after I started here, I went down with 'flu. I was off for a couple of nights.'

'So one could say that purely from your point of view, you were extremely lucky that you weren't working here Wednesday night?'

'I suppose so.'

'Although if you had been, of course, the assistant bartender would not have been bringing you any beer . . . Does it strike you as in any way significant that the sequence of events was as it was?'

'No.'

'I see . . . Well, thank you for your assistance.'

Thorpe was surprised by this abrupt ending to the interview, with the last question rather left in the air.

CHAPTER 7

The detective-constable smiled at the sister and was gratified when, for the first time in three days, she smiled back. He whistled under his breath as he made his way up the ward to the end bed, behind which the curtains had been half drawn across the floor-to-ceiling window to ward off the sun.

Adams, head still heavily bandaged, looked small and shrunken and petulantly resentful.

'How are things going, then?' asked the DC.

'All right for some, I suppose.'

The DC sat on the chair set between the two beds. 'I've come for another chat.'

'I didn't think you was here to hold me hand.'

'I will if you like.'

Adams was not amused.

'I want to go over one or two things again.'

'I've been over 'em already enough times to fill a book.'

'Let's call this the second volume.' The DC took a note-book from his pocket and asked a series of questions which Adams answered bad-temperedly. No one had ever asked him anything about his taking the beer to the vaults; he hadn't seen anything wrong in doing as he'd been asked; it wasn't any of his business if it was dead against the vaults' rules; he'd paid for the beer and put the money in the till and if anyone tried to say different, in particular the landlord, he was a bloody liar; of course he'd got a bit extra from the guard for delivering the beer—he wasn't Santa Claus; he hadn't noticed anyone in particular in the bar on Wednesday night, but there were always some faces he didn't know; he hadn't noticed the car following him—if he had, wouldn't he have done something about it? he'd been too browned-off at being ordered back to the pub to take much of a butcher's at any of the men in the car; they'd called him by his nickname and they'd said Bert wanted him back at the pub and it hadn't begun to occur to him that they were bleeding crooks who'd cosh him silly and leave him with a screaming headache enough to send a man crazy . . .

'What happened once you were in the car?'

'They knocked me around, didn't they?'

'Did you lose consciousness immediately?'

'Soon enough to make no bloody difference.'

'Were you able to notice anything about any of the men before you finally did lose consciousness?'

'Haven't I just told you?'

'Look, we've got to try and identify them. People get identified by funny little things—a scar on a thumb, a bit of a stutter, a habit of wearing plimsolls . . . D'you notice anything about the way they were dressed?'

'No.'

'What about the way they moved? Was one of 'em left-handed?'

'I didn't get around to shaking hands with 'em, did I?'

'Did any of 'em speak with an accent?'

Adams groaned. He touched the right hand side of his head. 'I keep telling the nurses it feels like someone's driving a six-inch nail into me skull, but they won't give me anything strong to kill the pain.'

Showing considerable patience, the DC commiserated with him, then said: 'Did you hear them talk?'

'One of 'em said something.'

The DC gave no indication that this was the first time Adams had referred to the fact that he'd heard them speak. 'What kind of voice did he have?'

'What d'you expect, soprano?'

'A Cockney accent; or Liverpudlian or West Country?'

'They'd knocked me three-parts silly and it was like hearing something from the other end of a tunnel; he could've been speaking Russian for all I cared.'

'What did he say?'

'Gawd knows.'

'It could be very important so have a real try to remember.'

Adams groaned again, closed his eyes. After a while, he said: 'It was something to do with telling someone I was hurt and to make it sound natural 'cause then the guard wouldn't suspect nothing.'

The operations room had been set up in divisional HQ; a couple of desks, outside telephone lines, an internal line through to the civilian secretary who had been assigned to the unit, a computer terminal, and a battered metal filing cabinet.

Bell, who had been working at some papers, looked up at the DC who had just entered. 'Any joy?'

'Could be something, sir.'

Bell picked up a pipe from the desk and put it in his mouth, but did not light it; his wife kept on insisting that he must cut back on his smoking.

'Adams's story remains the same except on one point— now he remembers that he did hear one of the men in the car say something. One said that one of the others was to say that Red had hurt himself—Adams is certain that the nickname was used—and to make it sound natural and then the guard wouldn't suspect anything.'

Bell took the pipe from his mouth, reversed it, and rubbed the bowl against his cheek. 'That seems to cut out the possibility that Vinay fed them the news and then got taken out to make certain he never confessed.' He put the pipe down on the desk.

'I don't suppose there's anything more to be got out of Adams, but might it be an idea to have another session with him tomorrow?' suggested the DC, remembering the sister in the ward.

Bell nodded. The DC left. Bell picked up the pipe and fiddled with it. If Vinay had not been the informer, then Fifield, Thorpe, Nithsdale, or Mrs Johnson had been. Almost certainly, one of the indirect consequences of the successful raid would be that the business would be forced to close—would Fifield have cooperated with the villains, knowing this? Whichever way one looked at Mrs Johansen, she made an unlikely suspect. Discreet inquiries had already established that she led the quiet, humdrum life to be expected of a quiet, humdrum woman, her only extravagance—admittedly a mind-stretching one—the ballet lessons. Nithsdale was an ex-policeman and Bell always held, until forced to accept otherwise, that once a policeman, always one. Added to which, Nithsdale was not a man of initiative. Which left Thorpe. An intelligent, ambitious man, working to enter a profession that was notorious for demanding heavy financial backing at the beginning . . .

On Monday morning, Mrs Harbuckle knocked on the door of Thorpe's bedroom. 'Two policemen to see you,' she said in tones of disapproval. Police visits were not respectable.

'I suppose it's to do with the robbery at the vaults.'

She sniffed, before leaving.

They were in the sitting-room. Bell shook hands with his usual quiet courtesy, Fuller merely nodded and although his manner was not antagonistic, neither was it friendly, as it had been before.

As soon as they were seated, Bell said: 'It's kind of you to break into your off-time to have a word with us.'

'Did I have an option?' he asked lightly.

Bell smiled. 'In a private house, we have fewer powers than a VAT snooper. But you must know the law on that much better than I do.'

'That's quite an assumption.'

'As a serving policeman, it always helps my morale to assume that lawyers and judges have a better knowledge of the law than I do.'

'Paul Fifield doesn't accept such an assumption.'

'Once you're retired, you can afford to discard those which are purely anodynes.'

Thorpe relaxed as he decided that he'd read far more into Friday's interview than there had been to read.

'I thought we'd clear up a few loose ends, Mr Thorpe . . . I think I should start by explaining that it now seems certain the villains had inside information. Do you know what I mean by that?'

Abruptly the tension was back. 'Of course.'

'They knew that Vinay would be on duty on Wednesday night, that he'd be on his own, and that he was in the habit of having beer delivered to him. On top of that, they had a very clear picture of the full security system and knew that if they could gain entry without an alarm being given, they'd have the rest of the night in which to rifle the strong-boxes. The only thing they didn't know was what were the contents of the boxes. Do the staff know that?'

'No.'

'There's no way, for instance, in which you could tell which boxes contained money or jewellery?'

'Sometimes we learn what a customer's depositing—they can get extraordinarily chatty—but normally we don't and often they take every possible precaution to make certain we don't get an inkling.'

'That's clear enough . . . Our immediate job is to identify the informer. Did you pass on details of the security system to anyone?'

'I am not a criminal.'

'As to that, it's not unusual to meet an informer who is shocked by any suggestion that he's a criminal.'

'I haven't passed on information to anyone.'

'When we had our previous chat, you told me that Mr

Fifield suggested you asked someone to do your night duty on Wednesday, but didn't specify which of them. Why did you choose Vinay?'

'As I told you then, because Mike had done the previous relief at the weekend.'

'Does Nithsdale go in for drinking beer on night duty?'

'As far as I know, no.'

'But you were aware that Vinay did?'

'I also answered that question before.'

'I'm afraid we sometimes have to ask the same ones over and over again.'

'Why? To see if the answers change?'

'Are you likely to change yours?'

'No.'

'You have a good memory?'

'I'm telling the truth.'

'That's reassuring.' He brought out his pipe and fiddled with it. 'When were you asked to the birthday party?'

'Roughly ten days beforehand.'

Bell said, in the vague tones of someone whose mind was ranging beyond his words: 'Plenty of time in which to organize the job after receiving the information . . .'

Thorpe roughly interrupted him. 'I didn't pass on any information to anyone.'

'Someone did.'

There was a silence.

'If it wasn't you, who do you imagine it was?' Bell asked.

'I haven't the slightest idea.'

Bell looked at Fuller. 'Have you anything to ask Mr Thorpe?'

'No, sir.'

'Then that's about it. Except . . .' He half turned and faced Thorpe once more. 'If, as you assure us is the case, you've not been guilty of passing on information about the security system of the vaults, I imagine you'll be willing to help us find out who has?'

'Yes.'

'Even if that means forgoing a little of your privacy?'

'I've been forced to do that already.'

'We've tried to be as discreet as we can be,' said Bell comfortingly. 'What we'd like to know now is whether you have a bank account and if so with whom and where?'

'The local branch of the National Westminster.'

'Outside of your bank, do you have any form of savings account?'

'Were I so lucky! This job doesn't pay on a par with merchant banking.'

'Not many do . . . Will you give us written authority to be shown the details of your accounts?'

'Why d'you want that?'

'In a case like this, the informant is usually paid for his information. The odd thing about money is how difficult it can be to hide it. So we'd just like to look through your accounts to confirm that no large sums have recently been paid into them while your normal withdrawals have continued.'

Thorpe spoke bitterly. 'If it'll help convince you I wasn't bribed and didn't have anything to do with the death of Dick, I'll give you the authorization.'

Thorpe, knowing that Mrs Harbuckle had no scruples about eavesdropping, left the house and walked down to the tube station and a call-box. He dialled the vaults. Trudy answered the call. 'It's Jim—can I have a word with Paul?'

'He's on the other line at the moment.'

'I'll hang on. How are things?'

'Rather troubled,' she said, in her careful manner. 'People keep demanding to know when they'll be compensated for their losses.'

'Has anyone worked out the total value of what's been stolen?'

'It's very difficult to be certain yet, but it does seem it

wasn't as much as we first thought. It's quite surprising how many boxes contained valuables that were discarded.'

'Are many people threatening to quit?'

'Quite a few, I'm afraid. Of course, they're all a bit angry at the moment and it doesn't mean they actually will when the time comes, but . . . Well, rather a lot of them are saying they will.'

'It couldn't have happened at a worse time.'

'No, it certainly couldn't . . . Mr Fifield's just finished on the other line, so I'm putting you through.'

He said to Fifield: 'I've just had the police along at my place asking more questions. They're convinced that one of us sold the security details to the gang.'

'I know.'

'It's bloody ridiculous.'

'I hope so.'

'You only hope so?'

'The mob knew about Dick and the beer.'

'They could have learned that at the pub from the man who always took it along to him.'

'They were certain Dick would be on his own and that once he was taken out they were safe.'

'For God's sake, you're talking like the police.'

'Is that so surprising?'

'It is surprising you don't seem to think it's all stupid.'

Fifield said nothing.

'They've demanded written permission to check my bank accounts to see if there's any unexplainable money in them.'

'That's normal routine.'

'Have they been on to you.'

'Not yet. But they will.'

'You don't sound very disturbed.'

'I told you, it's just routine. Check everything and everyone, eliminate, find out what's left.'

'Surely to God they've learned to judge whether or not a man's crooked?'

'If a policeman could ever learn to do that accurately, life would be a lot easier.'

'Their suspicions made me want to . . .'

'It's no good getting uptight, Jim. It'll all sort itself out in the end.'

He couldn't accept suspicion with such philosophical calm. He knew a bitter anger that anyone could seriously believe that he could ever be a party to theft and murder.

CHAPTER 8

The uniform PC turned into Arcadia Avenue. Not for the first time, he reflected that few roads could ever have been so inappropriately named. To the left was one section of the local comprehensive school and it was an unusual week when the several buildings did not suffer a case of vandalism, on the right was a small, disused factory whose every window within a stone's throw of the road was broken, while beyond on either side were terrace houses, huddling together in mutual misery. Only the number and quality of cars parked in the road suggested that the overall picture was not one of financial poverty, rather of a deprivation of soul.

When level with the school playground, he noticed the green light van, a Ford, which had been parked in the same place the night before; exactly the same place, he realized, when he saw the newspaper wrapped against its near-side back wheel. He came to a stop and peered into the cab. Nothing unusual there. A metal bulkhead and lack of rear windows prevented his seeing into the cargo compartment.

He walked round until he could check the licence. It was in date. The registration number, the present year's, was not a London one and, he seemed to remember, was from somewhere up north. Although there was nothing inherently suspicious about a newish van, registered outside London, being parked for two days in Arcadia Avenue, he had a hunch that there was something wrong about it. He used his pocket transceiver to ask the duty sergeant at the station to check out the registration. A couple of minutes later the duty sergeant told him that the van had been stolen from Manchester over the weekend and that a car from Vehicles was on its way.

A battered Metro which had obviously had a very hard life turned into the road and drew up alongside the van. The PC in the passenger seat climbed out. 'Couldn't you have waited, Mac? We'd just gone down to the canteen.'

'What's on the menu?'

'Bangers.'

'Not again?'

'Haven't you heard? The local factory had a whole load go wrong and couldn't sell 'em to the great British public, so our canteen got 'em cheap.' The speaker produced a large bunch of keys and tried them one after the other in the lock of the driving door. The lock turned. He slid open the door. 'OK, Fred, bring over the sheet and wheel clamp.'

'Fetch 'em yourself.'

'Pardon me for presuming.' The PC went round to the back of the van and used the same key to unlock the rear doors. The interior stank and he began to swallow quickly. On the floor, several sacks were draped over an ungainly shape and when he pulled some of these back he was faced by a body, drawn up in a foetal position.

The assistant bank manager read the handwritten note twice. 'It seems to be in order.'

'It is in order,' said Fuller impatiently.

The assistant bank manager, a man with little sense of humour as befitted someone determined to scale the heights of his career, said primly: 'In a matter like this, one has to check very carefully.' He stood, looked round the small office as if to make certain that nothing confidential was lying about; left. When he returned, he carried a file. 'Yes, well I'm satisfied that the signature on this letter matches the one on our files and so I have with me the details of Mr Thorpe's account.' He set the folder on the desk and opened it, took out several statements and handed two to Fuller, then sat.

Fuller studied the figures. Very much like his own, he thought. Only one step ahead of a nasty letter from the bank manager. No sign of sudden wealth, no sign of any cutback on spending. 'You'll keep these handy if we need another look at them?'

'They will naturally be on file.'

'And he's no other account with you?'

'None.'

'What about a trace on unclaimed credits covering the last three months?'

'Is that really necessary, sergeant? Any money paid in to his name would certainly appear in his account and . . .'

'We need to eliminate the possibility that he's tucked a reasonably large sum out of sight.'

'I've only met Mr Thorpe once, but I remember that I gained the definite impression that he was not that kind of a person.'

'I reckon we all are, given the chance.'

The assistant manager pursed his lips in strong disapproval of so slanderous a suggestion before he used the internal telephone to ask someone to check the frozen credit account. Inevitably, since money could be paid into an account without reference to, or the authority of, the holder of that account (and normally even without a check at the time that such an account existed) every bank received credits wrongly catalogued; these sums were put into a frozen credit account where they waited until inquiries by indignant customers identified them, whereupon they would be transferred to where they should have gone in the first place (without interest, of course).

They spoke in a desultory manner—two men with so little in common that in four minutes they found not one subject of mutual interest—until a clerk entered with a complete tear-off sheet. 'These are in our account at the moment.'

The assistant manager read the figures. 'We're holding a total of nine hundred and seventy pounds, fifty-six p. at the moment.'

'What's the highest single sum?'

'Two hundred and seven pounds.'

The clerk said: 'We think we've traced that; we're just awaiting confirmation.'

'Then you've nothing for me,' said Fuller.

He returned to the station and from there telephoned each of the local branches of the other banks, asking them to find out whether in the past two months there had been a fair-sized sum deposited which had ended up in the frozen credit account. Forty-five minutes later the branch accountant in the Midland Bank told him that the sum of one thousand five hundred pounds, paid in in cash, had been lying in their frozen credit account for the past ten days; the paying-in slip had listed the name of J.A. Turner.

Fuller found Bell about to leave the operations room.

'What are Thorpe's christian names?' Bell asked.

'James Angus.'

'The same initials. So that's probably the pay-off, tucked away until the heat's off.'

'Fifteen hundred quid—the price of a man's life,' said Fuller angrily.

'It's not much for a job of this size, is it?'

'He's an amateur.'

'I suppose. All right. Go ahead and see if you can prove he deposited the money.'

The van was driven into the vehicle bay at the nearest police station and the body was examined *in situ* by the police surgeon. He stepped out of the van. 'From the look of things, tortured and then murdered by garotting,' he said in his clipped manner of speaking as he stripped off the gloves he'd been wearing.

'Tortured?' said the detective-inspector, momentarily startled.

'Barbarically . . . Signs of mortification are beginning to set in, so when you contact whoever will be coming out to do the full examination you'd better stress that the sooner the better. And you can add that I've done no more than make a superficial examination so everything's been left intact . . . Have you any idea who he was?'

'Not yet. But ten to one's he's got form so as soon as we can take his dabs, we'll find out.'

Fuller and one of the local DC's arrived at Ponds End Road at six-ten that evening and spoke to Thorpe in the dimly lit hall. Thorpe looked at his watch. 'I'll have to start off to work very soon.'

'Ring up and tell 'em you may be delayed,' said Fuller.

Thorpe resented the way in which that had been said. 'Why should I be delayed?'

'Because we're making further inquiries.'

It was, he decided, ridiculous to let himself become too annoyed over the other's manner. 'How long do you expect your inquiries to take?'

Fuller shrugged his shoulders. 'No saying, is there?'

All right, thought Thorpe, however long it took, he'd convince them once and for all that their suspicions were ridiculous. He crossed the hall to the telephone, spoke to Fifield and explained what was happening. He replaced the receiver.

'Where's your bedroom?' asked Fuller. 'Up these stairs?'

'Why d'you want to know?'

'We want a butcher's at it.' Fuller crossed to the stairs and climbed them, followed by the DC, a morose man.

When he reached the landing, Thorpe attempted to regain a measure of authority. 'Why d'you want to see my bedroom?'

'To search it.'

'Like hell you do. You've no right . . .'

'The lawyer speaking!'

'I know enough law to be certain you can't search anywhere without my permission or a warrant.'

'That's right.'

'Then where's the warrant?'

'I'm looking to you to give us permission to go ahead.'

'Keep looking.'

'Did you sell the details of the security system to the mob who murdered Vinay?'

'I did not.'

'Then you can't be in possession of incriminating evidence, can you?'

'Well?'

'Then why object to us searching your bedroom when all the search can do is establish your innocence?'

'You want me to establish my innocence rather than that you have to establish my guilt?'

'Maybe you've not got as far in criminal law as I've been thinking. The police don't establish guilt, they only establish the facts; these are presented to the court and it's them who establish guilt—or, in the odd case, innocence.'

He wanted to hurl the mockery back at Fuller.

'We can always apply for a search warrant, but initially we try to work discreetly.'

If he forced them to apply for a warrant, they'd then carry out the search with the maximum degree of publicity. Mrs Harbuckle's sense of respectability would be outraged.

'So do we have your permission?'

The law books made it all so clear cut, with rights and duties exactly determined. The detective-sergeant had just proved that in practice rights could be rolled up and duties could be sidetracked . . .' Yes,' he replied bitterly.

He watched them search his bedroom. The bed was stripped and the mattress and base examined, then the bed was carefully remade. The drawer of the bedside table was emptied, the packet of aspirins opened, the back of the old pocket watch swung back after he'd explained how the catch worked. All the clothes in the rickety cupboard were lifted out and the pockets checked. The toes of the shoes were examined. Each drawer of the bow-fronted chest-of-drawers was put on the wicker-bottomed chair, emptied, and then repacked. The papers in the desk, the law books, and the few paperback novels, were examined page-by-page.

'Are you satisfied?' Thorpe asked sarcastically.

'There's just one more thing.' Fuller produced an envelope and from this brought out a form which he put on the desk. 'Fill this in as if you were paying in a thousand quid's worth of fifties and five hundred of twenties; the date is the fifteenth of this month; name of account is J.A. Turner and name of person paying in is the initials K.C.G.'

Thorpe went over to the desk and saw that the form was a paying-in slip, of the kind to be found on bank counters for general use and not personalized for a customer . . . 'What's this about?'

'On the fifteenth, someone at the local Midland branch paid fifteen hundred in cash into the account of J.A. Turner. There's no J.A. Turner banks there. Paying into a non-existent account is a handy way of losing money.'

'I still don't see why you want me to fill this slip in.'

'You're not very quick, are you? . . . We're going to check your handwriting with the paying-in slip that was used to deposit the money.'

'You . . . you reckon I paid in that money?'

'Now you're there.'

'Where would I get fifteen hundred pounds from?'

'The mob who murdered Vinay.'

'You're sick.'

'Sick of people who murder ex-cops,' snapped Fuller and there was a hard, ugly expression on his normally cheerful face.

It was no good arguing with them right now, Thorpe thought. Their absurd, twisted suspicions were stronger than logic. He sat at the desk and filled in the slip. Fuller took it and returned it to the envelope.

When Thorpe finally reached the vaults, Fifield made his angry annoyance obvious.

'I'm sorry, Paul,' Thorpe said, 'but the police didn't leave my place until after eight.'

'You told 'em you had to relieve me?'

'Several times. It didn't make any difference.'

'Selfish bastards! . . . What was the trouble?'

'They searched my bedroom.'

'D'you find out what they were after?'

'A paying-in slip, made out in a false name. They said that sometimes someone wanting to hide money safely will pay it into a fictional account . . .'

'Yeah, I know the drill. What name was on the slip?'

'J.A. Turner. And there's no way anyone's going to be able to tie in that name with me.'

'Then you haven't realized . . .' He stopped.

'Realized what?'

'The initials are the same as yours.'

'No, I hadn't. But so what?'

'People taking up false identities very often use the same initials. It makes it easier to remember their new identity and explains away things like initialled cigarette cases. What was the name of the payer-in?'

'There were only initials—K.C.G.'

'Could they have any direct connection with you?'

'Not in a thousand years.'

'You are quite certain? The police will be checking the initials of all your friends and relations.'

'They can check from now until the Bomb goes off . . .'
He stopped.

'You've thought of someone?'

'My . . . my mother's maiden name was Grantham and
her initials were K.C. . . . It's a pure coincidence. There
must be thousands of K.C.G's in the country.'

'Who are directly connected with a J.A.T.?'

'Paul, you're making it seem . . . You sound as if you
could believe they might be right.'

Fifield stood.

'For God's sake, you've known me long enough to be
certain I couldn't have sold that information.'

He went round his desk and over to the stand; he lifted
off his mackintosh. He crossed to the door.

'Well?'

'Do the door, will you? I'm in a hurry to get home.'

'What you're really saying is, you're beginning to think
like the police . . . What is it? Once a policeman, always a
policeman, and a police mind gets so sandblasted it can't,
or won't, see a person as he really is?'

'Would you open this door.'

'What's your guiding motto? A man's guilty until he's
proved himself innocent?' He went to the larger desk and
pressed the button to activate the door.

Half a minute later he watched Fifield walk up the road.
It was conventional wisdom to hold that in Britain justice
was just. Occasionally, one read of a policeman who'd
pursued a case too vigorously by helping the evidence along,
but it was always obvious that he'd only done that because
he could be quite certain of the accused's guilt. But here the
police were pursuing him without any justification, intent
on proving him guilty in the face of his innocence. He was
frightened. When there was no justice, there was nothing.

CHAPTER 9

The mortuary had been built six years before and in its tiled asepticism it resembled an operating theatre. Against the walls, fixed or free standing, were working surfaces, a double sink, a glass-fronted cabinet which contained instruments, a solid-fronted cabinet in which were containers of different sizes for storing specimens, a sterilizing unit, a refrigerator, and a plastic-lined disposal bin. In the centre was a table on a stand which could be tilted in any direction.

Detective-Inspector Simmonds tried to block out the sights, sounds, and smells by thinking of last year's summer holiday in the Algarve. He failed. He wished he could summon up the phlegmatic indifference of the coroner's officer, a PC who was so obviously unaffected by what was going on. An old sweat had told him after his first post mortem, when nausea had threatened to overwhelm him, that after a while he'd think no more about it than seeing a butcher saw off a pork chop; the old sweat had been quite wrong and additionally it had been years before he had again been able to eat a pork chop with any pleasure.

'That's it, then,' said the pathologist, a plump, cheerful, extrovert who'd chuckled heartily when, one afternoon, he'd overheard himself referred to as Old Breakbones. He walked over to the disposal bin which his assistant was keeping open by using the foot-pedal, stripped off the gloves and dropped them into the bin. He took off his green apron and this was bundled into a large plastic bag for laundering. He crossed to the double sink, his wellington boots clopping on the tiled floor which sloped towards a drainage hole, and washed his hands with antiseptic soap. His assistant handed him a towel as Simmonds came over. 'Crushed fingers and toes, torn-off nails, burns to the face, neck, feet, and genitals,

three broken ribs, overall bruising, and marks around the
top of his head which suggest that a length of knotted cord
was slowly tightened, a form of torture well known in Tudor
times which, as far as I can remember, was known as the
angel's haircut. Death was finally caused by garrotting.'

As a recital of facts, thought Simmonds, it was horrifying;
as the framework on which to hang a vicariously active
imagination . . . 'Can we take his dabs now?'

'He's all yours. When you've finished, tell my assistant
he can tidy up.'

Unfortunately, Simmonds knew exactly what was meant
by tidying up. He turned to the detective-sergeant who'd
been standing by the near wall, patiently waiting. 'OK,
Stan, you can get cracking.'

He went over to one of the working surfaces on which the
dead man's clothes had been laid out and searched through
them. He found the key in the left-hand inside pocket of the
good quality Harris tweed jacket.

Bell, telephone resting on his shoulder, stared out of the
window at the van which had just drawn into the courtyard
below; a man climbed out of the cab, went round to the
back and opened the door and let out an Alsatian. At a
word of command, the dog sat and waited. Bell thought that
dogs were often to be preferred to humans and wished he'd
gone into the dog section.

'Sorry to keep you waiting,' said the DI on the other end
of the line, 'but I had the old man on the other blower,
shouting his head off . . . As I began saying, we identified
the dead man half an hour ago; Vernon Watson, more
usually known as Prof Watson or just The Prof. Does the
name say anything to you?'

Bell searched his memory. 'No.'

'Quite a good background, well schooled, but a weak
character. Fiddled the petty cash of the first firm he worked
for and never looked back. One conviction for fraud and

three for housebreaking; last out of stir just over three years ago. Turned into a bit of a specialist on large country houses and had quite a run of luck; should have been done for several jobs, but never quite enough hard evidence to land him . . . Now, the reason I'm on to you is that his clothes contained a key bearing the name of Fifield Vaults. Thought you'd be interested.'

'I am. What's the number?'

'One five six.'

Bell wrote down the figures. 'And you said you've no idea why he was tortured and then murdered?'

'Nothing direct, no. But as soon as I found that key, I naturally began wondering whether he's somehow tied in with your job.'

The door rolled open and Fuller stepped into the main vault which held the strong-boxes. Behind him, the door slid shut. Like being locked inside, he thought. He walked along the right-hand side to box 156. The records said that the box was hired by a man called Wilkins and that he'd been one of the first to turn up after the robbery to check whether his box had been broken into. It had been. When asked what he'd lost, he'd said some papers of purely personal import-ance. Now that they presumably knew his true identity, they could postulate the fact that the box had contained cash and/or jewellery from some of his thefts and he'd dared not report their loss . . . But then why had he been tortured after the robbery?

Fuller unlocked the door with the key found in Watson's coat and examined the interior with meticulous care. He found, in the far bottom right-hand corner where it had been squeezed by the wire-mesh container, a short length of wool coloured navy blue.

Thorpe sat on the ege of the smaller desk in the office. 'When I rang Trudy at lunch-time to check that Mike can do the weekend nights, she told me the police have been here again. What was it this time?'

'They found the key of box one-five-six on the body of a man who's been murdered,' Fifield answered. 'The detective-sergeant wanted to look inside it.'

'God Almighty! what the hell's going on?'

'Your guess is as good as mine.'

'It can't be. You were a policeman. They'll have talked to you.'

'They're not going to be loose-lipped in the circumstances, are they?'

'What circumstances?'

'That someone here passed on the information on the security system.'

'That's what they keep saying, but they've got to be wrong.'

'Have they?'

'I know it wasn't me, you were hardly going to do something that would result in the business being hit for six, Dick wasn't going to commit suicide, Mike's far too genuine, and anyone who names Trudy needs to see a psychiatrist.'

Fifield checked that the papers on top of his desk were of no consequence and then stood. He crossed to the stand and lifted off his mackintosh.

'You're not believing me, are you?' said Thorpe, his voice belligerent because of his fear.

'Right now, it's not up to me to believe or disbelieve you.'

'Not as a friend?'

'This sort of question isn't for friendship.'

'D'you know what you're saying now?'

Fifield didn't answer.

'You're saying I'm a liar.'

Fifield walked over to the door.'

'If you're so convinced, why don't you sack me?'

'The police have asked me to make certain that for the

moment nothing is altered. Now, will you please open the door.'

Thorpe watched him leave. According to the textbooks, circumstantial evidence was good because although witnesses could lie, circumstances couldn't. Couldn't they?

Mrs Harbuckle hammered on the door of Thorpe's bedroom. 'Are you awake?'

He rolled over, opened his eyes, and looked at the bedside digital alarm clock. The alarm was set to go off in fifteen minutes' time; he resented losing those fifteen minutes of sleep.

'There's two more detectives to see you.' Her disapproval made her sound as if she were sucking a slice of lemon.

Why were they crowding him like this? What value the image of the British policeman as being scrupulously fair? Or was that image only for the minds of those who'd never had to come into close contact with them . . . ?

Detective-Inspector Cartwright was in the sitting-room, together with a uniform PC whom he did not bother to introduce. 'Sorry to have to wake you up.' His hair was as unruly as ever and in a broad-check sports jacket he looked far more like a farmer in town for the day than a detective. 'I need to know if you ever have occasion to go into the room in the vaults in which the strong-boxes are?'

'Normally, no. The only time I might is if someone has trouble in opening or closing a box.'

'When you'd help?'

'I'd do what I could, but if it's a question of locks, I call in someone from the firm of specialist locksmiths we use.'

'Are there spare keys in the office for all the boxes?'

'No.'

'Have you had occasion in the past month to help anyone with a box?'

'No.'

'Over the past month you have not put anything into a box, or taken anything out of one?'

'I haven't been in the box-room for well over a month.'

'Do you possess a navy blue woollen sweater?'

'Yes.'

'I'd like to see it, please.'

'Why?'

'A small length of navy blue wool was found at the back of box one-five-six. We want to establish where it probably came from.'

'One-five-six . . . That's the box for which the key was found on a murdered man's body?'

'That's right.'

'I haven't been near that or any other box.'

'May we see the sweater, please?'

'Just tell me one thing. If my name were Jehovah, would you try to believe me?'

'It would depend on the circumstances . . . Have you any objection to showing us your navy blue sweater?'

'I object to being treated like a criminal.'

'Criminals, Mr Thorpe, are told, not asked.'

'Which are you doing?'

There was no answer. Thorpe turned towards the door.

'Phelps will go upstairs with you.'

'I am just capable of managing on my own.'

'We wouldn't want you to overlook anything.'

As he began to climb the stairs, Thorpe saw Mrs Harbuckle in the doorway of the kitchen. Her expression was sour and angry. Much more of this and she'd tell him to leave. She liked the extra money of his rent, and at times his company, but she liked her respectability more.

On Saturday afternoon Fuller found Bell down in the courtyard by his car, enjoying a moment's pause in the sunshine. 'I've just had the DI in the Watson case on the blower.'

Bell, with a gesture of tiredness, rubbed his forehead with the back of his hand; the sunshine glinted on a few hairs on the side of his cheek which his electric razor had missed over several days.

'They've been picking up smoke signals. After the raid on Fifield Vaults, Watson was shouting that he'd lost his pension.'

'Pension?'

'That's the word. And there's something more. The mob who tortured and murdered him was the same mob who did the vaults job.'

'That doesn't make sense.'

'That's what I said to the DI.'

'What was his reply?'

'It was our worry, not his.'

Bell put his hands in his pockets and jingled some coins. '"Pension" would be a new way of describing loot nicked from the houses he'd been screwing . . .' He stopped jingling the coins. 'We'll accept it was the same mob. Then the fact they tortured Watson before they killed him must mean they needed to know what he was shouting about because they'd not found any "pension" in box one-five-six. But Watson lost the contents or he wouldn't have been shouting. Where's whatever was in it vanished to?'

Fuller, not known for a sense of tact, said: 'Are you forgetting the wool?'

'No.'

'We haven't had confirmation yet, but I'll give you a hundred to one it came off Thorpe's sweater.'

'We seem to be moving into uncharted waters,' Bell said.

Thorpe dialled Melthorpe Avenue and Susan answered the call. 'I've had an idea that puts me straight up into the Mensa class. Instead of my coming round to your place, why don't you and Paul have dinner with me tonight? There's a—'

'I was going to ring you,' she cut in. 'I'm sorry, but I can't see you tonight.'

'But we'd arranged ... All right, then let's make it tomorrow instead. Quite a few places are open on a Sunday evening, particularly if one likes Pakistani or Chinese food —and you do, don't you?'

'I'm returning home tomorrow.'

'Then I'll just have to make the supreme sacrifice and get up early and we'll have lunch ...'

'No.'

'Why not?'

'I'm too busy.'

'How d'you know now that you'll be too busy tomorrow?'

'Why can't you realize ... Just leave it, will you?'

'Exactly what is it that I've got to leave?'

'Arguing. I'm too busy.'

'Not for you the conventional previous engagement? ... What's really the trouble? Has Paul been telling you that the police can't get it out of their heads that I might be the traitor?'

She didn't answer.

'You're not going to tell me that you believe there could be some truth in that?'

'No.'

'But Paul does?'

'He's had a rough time of things.'

'Recently, my life hasn't been a bed of roses.'

'You haven't put all you possess into a busines which is on the point of collapse.'

'But I have had a succession of thick-headed policemen make it all too clear that they reckon I'm the traitor ... Let's go out together. I'm sure I can persuade Paul how ridiculous he's being ...'

'You just don't understand.'

'Don't I?'

'Father just wouldn't go out with you, to anywhere. Because he was in the police, they've told him some of what's going on. You can't blame him when they make it seem so certain . . .'

'I can blame him on the grounds of friendship.'

'You know he often says that a policeman can't afford friends.'

'Can't or won't?'

'If you're going to be like that . . .'

'How else d'you expect me to be? Delighted? . . . Look, I'm sorry if I seem to do nothing but snap at you, but it's getting me down. Be an angel and change your mind, qualify for a good Samaritan, first class, and come out and cheer me up.'

'I'm sorry, but that'll make things impossible with Father. Goodbye.'

He stared through the side of the call-box. She was obviously in the middle of an emotional tug-of-war, but even so he would have hoped she could have shown him more open sympathy. All right, Paul as an ex-policeman was automatically accepting the police's interpretation of events, had become convinced that he was the traitor, but she knew him well enough to be absolutely certain that he could never, ever, in any circumstances, be a party to theft or murder . . . But now it was he who was being unfair through making wrong judgements on an emotional level. Convinced of his innocence as she must be, she could hardly say so over the telephone if her father were within earshot because that would be to evoke a row over her divided loyalties. She'd write when she got back to Oxford and explain . . .

In the meantime, he was left with a lonely weekend, made bitter by events. He wondered how many of the passing people led, behind their masks, lives of ever-increasing bitterness? The fat woman, leading a Pekinese, the distinguished-looking man who almost tripped over the lead as the fat woman suddenly changed course, the young and attractive girl waiting with a growing uneasiness for her boyfriend to turn up, the short, thin man with a forgettable face who for no specific or immediately identifiable reason reminded him of his father, the couple, arms about waists, egotistically interested only in themselves . . .

CHAPTER 10

Although the Fifield Vaults murder was the most serious case under investigation, there were a number of others with which Bell had closely to concern himself and on Wednesday, July 4, he didn't reach divisional HQ until after midday. As he parked next to the divisional superintendent's Escort, he reminded himself that, catastrophes notwithstanding, he had on pain of matrimonial exile to be home by eight in order to take his wife to the Independence Day party some American friends were giving. It struck him as slightly ironic that they should be proposing to join in celebrating a time when the British had been given their marching orders, but he rationalized events with the comforting thought that a large proportion of the troops had been German mercenaries.

There were two reports on the desk in his office, one referring to the paying-in slip which Thorpe had filled in at the direction of Fuller, the other to the woollen threads found at the back of the strong-box. Bell read through the first one, after putting on his half-spectacles. The writing on the comparison slip showed a very close similarity with that on the control one, but there were also small but marked differences. Because the sample of writing was so limited and episodic (some of it consisted of single capital letters), it was impossible to give a worthwhile opinion on whether the slips had been filled in by two hands or whether the differences were no more than those frequently to be found in one person's writing.

Bell picked up the second note. The forensic laboratory's report, a précis of which had been phoned through for the sake of speed, was that the two woollen threads were very similar. He removed his spectacles and put them down on the desk, phoned the laboratory. 'Then you can say that they did come from the same sweater?'

'No, we can't go that far.'

'Why not?'

'Because we can't be any more specific than we have been in our report.'

'But if the threads are very similar . . .'

'Very similar, Superintendent, but not identical.'

Bell finally allowed his exasperation to surface. 'If one of you blokes ever wakes up in heaven, you'll demand further proof before you'll believe yourself dead.'

The man on the other end of the line seemed to regard that as a compliment.

Bell rang off. Two leads, he thought angrily, which weren't going to lead very far. He picked up a pencil and began to doodle. It was time to have Thorpe along to the station for questioning.

The interview room was square, painted in two shades of green, and it had a single window set high up and protected by bars; it was furnished with a table, six chairs, and a framed copy of the rights of persons being questioned.

Bell was pleasant, at times almost paternal, Fuller was at his sharpest.

'I know what the Superintendent said; he's a very cautious man.' Fuller spoke with careless criticism. 'But I also know what even the stupidest jury's going to say when they hear the scientific evidence.'

'I didn't open that strong-box,' Thorpe said yet again.

'Perhaps you're claiming the wool got there by magic?'

'I don't know how the hell it got there.'

'From off your sweater.'

'You said yourself that you can't prove for certain that it did.'

Fuller smiled sardonically. 'Never give up, do you? Never say to yourself, if I'd half an ounce of common sense I'd admit the obvious?'

Bell said quietly: 'Mr Thorpe, we're trying to establish exactly what happened. If there's an explanation that doesn't bear directly on recent events, if you went to that box for a reason totally unconnected with the robbery and murder, tell us what that reason was and we'll check it out and confirm you're correct. Then that'll put an end to it.'

'The only explanation is the one I keep giving and you refuse to accept. I've never opened that locker.'

'But the wool was inside it.'

'So you say.'

'I assure you it was. And it does seem it came from your sweater.'

'You can't prove that.'

'You've got to be certifiable to think it could have come from anywhere else,' said Fuller angrily. 'Are you certifiable?'

'I'm beginning to wonder . . . The whole thing's become Kafkaesque.'

'So what the hell's that supposed to mean?'

'An author,' said Bell, 'who mixed-up uncertainty and unreality with pea-souper fogs.'

Just for a moment Fuller looked nonplussed.

'Why did you say it's like Kafka?' asked Bell.

'Because I don't know a damn thing about what happened, I'm not even certain I understand what did happen, but from the beginning you've reckoned I'm guilty and have kept producing so-called evidence which has been twisted and slanted and I can't untwist or unslant it because all I know is the truth . . . And because you refuse to understand what kind of a person I am, which would tell you I couldn't have anything to do with robbery, far less murder . . . And because I'm caught up in a nightmare and the more I struggle to get out of it, the harder it presses down on me.'

'Quite a speech,' sneered Fuller.

'I'm innocent,' he shouted.

'Funny thing is, I've never met a villain who didn't claim that.'

'If you're innocent,' said Bell, 'why won't you help us?'

'What d'you think I've been trying to do?'

'Then now tell us the truth.'

'Oh, Christ, what is the truth?'

'The truth is what actually happened,' replied Fuller, completely missing the point of Thorpe's anguished cry.

When Thorpe arrived at the vaults, only Trudy was there. 'Mr Fifield was feeling so rotten with his asthma I suggested he went home early and I said I'd stay on until you arrived. I made him take a mini-cab back instead of the tube.'

'He seems to have been ill a lot recently.'

'It's no wonder . . . We've had six more cancellations today on boxes rented by the month.'

'How many in all have quit?'

'We're an awful long way under fifty per cent occupation now. I don't see how we can go on much longer, especially when the rent goes up. It's terrible for him.'

'It's not much fun for you.'

'But it's not as if I'd put all my money into the business.'

He wondered if she'd be able to find another job? She was intelligent and efficient, but there was so much unemployment and at her age intelligence and efficiency were often not enough.

'As my mother used to say, these things are only sent to try us.' She smiled wanly. 'Unfortunately, I've never understood why there should be any comfort in that fact.' She picked up her black handbag and checked something inside, closed it with a snap. 'Good night, Jim.'

Nothing in her manner suggested she'd heard the rumours concerning his guilt, but she was the kind of person who'd remain loyally friendly until the very last moment . . .

'Would you work the door, please.'

'Sorry, I was miles away.'

He watched her on the TV screen climb the steps to street
level, turn left, and walk along the pavement with a brisk
stride that was almost masculine in quality. Half way to the
corner she passed a man who was coming in the opposite
direction and because there was something about him which
seemed familiar, Thorpe switched his attention. After a
while, he began to think he must be mistaken. The man was
short, middle-aged, narrow-shouldered, dressed shabbily.
Mr Suburbia on his way home after a dusty day's work and
a couple of drinks at the pub. Then the face came into sharp
focus and the sense of *déjà vu* returned. A distant echo of his
father's face . . . The man he'd seen from the call-box after
he'd phoned Susan on Saturday.

He might still have accepted this second sighting as a
coincidence if the man had not suddenly noticed the TV
camera and immediately looked away, in sharp contrast to
the majority of people who stared at it with interest, some
even waving and making ridiculous faces. The man walked
on. A policeman? But he didn't look large enough ever to
have been recruited. If not a policeman, who in the hell
could he be?

By Saturday, Thorpe had forgotten all about the man,
having finally dismissed as ridiculous the possibility that
the other might have been keeping some sort of a watch on
him. He left Ponds End Road to walk to friends who lived
on the borders of West Ealing and half way there took a
short cut which was an alley that ran between the back
gardens of two rows of houses and normally saved five
minutes but which, he discovered on rounding the bend half
way along, had been dug up for the last two hundred yards
for repairs to a gas main. He visually checked whether it
would be possible to clamber over the stacked earth, decided
the risk of getting coated with the yellow clay was too great,

and turned back. As he rounded the bend, a man entered
the alley. The man saw him and came to an abrupt halt,
then turned and retraced his steps to go out of sight. Someone who'd realized from his own actions that the alley must
be impassable? Yet although the jumbled pattern of sunlight
and shadow had made it impossible to see the other's face
with any clarity, he had been reminded of that insignificant
little man ... He hurried to the end of the alley and
stepped out on to the pavement. The man was on his right,
approaching cross-roads. Thorpe called out and the man
increased his rate of walking. The normal reaction of a
meek, law-abiding citizen who was suddenly scared? Or the
reaction of a man who was anxious not to be cornered?
Thorpe began to run. At the sounds of his pounding feet,
the man looked back before himself starting to run and in
that brief moment Thorpe identified him.

The man turned right at the cross-roads and disappeared.
Beyond, Thorpe knew, there was a maze of roads, that
would make escape easy. He tried to run faster, telling
himself that he wasn't as out of condition as his body insisted
he was. As he came up to the cross-roads, there was
the sudden squeal of brakes which ended in the thump
of a collision and the harsh, ugly clatter of shattering
glass.

Two cars had collided, the one hitting the other broadside
on, and several feet from the point of collision a man lay
sprawled out on the road. Along the pavement to the right
of the accident a woman with a wheeled trolley had been
shocked motionless and well beyond her two boys were
beginning to run.

Thorpe reached the injured man and knelt by his side.
The unremarkable face was twisted with lines of growing
pain; his eyes were closed and he was groaning at a low,
unvarying pitch; a thin dribble of blood was starting to roll
down from his mouth; his coat had been flung open and the
right flap was folded back to reveal the breast pocket and

the leather wallet that was half-spilled out of it.

For Thorpe it was as if time suddenly stopped for the rest of the world but not for him. The two drivers, the woman, and the boys, stayed where they were, there was no other movement, yet he could carefully appreciate all that had happened, see the opportunity in front of him, gauge the advantages and dangers of accepting that opportunity . . . This man, half conscious at best, had been following him and the reason for this must be connected with the vault robbery and murder. He'd hoped to corner the man and persuade him to explain his actions because the answer might help to prove his innocence. But now the man was beyond explaining anything . . . That wallet, lying half out of the breast pocket. There might well be papers in that which would identify him, perhaps even go some way to explaining what and why? But how to find out? . . . Just for the moment, he was shielded from everyone else and could probably remove the wallet without being observed. Theft. Theft from an injured, perhaps dying, man. One of the most contemptible forms of theft . . .

Time slipped back into gear as he picked up the wallet and slipped it into his own breast pocket. Feet pounded up to where he knelt. 'Christ, how bad is he?' asked a hoarse, shaking voice. He looked up. The driver of the second car, middle-aged, overweight, was ashen-faced, his shock so great that even if he had actually seen the wallet pocketed there was every chance that his brain would not have recorded the fact. Thorpe said: 'Call an ambulance.'

Some vehicles were stopping, others were accelerating past, their drivers determined not to be caught up in the trouble. People, alerted by the sounds of the crash, had come out of nearby homes and were grouping round the injured man.

The driver of the second car had not moved, but was still staring down with shocked horror. 'Someone call an ambulance,' Thorpe called out.

'I will.' A man turned and sprinted back to his house, a hundred and fifty yards away.

'He ought to have a blanket over him,' said Thorpe.

'I've one in my car,' said a woman. A moment later he was handed a travelling rug which he spread out over the man.

The driver of the first car came up. 'I couldn't help it,' he said wildly. 'I swear I couldn't. He just came straight out in front of me.' He looked round at the watchers. 'Can't you understand? There wasn't anything I could do. It all happened too quickly. If I'd seen him . . . Oh my God! . . . Is he dying?'

'You need a hot drink,' said the woman who'd provided the travelling rug. 'Is there someone here who lives close enough to make this man a hot drink?' She spoke with the voice of authority; someone used to handling bewildered people.

A man called out that he was a doctor and he pushed his way through the crowd. He knelt and examined the injured man. A two-tone siren became audible and rapidly grew louder. The ambulance braked to a halt and three men, two carrying a stretcher, came through. A police car, siren sounding, blue light flashing, drew up. The observer came across, the driver set out emergency cones in a rough ellipse. The observer said: 'Does anyone know who he is?' He waited, then asked those who had witnessed the accident to stay and everyone else to move on. The driver of the first car hurried up to him and in a garbled voice, almost as if he had been drinking heavily, kept repeating that the accident hadn't been his fault and there'd been no way of avoiding the man. The observer calmed him down with a few brisk words, went over to the ambulance crew who were just about to lift up the stretcher. He checked the pockets of the injured man's coat. 'Nothing to say who he is. We'll have to identify him later.' The ambulance crew carried the man over to the ambulance.

The wallet in Thorpe's breast pocket felt as if it were filled with lead, weighing that side of him down so that his guilt must be obvious . . .

'You were quick on the scene, then?'

The observer's words cut through his fears. He waited to answer until the ambulance had driven away, siren sounding. 'I was just round the corner when the cars collided.' His voice sounded strained even to himself, but the observer seemed not to notice or, if he did, imagined it to be the result of shock, not panicky fear.

'So you didn't see what actually happened?'

'The first I saw of it was the man sprawled out on the road.'

'Can you say where the two drivers were?'

'One was still in the car, the other was climbing out on to the road.'

'Were any other vehicles around?'

'Not immediately, but there soon were. Some of them stopped, most of them kept going.'

'And what about people; who was nearby?'

'I saw a lady with a shopping-bag and two boys, but not anyone else.'

The observer looked at the people who waited on the pavement. 'Is the lady you're talking about over there?'

'Standing on the left, with that shopping trolley on wheels . . . And I think those are the two boys.'

'That's right. I've had a quick word with them already . . . So you came round the corner of the cross-roads after the accident had actually happened and then did what you could to help?'

'That's right.'

'I'll just have your name and address in case there's any need to get back on to you, but seeing you didn't witness the accident I don't suppose there will be.'

He gave his name and address and the observer wrote them down.

'Thanks for giving a hand, Mr Thorpe. It's not everyone willing to do that.' The observer turned away.

Thorpe wanted to run, to escape as quickly as possible, but he forced himself to walk calmly past the driver of the police car who'd persuaded an onlooker to help him take some measurements. He approached the cross-roads, dreading the call to return to face questions raised by the evidence of someone who'd seen him pocket the wallet . . . At the cross-roads, he turned right in the direction of his friends' house. As he passed out of sight of the police, he reached up with his left hand inside the coat and felt the wallet.

In his bedroom, he sat at the desk, took the wallet out of his pocket, and examined the contents. Twenty-three pounds in notes, one bank and two credit cards in the name of George M. Smith, a shopping list with three items crossed off, four small, folded sheets of paper, each with a heading and underneath a series of times, and several business cards bearing the name Harrison & Carmichael, Private Investigators.

He spread out the four sheets of paper. The headings consisted of two or more initials, written in pen in a careful, old-fashioned style that was nearly copperplate. The times were listed in three columns, in twenty-four-hour notation, and it needed little intelligence to appreciate that in every case the third set of figures was the difference between the other two on the same line. Smith presumably worked for a firm of private detectives so it would be necessary for him to keep a note of the hours he worked on each case in order that accurate accounts could be made up. Were these such notes? One way of checking was to find out if any of the times conflicted—although if Smith and his firm were less than honest and it was the habit to charge two clients for the same time, they might. None of the times conflicted. The initials, then, were those of the clients. For which client had he been working when he'd been knocked down? Under the heading of H & WH Ltd., there was an entry in the first column but none in the second or third—all the other entries were complete.

H & WH Ltd. A firm. How on earth was he going to identify them? And why should a firm be interested in the robbery and murder?

CHAPTER 11

When in the fifth form, Stewart Morley had been described by his housemaster as intelligent but lazy and lacking in ambition; which only confirmed the fact that the average housemaster was a very poor judge of character. By the time he was twenty-five, he had built up from scratch a business which was successful and which would, before long, make him a wealthy man.

Thorpe met him in his office in a renovated warehouse in West Croydon at eleven o'clock on Monday and for a while they talked generalities, catching up on the three years since they had last seen each other, then he said: 'I've come to ask you to do me a favour.'

Morley chuckled. 'And there was I thinking that the visit was solely in the name of old friendship!'

'I need to identify a firm from its initials. Since you told me last time that one of the jobs your firm does is compose lists of businesses of all sizes and types for mailing lists, I thought you might be able to help?'

'We probably can, always provided, of course, that the firm is on our tapes—we haven't yet attained blanket cover-age even if we are approaching it . . . Anyway, let's have the details. What are the initials?'

'H & WH Ltd.'

He wrote. 'And their line of business?'

'I don't know.'

'That always helps! What town's it in?'

'I've told you all I know.'

He looked up, his round face, owlish in design, showing his surprise. 'Are you asking for a blanket search?'

'If that's what you call it. But surely you have computers?'

'We have the best computing power that the bank's money could buy, but to programme the work you want would take hours. And I'd hate to scare you with the details of what every hour would cost. I'm sorry, Jim, I'd like to help, but . . .' He shrugged his shoulders.

'I can raise a bit of cash . . .'

'I'm afraid we'd have to talk about a lot.'

'Then that seems to be that,' said Thorpe dully.

Morley removed his glasses and polished them with a handkerchief. 'It sounds as if it could be important?'

'It is.'

'How important?'

'I'm trying to prove I had nothing to do with a theft and a murder.'

'Good God! Surely the police can judge you aren't that kind of a chap?'

'They don't recognize such distinctions.' He stood. 'Anyway, thanks for listening. And if I don't end up behind bars in the next couple of weeks, how about a lunch together?'

'Is it really that serious?'

'Yes.'

'And knowing the name of the firm might help?'

'It could make all the difference.'

'Then give me your telephone number and I'll get in touch when I've run the programme.'

Morley rang on Tuesday morning. 'It's Stew here, Jim. We've just finished.'

'With what result?' Thorpe asked, his voice strained.

'We've come up with three names, one in London, one in Cardiff, one in Inverness. I reckoned you'd like a bit of a run-down on them. Haysair and Waites Holdings are in the City and they are Sir Thomas Barnham's personal little baby. You'll know who he is?'

'The name seems to strike a bell.'

'He's big business and an MP and was recently in a rumpus in the House when he denied any connection with a local government official convicted of corruption. You'll find a lot of people in the business world who'll admit to being very sorry that he escaped any form of censure. But then nothing's so unpopular in the City as someone else's success ... He's a genuine financial wizard—or demon, depending on your viewpoint—fingers dabbling in dozens of streams, turning up where least expected, making strategic takeover bids, greenmailing, and generally keeping everyone on his toes because he's the hungriest shark in the whole of that shark-infested sea. Haysair is the holding company and stretching out from it is a maze of interlocking companies which probably leave the Inland Revenue boys puffing.

'Number two is Hewart and Wayne Hape and they're ships chandlers based in Cardiff. Originally they were concerned solely with commercial shipping, but they saw the light early on and realized before a lot of other people did that container ships and supertankers were drastically cutting the number of vessels at sea and they branched out into leisure boating. They're not big, but they're sound— the shareholders will be kept in bread and butter and a worthwhile spread of jam.

'Number three is something of a question-mark. Hyslop and Walter Hitchcock were formed seven years ago with the object of promoting tourism in the Highlands, but seem to have done very little about it. It's a private company with all the power in the family and I'm told they own a lot of land between Inverness and Cromdale. It seems they projected a tourist complex but failed to get planning permission. Could be they're sleeping on the idea and will wake up and have another try when they reckon the atmosphere's better.

'Those are the only three on our tapes. But don't forget that our files aren't complete yet. We might have no record as yet of the firm you're interested in.'

'I'll keep my fingers crossed that you haven't,' said Thorpe tightly.

'Good luck. And if I can help again, shout.'

Thorpe thanked him, said goodbye, replaced the receiver. He returned upstairs, sat at the desk, and looked down at the notes he'd just made. One financial expert, one small to medium-sized business, one moribund family firm. Had one of them hired Harrison & Carmichael to investigate him?

The natural thing to do from a geographical point of view was make what inquiries he could at the London company first, then try Cardiff, and lastly Inverness. It was difficult, though, to believe that a highly successful concern, run by a well-known and clever businessman and MP, could have any connection with a robbery and murder. But equally, why should a ships chandlers? Or a landowning family? . . . In the bleak light of logic, it looked as if he were on a wild goose chase. But one of the things his parents had taught him was that if one believed something was worth doing, one did it, whatever the obstacles or cost.

'Sir Thomas Barnham? There'll almost certainly be an entry in *Who's Who*,' said the librarian in the reference section of the public library. She scratched her chin. A woman of indeterminate age, but surely over forty-five, she was dressed in a puce twin set and a pleated skirt. 'Isn't he . . .' Her voice died away.

Thorpe, standing by the side of the desk, waited.

'I'm sure I've read . . .'

'He's an MP.'

'Then you'll find a reference in Grosse's Members of

Parliament. That's on the third shelf on the right. If the girls haven't . . .'

He didn't learn what it was the girls might have done. He went past the central table to the shelf she'd indicated and found the thick, leather and cloth-bound book. He sat, on the opposite side of the table to a girl in her teens who was researching some work.

Sir Thomas Barnham. Aged 56, married to Lady Ottway, only daughter of the 4th Earl Royslon. Two sons. Educated Casterham Primary school, The Roy Blagdon Grammar School. First elected to the House with a majority of 7,325 twelve years before for the constituency of Highwarm and Laydon, succeeding Mr Bernard Avory who had held the seat for the Conservatives for the previous twenty-two years. Recent boundary changes had altered the nature of the constituency and turned it into a marginal seat. Majority at last election, 1,221. Offered a position in the present government, but refused it on the grounds of pressure of business. Elected chairman of the New '82 Committee . . . An active backbencher. A thrusting speaker, always in command of his subject . . . Considered by his opponents to be intellectually arrogant and by some of his own party to lack a sense of tact . . . One of the new Conservatives, a man who by his own initiative and skill had worked his way from humble beginnings to position and wealth . . .

He replaced Grosse with *Who's Who*. The only additional information he gleaned from this was that Barnham listed his hobby as work. He'd always mistrusted people who claimed that.

The librarian tiptoed up to where he sat, an exercise spoiled by the fact that her right shoe squeaked. 'I knew I'd read . . .' She put a magazine on the table in front of him, squeaked her way back to her desk.

It was a months old copy of the *Sunday Telegraph* Magazine and in it was an article headed 'The Barnham and Barber Circus.' There were photographs of both Sir Thomas

Barnham and Phillip Barber. Barnham's was a studio study and he looked suave and strong, a builder of financial empires; perhaps by chance, Barber's photograph was a family snapshot which had been taken out of doors and with the sunlight slanting across his round, thickset face to make him look self-satisfied, evasive, and weak. Barber, until his conviction the chief executive of a large county council, had been arrested and charged with bribery and corruption. At his trial, evidence had been adduced of his systematic corrupting of other local government employees who were in a position to influence the granting of contracts and the issue of building permissions. Despite the overwhelming weight of the prosecution's case, it seemed that the verdict of guilty had come as a complete surprise to him and when he was asked if he had anything to say before sentence was passed he made a wild outburst in which he swore that there were any number of people who were in high positions who were just as guilty as he and why should he alone have to suffer. When asked to name those persons, he had refused. Inevitably, rumours had spread and one of the names frequently mentioned had been Sir Thomas Barnham whose career had begun in the property field in the North and therefore he could quite clearly have had direct contact with Barber. In the House, a member of the Opposition—in the name of public interest, naturally—had put a question which, by inference, suggested that Sir Thomas had, in fact, at the beginning of his career worked with the now discredited and jailed Barber. Sir Thomas had made a statement to the House. He had never had any dealings of any nature with Barber and to the best of his knowledge and belief he had never even met him. And if anyone repeated the monstrous allegation beyond the House, and hence beyond the bounds of absolute privilege, he would immediately institute proceedings for defamation of character. The House had accepted his assurances.

Thorpe stared into space. Sir Thomas Barnham had been

accused, by inference, of complicity with crime. Admittedly this connection dated back many years and there was no proof, only innuendo . . . But surely it had to be more than a coincidence that now one of the three firms which might have employed Harrison and Carmichael was run by him . . .

Eston House, a twelve-storey slab building of concrete and glass, was Philistine in concept and built to honour Mammon. The offices of Haysair & Waites Holdings were on the eleventh and twelfth floors; reception was on the eleventh.

An attractive but rather bored receptionist said: 'Do you have an appointment with Sir Thomas?'

'No, I don't,' replied Thorpe.

'Then he won't see you.'

'It is very important.'

'He never sees anyone without an appointment.'

'Then perhaps you'd have a word with his secretary?'

She hesitated, finally spoke over the telephone. 'Miss Ewing will be along in a minute.'

He sat on one of the luxuriously soft armchairs, picked up a glossy magazine on mining, and flipped through the pages of photographs of machines which he couldn't identify and statistics which for him were meaningless . . .

'Mr Smith?'

The thick pile carpet had deadened any sounds of her approach and her question startled him. Hurriedly he came to his feet. Her face was long and bony and both her nose and lips were too heavy so that she was misproportioned; a caricaturist could have caught her likeness with cruel accuracy with only half a dozen strokes of a pencil; sometimes an ugly person could be attractive, but her heavy features precluded this; only her large, soft brown eyes, as tender as a leveret's, held beauty and because they did they seemed not to belong.

'Mr Smith, Sir Thomas never sees anyone without an appointment.' Her voice was soft and musical. 'All I can suggest is that you write a letter explaining why you would like an appointment with him.'

'The matter is very important.'

'I'm sorry.'

Thorpe brought out his wallet and from it extracted one of George M. Smith's business cards. 'Would you show that to Sir Thomas and tell him I'd like a quick word.'

She studied the card when he'd handed it to her, looked quickly at him with curiosity, said: 'Will you please wait here and I'll see if I can speak to him.' She walked away, her movements graceful.

When she returned, she said: 'Sir Thomas can spare you a minute. Will you come with me, please.'

He followed her along a corridor and up a flight of stairs to the twelfth floor. They passed an office in which a dozen people worked, many of them with video screens on their desks, and came to a small square which was heavily carpeted; on two sides there were indoor plants, in elaborate glazed pots, and on the third side was a large tank of multi-coloured tropical fish. Three doors led off the square and the nearer one was open. Beyond the open door was her office, large, well furnished, on the far side of which was another door. She knocked on this, opened it and went out of sight for a moment, returned and motioned to him to enter.

Sir Thomas Barnham was several years older than he had been in the photograph; those years had added more self-assurance and power to what had already been a face of strength. Success had branded him.

'Thank you, Miss Ewing,' he said, by way of dismissal. He waited until she'd closed the door behind herself, then he said: 'Why exactly have you come here?'

'To ask you a question,' replied Thorpe.

'Which is?'

'Why have you instructed Harrison and Carmichael to have me followed?'

'You are not a member of that firm, as your card would suggest?'

'No.'

'Who are you, then?'

'My name is James Thorpe.'

Barnham picked up the business card from his desk. 'Where did you get this?'

'That doesn't matter.'

Barnham pressed down one of the switches on the intercom. 'Would you come in here, please.'

The door opened and Miss Ewing stepped into his office. 'See that this man leaves immediately. And in future, before you introduce someone into my office, make certain of his identity.'

She flinched at the tone of his voice. 'Mr Smith said . . .'

'His name, so he now claims, is Thorpe.'

'But how could I . . .' She stopped, half turned. 'Mr Thorpe, please come along . . .'

Thorpe went up to the desk. 'What's the answer?'

Barnham picked up a pen and signed one of the many papers on the desk.

'Please come along,' she said, in a flustered voice.

'Why?' Thorpe demanded violently. 'What does it matter to you who the hell I am or what I do?'

Without looking up, Barnham said: 'Miss Ewing, ask someone to come in here and help remove this man.'

She was obviously at a loss to know what to do.

'Perhaps it will be simplest if I call the police,' said Barnham.

One of the first things the police would ask, Thorpe thought, would be how had he come into possession of that business card. Which would lead to a charge of theft from an injured man . . .

'Just leave immediately,' said Barnham, making it obvious that he had not missed the fact that the mention of the police had sharply undermined Thorpe's determination.

'Please do come along,' pleaded Miss Ewing.

Thorpe turned away, crossed the office, and went through the doorway. As Miss Ewing shut the door, she said: 'That was a very stupid way to behave.'

'Was it? One becomes stupid when one's desperate.'

'Why did you say your name was Smith?'

'To match the card.' He added sardonically: 'And it was nice and anonymous.'

'But you've caused an awful lot of trouble. Sir Thomas has such a temper.'

'He struck me as being ice rather than fire.'

'When he becomes really annoyed . . .' She realized she ought not to be talking to him in such terms. 'You must go. Now.'

He left the building and walked along the pavement and when he came to a sandwich shop he went inside and bought a cup of coffee. He squeezed into a seat at one of the empty tables, spooned sugar into the coffee. Sir Thomas Barnham might not have admitted it was he who had engaged the private detectives, or had authorized such engagement—come to that, he'd said practically nothing beyond 'get out'—but the fact that, when the business card had been handed to him, he had broken his rule never to see anyone without an appointment must surely argue that he had known it was possible someone from Harrison and Carmichael might conceivably contact him? And he could only accept that if he knew that they had been engaged to investigate James Angus Thorpe . . . He'd struck oil first time and had identified the company and the man who'd employed the detective agency. So now he had to find some way to break through that defence of ice which Barnham had built around himself . . . No man was a hero to his valet, equally no boss was an enigma to his secretary.

Miss Ewing, wearing a smart lightweight coat despite the fact that the evening was warm, stepped out of Eston House, turned right, and walked briskly along the pavement.

Thorpe came up behind her. 'Miss Ewing.'

She looked sideways at him, then increased her already rapid rate of walking.

'I promise you that my intentions are strictly honourable.' He saw the quick twitch of her lips and was glad to discover that she had a good sense of humour. 'Won't you slow down a bit?'

'Go away.'

'Slow right down and have a drink with me?'

'Please leave me alone.'

'I can't. I've got to talk to you. It's a matter of life and death.'

'Whose?'

'Mine, unless you stop running a marathon.'

She came to a stop, forcing the hurrying people behind her to pull out and go round; one woman angrily said something that was unintelligible. 'Why are you bothering me?'

'Because I want, honourably, to buy you a drink.'

'I don't drink at this time of the day.'

'Nor do I, except in cases of emergency.'

She resumed walking and almost immediately they were separated by the press of people and it was several seconds before he could draw alongside her again. 'Do you know of a pub around here?'

She didn't answer.

'If you're waiting for references, I'm afraid I left them at home.'

'I'm not surprised.'

'Why not?'

'You told me your name was Smith; you told Sir Thomas it was Thorpe.'

'If I hadn't said I was Smith when I gave you that card, I'd never have got in to see the great man.'

'It would have been much more pleasant for me if you hadn't.'

'Did he give you a real roasting after I'd gone?'

'He made his feelings known.'

'It wasn't your fault I gave a false name.'

'I was inefficient. He doesn't like that.'

'You can tell him he's been very inefficient somewhere along the line since he's had to employ a private detective agency to pry into my life.'

She came to a stop for the second time. 'Are you from the Press?'

'Why d'you think I might be?'

'Because we've had a number of reporters trying all sorts of strategems to gain an interview with Sir Thomas since that criminal case and the repercussions to it in the House.'

'I'm not a reporter.'

'Then who are you?'

'That's what I want to tell you over a drink. But as I don't know where the nearest bar is, I can't lead the way.'

She studied him for a moment, then said: 'All right.' She resumed walking and, a couple of hundred yards on, turned right into a side street. Half way along was a public house.

It was one of the few bars left in London which had not suffered modernization. Long and thin, on the left-hand side was the bar, on the right were individual booths separated by wooden screens on which were hung sporting prints. He led the way to one of the nearer booths. 'What can I get you?'

For the first time she smiled and her craggy, awkward features softened. 'I suppose that if I'm ready to break my principles, I might as well break them thoroughly. May I have a Ricard, please?'

He went across to the bar and ordered a Ricard and a sweet Martini with soda. He carried the two glasses and a packet of crisps back to the booth. She'd taken off her coat and hung it on one of the hooks and was now seated. A small, elegant silver cigarette case was on the table. 'Do you smoke?'

'Thanks, but that's one vice in which I don't indulge.'

'The inference being that you enjoy all the others?'

'Who was it said that nothing is such fun as excess?'

'I don't know. Unless you're mixing up Wilde's nothing succeeding like excess?'

'Probably. My English lit. teacher once told me that failing everything else I might get a job working on a dictionary of misquotations.'

'English literature teachers have a habit of being ped-antic.' She lit a cigarette with careful, economical move-ments, replaced lighter and case in her smart leather handbag. She added water from the carafe to her glass.

'Let's drink to both success and excess,' he said.

She sipped her drink, replaced the glass on the table which bore the scars of generations of drinkers. 'Are you going to tell me who you really are and why you've asked me here for a drink?'

He thought that there had been a note of wistful bitterness in her voice. Was she never asked out solely for the pleasure of her company? Did she sometimes look in a mirror and wonder how fate could have been so cruel as to place such beauty in her eyes while completely forgetting her face? 'Did you read in the papers or see on the television any-thing about the raid on Fifield Vaults roughly three weeks ago?'

She thought, her high forehead furrowed. 'I'm sure I did, because I recognize the name, but I don't remember any of the details.'

'The vaults, containing strong-boxes, were broken into by a gang who severely injured the night guard. He died a couple of days later.'

'Yes, I do remember now. I felt so sorry for the family . . . These days, terrible things are always happening. It sometimes seems one can't open a paper without reading about an old woman mugged and robbed, in her own home. Someone in the government was talking the other day about the uncaring society. Can't they realize that it's up to the government to make certain it becomes a caring society once more, to try to stop such things happening, to have the moral courage to make certain convicted criminals are punished sufficiently hard to make others think twice . . . I'm sorry, I've been on my soap box. But I get so angry when life becomes more and more brutal and no one has the courage to contradict the liberals and their cry that it's the fault of society, not the individual.'

'Most of the people who make and administer the laws live above the mud; that makes one hell of a difference. It's only when you get your feet dirty that you know how difficult it is to clean them.'

She said slowly, as if she were uncertain whether or not she should speak: 'You sound as if you've got your feet dirty?'

'I haven't. But I can't persuade other people that I haven't.'

'I don't understand.'

'I work at Fifield Vaults and the police are convinced that I had something to do with the robbery.'

She looked dismayed.

'I had nothing whatsoever to do with it.' Quickly, he gave her a résumé of the facts and the reason for his visit to the offices of Haysair and Waites Holdings. 'I'm certain Barnham paid the firm of private investigators to have me followed. I must know why.'

'But you're suggesting . . . Well, that Sir Thomas might

have had some connection with the robbery and murder.
That's ridiculous.'

'Why is it?'

'Because . . . because of his position, because of the kind
of man he is.'

'What kind of a man is he?'

'Successful, rich. His wife's very well placed socially and
they entertain all sorts of important people. Why on earth
should he have anything to do with a nasty, vicious crime?'

'I once heard big business defined as crime made legal.'

'That's the kind of ridiculous nonsense that people who
don't know anything about the City say because they think
it sounds clever.'

'Nevertheless, in the past successful, rich, and socially
acceptable businessmen have turned out to be crooked.'

'There's always likely to be one rotten apple.'

'How do you know Barnham isn't the one?'

'You've no right to suggest that.'

'If he's as pure as the driven snow, why did he have me
followed?'

'I'm certain he didn't do anything of the sort.'

'You told me that he never saw anyone without an appointment. Yet after you gave him that card, he saw me.
Why should a very important, very busy man agree to see
me unless he knew someone from the detective agency might
well be getting in touch with him? And he could only know
that if somehow, somewhere along the line, he's tied in with
the robbery and murder.'

She lit another cigarette. 'He must have presumed that,
even though he'd no idea what it was, you had a valid reason
for wanting to speak to you.'

'Miss Ewing, I had one hell of a valid reason. I told you,
the police are doing their damndest to charge me and the
evidence keeps seeming to prove I'm guilty. I've got to fight
to prove my innocence . . . Will you help me fight?'

'I don't see how I can possibly help.'

'Tell me everything you know about his life; his business interests, his financial position, his social contacts—anything which might give the clue as to why he's so interested in me.'

'You're asking me to betray him.'

'I'm asking you to help me prove my innocence.'

She stood. 'I made a terrible mistake coming here,' she said, as she reached for her coat.

'You've got to understand . . .'

'I understand one thing, you're asking me to be the vilest of all people, a traitor.' She left the booth, her face set in angry, bitter lines.

He arrived at the corner of Devreux Road at a quarter to eight, early because his train connections had been smooth. A car drew up alongside him and a man said: 'Excuse me.' He stopped. 'Can you show me on this map the quickest route to Barnet?' The rear door opened and a map was held in such a way that he had to bend down and forward to look at it more closely. A savage blow on his head blasted his mind into chaos. The shoulder of his coat was grabbed and he was hauled inside, his right knee slamming into the sill to send pain skittering through his leg. He knew he should struggle, but could not. The sleeve of his coat was dragged up as far as it would go, he felt a sharp prick of pain in his forearm, there was the sensation of heat rising up towards his shoulder, and then he lost consciousness.

CHAPTER 13

He dimly became aware of the world just before he was sick. After a while he ceased vomiting. He heard sounds. He was rolled over and whatever he had been lying on was pulled from under him.

'Christ, what a stink!'

'Wake up, beautiful,' said a second voice.

His shoulder was shaken heavily. Fresh waves of nausea swept through his body.

'Look out, he's going to spew again.'

'We'll have to leave him.'

He slid back into nothingness.

The next time he regained consciousness, his mind was functioning correctly once more. Why had he been attacked and bundled into the car? Where had he been brought? What were they going to do with him?

The door opened and two men entered. Both were dressed casually, one in T-shirt and jeans, the other in a jersey-shirt and flannels, both had brightly coloured ski masks over their faces.

The taller of the two hauled him up into a sitting position and for the first time he studied the room. Rose-patterned wallpaper was peeling away in several places, the ceiling was badly cracked, the floor was carpetless, the furniture consisted only of the bed he was on, a wooden chair, and a battered chest-of-drawers which leaned drunkenly to one corner.

'Are you a sensible man?'

He stared up at the red and black ski mask.

'Well, are you?'

'Yes.' It was difficult to speak; his mouth felt as if it were half filled with cotton wool which had been soaked in something foul.

'Good. Then tell us where it is, we'll pick it up, and you can go.'

'Where what is?'

'I thought you said you was sensible?'

'But I don't know what you're talking about.'

The man was silent for a while, as if debating with himself, then he said: 'Where's the letter?'

'What letter?'

'The letter that was in the strong-box; that you nicked before the raid.'

'Let's get started,' said the second man, with angry impatience.

'Give him a bit of time. He's probably still thick-headed.' He turned to Thorpe. 'Where is it?'

'I don't know anything about a letter.'

'That's not what the splits think.'

'If you mean the police, they're so wrong . . .'

'Look, I'll make it simple for you. Someone offered us news on the security set-up in some vaults. Sounded good, except we didn't know who was telling because he did all his talking over the blower. He had to be someone working in the vaults to give us so much information, but he was shy. We didn't like not knowing, so suggested a face-to-face, but he wasn't playing; said if we didn't want to do it his way, he'd find someone what did. We weren't in no position to argue. He told us there was two hundred and fifty-two boxes and well over three-quarters of 'em was occupied and some of 'em was rich; at night there was just one guard and sometimes this was an ex-cop who liked his beer and even for an ex-cop he was soft upstairs and let the man bring the beer right into the vaults.

'The lads—' he jerked his thumb in the direction of his companion— 'they got to worrying that maybe it was all a load of cobbler's. I thought different. A bloke doesn't go to so much trouble just to be funny. I said we'd keep listening and in the end he gave the place and time; Fifield Vaults, Wednesday. Don't case the joint, he said, there's a TV camera looking for the likes of you . . .' He indicated his companion once more. 'That had 'em running scared.'

'It didn't sound right,' said the second man resentfully.

'It made sense to me. So then we did the job, all neat and tidy . . .'

'Tidy? You murdered Dick,' interrupted Thorpe.

'It happens,' said the man with casual indifference. His voice became hard. 'So we did the job, all neat and tidy, and it paid but not like we'd thought ... And then we started hearing how Prof Watson was shouting his head off about how he'd lost his pension in the raid and what he'd like to do to the mob.'

'Him and whose army?' sneered the second man.

'We reckoned it would be an idea to get hold of the Prof and find out what he was on about. Funny thing about the Prof, he looked as weak as water and yet we had to work and work on the stupid sod before he'd tell us about the letter that he'd been keeping in the strong-box and which had been nicked along with everything else ... Only we knew we'd never seen no letter. That had me thinking. Wondering if we'd been played for suckers and our job had really been a cover-up for the nicking of this letter. Work things like that and no one would ever guess that someone in the Vaults had done himself a good turn ... So now we want that letter. Where is it?'

'I don't know anything about a letter,' said Thorpe.

'Don't be a right mug.'

'I swear that's the truth.'

'Give over, you stupid bastard. D'you think we're soft? The splits didn't take long to decide someone on the inside had been feeding facts to whoever did the job and they put the finger on you, didn't they?'

'But they've got it all wrong. I've never passed any information on to anyone ...'

The man turned and said angrily: 'Tell him to come up with his box.'

The second man left the room, to return in under a minute with a companion who carried a small suitcase. From the suitcase was brought out what appeared to Thorpe to be a transformer with two electrical leads.

'It's your last chance to tell us,' said the tallest of the three.

He tried to make them understand that he'd told the truth, but they slapped his mouth to shut him up and then stripped and spreadeagled him, face upwards, across the bed, securing his wrists and ankles to the corners with leather belts. They gagged him, plugged in the 'transformer' to a wall socket, then clamped the two leads to his testicles. The current was switched on and white-hot pain racked his body.

After a time—it was impossible for him to judge how long; time had lost all form—they ungagged him and asked the same questions as before. Desperately, he swore that he knew nothing beyond what he'd told them. They cursed him for his stupid stubbornness and the torture was resumed; unbelievably, its severity increased.

When next they questioned him, he said anything and confessed to everything in a frantic attempt to escape still further agony. His jumbled, distorted words provoked an argument. One man said they were wasting their time and the only thing left to do was to get rid of him, another said something about thinking smart and working out how to use him . . . He lost the thread of what was being said as the fear in his brain screamed louder and louder . . .

He didn't feel the hypodermic needle go into his arm, but he did feel the pain and the fear recede and the warmth advance; gratefully, he let himself fall forward into the warmth.

He regained a degree of consciousness. It seemed he was slumped in the front seat of a car and a man was demanding to know what had happened; he didn't try to explain, it was all too confused and called for far too much mental effort. He retreated back into the warm nothingness from which he'd so briefly emerged.

The hospital room was roughly the same size as the bedroom in which he'd been tortured, but there any similarity ceased;

the walls were painted a light pink, the fittings were new and clean, the bedside rug was filled with bright colours, and through the window he could see oak trees and part of a park in which people walked their dogs, children played, and life was normal.

The morning after he'd been admitted, Bell and Fuller came into the room. Bell sat down on the bedside chair, Fuller went over to the window and leaned against the frame.

Bell, in his normal, friendly manner, said: 'How are you feeling now?'

'Battered. Bloody.'

'From what I've been told, that's hardly surprising. Like to say what it was all about?'

'If I knew, I would.'

Fuller said: 'Don't you ever learn?'

'Who were they?' asked Bell. 'The mob who did the Vaults?'

'I don't know.'

'You know who you sold the information to,' said Fuller.

'I haven't sold information to anyone.'

'You just don't understand.'

'That's what I keep trying to tell you, for God's sake; I don't understand.'

'When a mob gets as rough as they did, it's because they know.'

'But know what?'

'Jesus! It's a pity we aren't allowed to carry on from where they left off.'

'That's enough of that talk,' snapped Bell.

'How else d'you get through to someone so thick?' retorted Fuller. He turned back to the bed. 'They wouldn't have worked you over if you hadn't sold 'em information, after which something went wrong. That they did, proves you were the traitor.'

'Know something really ironic? You're saying you're convinced I'm guilty because they were so certain I was. They were so certain because the police were. Is that a vicious circle, a catch twenty-two situation, or just plain lunacy?'

Fuller pushed himself away from the wall with his shoulder and crossed to the side of the bed. 'Who are they?' he demanded harshly.

'For the umpteenth time, I don't know.'

'Stop handing out that crap.'

'I told you, they had ski masks over their faces.'

'Is that likely, when you knew who they were?'

'I didn't and it's what happened, goddamn it.'

Bell said: 'What was the reason for their torturing you?'

'They were trying to make me tell them where the letter was.'

'What letter was that?'

'The one they said had been in a strong-box.'

'Why did they think you would have known anything about it?'

'It was stolen before their robbery.'

'By whom?'

'They reckoned, by me.'

'Was it you?'

'Of course it damn well wasn't. Don't you understand what I've been saying?'

'What's the letter about?' demanded Fuller.

'I don't know.'

'Who are you blacking with it?'

'What's that supposed to mean?'

'I'll make it simple. Who are you blackmailing with that letter?'

'Blackmail—on top of robbery and murder? Why not add simony and misprision for a little light relief?'

'Haven't you brain enough to understand you're in no position to get smart-arsed . . . Who are you blacking?'

Bell, his voice calm and quiet and in increasing contrast

to Fuller's, said: 'Did you eventually tell them where the letter was?'

'Once more: I didn't know a bloody thing about it.'

'I see . . . How did you end up in the car in which you were found?'

'God knows. I don't.'

'You must have some idea what happened after they stopped torturing you.'

'They had an argument and then they gave me an injection of something which put me right out.'

'An argument about what?'

'Whether to kill me.'

'They obviously decided not to—why?'

'One of them said . . .' He stopped.

'Said what?'

He shook his head. 'I can't remember; it's gone.'

'Think back harder.'

It was like trying to look down a dark tunnel which half way along had a right-angle turn in it.

'You can't suggest why they eventually killed Watson, but not you?'

'Watson?'

Bell said without emphasis: 'You've heard the name before?'

'I think so. But there was another name as well . . .'

'Prof Watson, perhaps?'

'That's right.'

'How was he mentioned?'

'Something to do with . . .' Thorpe thought back and this time his memory began to cooperate. 'One of them said Prof Watson had kept shouting his mouth off about how he'd lost his pension in the raid and they'd forced him to tell them what he meant and he said he'd lost a letter in the raid, but they hadn't found a letter.'

'You're quite certain they said they hadn't found one?'

'Yes.'

'You know bloody well they couldn't have found it,' said Fuller. 'You'd taken it.'

'Why won't you understand? I didn't take any letter; I didn't know it even existed.'

Bell said: 'Let's return to when the men were arguing over something. What happened once they stopped arguing?'

'That's when they gave me the injection which knocked me out.'

'So it's blank from then until you momentarily regained consciousness in the car and then another blank until you woke up here, in hospital?'

'Yes.'

'When they were torturing you, what did you tell them?'

'At first, the same as I keep telling you. That I didn't know a damn thing.'

'Why d'you say "at first"?'

'Because . . .' He stopped.

'Later on, you changed your story?'

'Yes.'

'To what?'

He stared at the far wall, his expression strained. 'In the end . . . In the end, it got so bad I tried to tell them whatever it was they wanted to know.'

'In other words you made out that you did, after all, know about the letter?'

'Yes,' he mumbled.

'And they believed you?'

'Not . . . not after a bit.'

'But they did stop torturing you?'

'Yes.'

Bell was silent for several seconds, then he said: 'I don't think we need bother you any more for the moment . . . But there is just one more thing. Would I be right in thinking that now you feel ashamed that you broke down under the torture?'

He didn't answer.

'Remember something. There's not one of us wouldn't have done the same and probably a lot sooner.'

Thorpe stared at Bell, his surprise obvious.

Bell stood. 'We'll leave you in peace now. I hope you'll soon recover completely.' He led the way to the door.

Thorpe lay back and closed his eyes. Immediately, he suffered the frightening conception that the hospital was only a delusion and reality was the bedroom in which he'd been tortured. He had to open his eyes and look around himself to be reassured that he was now safe.

Fuller managed to remain silent until they left the hospital and walked towards the car park, then he said pugnaciously: 'You went soft on him.' After a while, he managed to add, 'Sir.'

'Did I?' replied Bell easily.

'A bit more pressure and he'd have confessed.'

'But confessed to what?' The light wind plucked at Bell's hair, underlining his growing baldness. 'Have you thought about the fact that when the mob had learned what they wanted to know from Watson they murdered him, but that they didn't murder Thorpe? Was that because they hadn't learned all they wanted to know?'

Fuller said, not quite keeping the amused scorn out of his voice: 'If that were so, they'd have gone on torturing him.'

'Surely not, if they'd become convinced he really couldn't tell them any more?'

'That's suggesting he could be innocent.'

'It's a thought.'

'For my money, not much of a one.'

'No? Just remember one or two facts. The writing on the paying-in slip was very similar to Thorpe's, yet there were some differences; in other words, it could have been a forgery, not all that skilfully carried out. When Thorpe was first questioned, he was quite adamant that Fifield had no idea Vinay had been brought in to the Vaults when on night duty; but if he were guilty, wouldn't he have tried to suggest that Fifield must have known? And surely even a rank amateur could have judged that the contents of the strong-boxes would be worth a considerable sum of money so that the pay-off—assuming the money at the bank to be that—was very small beer indeed.'

'Remember all that, but the fact remains, the informer had to be someone working at the Vaults.'

'Well?'

'Who but Thorpe could it have been? The robbery was bound to hit the business hard and like as not finish it, so Fifield wouldn't have helped to cut his own throat. You can forget Mrs Johansen, and Mike Nithsdale's too thick to think up such a job.'

'When you say Fifield wouldn't have set it up because of the financial aspects, you're forgetting the letter. Watson reckoned it was worth a fortune. Far more, perhaps, than the business, which was looking very rocky. And one final point. How could Thorpe have begun to discover about the letter? But Fifield could easily have found out. He was an ex-cop and therefore in a position to identify Watson as an ex-con. If he had identified him, wouldn't he have wondered just what in the hell Watson had tucked away in the strong-box? And to go from wondering to finding out called for opening up the box, and who was in a better position to bring in a locksmith on the grounds that the customer had lost the key? Or even to get hold of the key temporarily from Watson on some pretext which wouldn't arouse suspicion and to take an impression of it and then make up a duplicate —we learn some odd skills in our job.'

Fuller was silent for several paces, then he said, in tones of sharp annoyance: 'What could be in that letter to make it so valuable?'

'That's a question to which I'd give a lot to know the answer.'

Fuller shook his head. 'It's not that complicated. Thorpe's

a cheap-jack grasser who helped an ex-cop get murdered.'

They reached the car. As Bell settled behind the wheel he decided, not for the first time, that the younger generation so often wore blinkers.

CHAPTER 14

Thorpe put down the book, chosen that morning from the trolley wheeled round by a voluntary hospital worker, and stared at the far wall. Considerations about the effects of nuclear war were referred to as thinking about the unthinkable; for days now, he'd been trying not to think about his unthinkable . . .

The men who'd tortured him had confirmed something which the police had always claimed to be fact, but which he had refused to accept: among those who worked in the vaults there was a traitor; Fifield, Trudy, Nithsdale, Vinay, or himself. He knew he wasn't the traitor. It was impossible to think of Trudy betraying anyone. Nithsdale was surely far too unimaginative. Vinay would have known that to make the raid realistic he would have to suffer assault and this could lead to his death if the mob had decided to protect themselves from a further betrayal. Which left Paul Fifield.

Fifield had put all his money into the business, had worked like hell to make it a success, only to see outside forces over which he'd no control threaten to destroy it. He'd been faced by bankruptcy. He was a man of imagination and initiative; he'd known about frozen credit accounts. It had been he who'd suggested that on the Wednesday night on which the vaults were robbed Thorpe swapped duties—which meant Vinay was on watch—although normally he demanded routine be strictly adhered to . . .

Susan would naturally treat with furious scorn any suggestion that her father was a crook. Yet the only way in which he could prove to her that he was innocent was to show that the guilty man was her father . . . A knock on the door interrupted his bitter thoughts.

Miss Ewing entered. She was dressed in a beautifully cut, gaily patterned cotton frock that emphasized with great tact her shapely body; until one looked at her face, she might have been a fashion model.

'Good morning . . .' Her nervous voice died away and she remained standing just inside the doorway.

'Come on in. What fun seeing you!'

'Are you certain it's all right? I mean, my coming here?'

'Couldn't be more so.'

She stepped right inside and closed the door. 'How are you now?'

'Recovering quite rapidly.'

'Are you sure?'

'Cross my heart and hope to die.'

'I really don't think you ought to say something like that.'

He smiled. 'Couldn't say it in a more appropriate place should someone hear and decide to do something about it . . . Come and sit down.'

She crossed to the bed. She held a paper bag as well as a handbag in her right hand and she separated the two. 'Do you like grapes? I know everyone brings them to people in hospitals, but these looked so nice and the man promised me they were really sweet. If you've become sick of them . . .'

'Far from it. The only fruit I've seen here were some tired apples.'

She was delighted, but a little surprised and even suspicious that he was bending the truth on her account. 'Haven't your friends brought any?'

'My only visitors have been the police.'

'But your family?'

'Both my parents, who are dead, were only children and I'm an only child; blood relations are so thin on the ground as to be invisible.'

She handed him the paper bag, then sat on the upright chair. He opened the bag. 'What enormous grapes! D'you think they were reared on hormones?'

She laughed. 'The man said they came from somewhere on the Italian Riviera. I seem to remember seeing a lot of vines on the slopes behind Bordighera and being told they were special dessert ones; maybe they came from there.'

'You couldn't have brought me anything more welcome.'

She was plainly delighted. 'I am so glad.' Then she clasped her hands together and showed signs of nervousness. 'I've come because . . . I read in the paper that a man called James Thorpe had been found badly injured and, it was believed, tortured. I just had to know if it was you, because if it was . . .' She stopped. Then she said in a rush: 'I had to apologize.'

'Apologize for what, for heaven's sake?'

'Please tell me, did it happen because it was something to do with the robbery and murder you told me about?'

'Yes.'

'I . . . I was sure it did. And that made me feel terrible because if I had tried to help instead of . . . But when you asked me to tell you everything I knew about Sir Thomas, all I could think was that you were insulting me by suggesting I could ever do such a thing.'

'I didn't mean to do that, but of course it was very insulting of me, Miss Ewing.'

'Please, my name's Pamela.'

'And I was christened James but naturally am always called Jim. You were absolutely right in refusing to tell me anything. But I was getting desperate because I couldn't think what else to do.'

'When I read the news, it made me feel sick. Especially when I remembered telling you how much I hated violence and how no one seemed to care what happened, unless it happened to them . . . But when you came and tried to involve me, I refused to do anything and because of that you've suffered most terribly.'

'It wouldn't have mattered what you told me, it couldn't have altered anything.'

'It must have done.'

He shook his head. 'They picked me up the same evening, so there just wasn't time.' He brought the bunch of grapes out and laid them on the flattened bag. 'Let's try these and forget all that happened.'

'I can't.'

'Forget it or eat grapes?'

She refused to respond to his air of light-heartedness. 'I started by trying to tell myself that there was nothing I could do about what had happened. But I knew that that was just being a coward. I could come and tell you.' She untwined her fingers. 'Does the fact that you were so terribly injured mean that what you told me is true?'

'Some of the things I said have to be, yes; others are still conjectures.'

'What are true?'

'There is in existence a letter which has been used to blackmail whoever wrote it. Almost certainly, the person blackmailed is very wealthy and in the kind of social or business position where he cannot afford any unsavoury revelations. Two men have been murdered because of the letter. It's also a fact that I was followed by a private detective, working for the firm of Harrison and Carmichael. But it's conjecture that the reason for my being followed was the blackmailing letter; conjecture that the writer of it is desperately trying to find out who now has it. It's also conjecture, even if based on facts, that Sir Thomas Barnham hired the private detective which therefore means he is almost certainly the writer of the letter.'

'But . . . but I just can't believe he could be mixed up in a robbery and murder.'

'It seems that the letter was stolen from the original thief and then the robbery at the vaults was set up in order to conceal this.'

'I don't think I understand.'

'I'm sorry, but I can't explain it more coherently at the moment because I'd have to name names and I'm not going to do that while there's still the possibility of doubt.'

'But you are saying that Sir Thomas is connected with the robbery and murder through a letter he once wrote?'

'I am, yes. But the connection is indirect. I'm sure he had absolutely no idea that the vaults robbery was planned and he knows nothing about the murder of the second man, the criminal who originally stole the letter.'

'But what could be in the letter? What could lead to such appalling violence?'

'I can't answer that.'

'Sir Thomas is so . . .' She laced her fingers together once more. 'I've worked for him for twelve years and during that time I've never known him to do anything that wasn't completely ethical from a business point of view.'

'You'd know quite a bit about his business dealings?'

'Yes, of course.'

'And his private life?'

'He's a man who keeps his two lives as separate as possible. But once or twice he's had a lot of urgent work and he's asked me to spend the weekend at his house to get it done.'

'What kind of man would you call him?'

'Well, he's always very correct in his behaviour. But there's not really much contact on a personal level, if you know what I mean?'

'What's his family like?'

'His wife is rather conscious of her position, but I suppose if you're from her sort of background and you're married to a very wealthy man, you're likely to be.' Then she added quickly: 'But I'm not suggesting for one second that she was ever unpleasant.'

'You've never seen any hint of domestic trouble?'

'Nothing at all.'

'No sign of other women?'

'No.'

'Not that, I suppose, in this day and age an affair would lead to blackmail; more likely an offer for serial rights from one of the Sunday populars.'

She spoke hopefully. 'Perhaps you could be wrong about Sir Thomas and the letter wasn't written by him.'

'Perhaps, but I wouldn't put any money on that.'

'I hope you are wrong.'

'You're very loyal.'

'I've always tried to be . . . But now, I just don't know where my loyalties lie.'

'In what way?'

'I don't know whether I ought to be loyal to him or to my principles.'

'Doesn't the one automatically lead on to the other?'

'I'm his personal assistant, which means that everything I learn about his business affairs should remain utterly confidential. But I've always believed that no one should ever let herself become an island, that she should make certain the bell tolls for her. So if there's something wrong and she could help to right it, she should and not turn her head aside . . . What I'm trying to say, only I'm finding it terribly difficult to do so, is that if you still want me to help and I can, I will.'

He left hospital on the Wednesday afternoon, roughly a week after he'd been admitted. He limped slightly as he made his way down to the bus stop. He'd suffered no broken bones or torn muscles, but the bruising was taking its time to disperse. However, the prognosis was that he'd soon be fit once more. One of the doctors had told him he'd been very lucky. He'd have considered himself luckier if it hadn't happened in the first place.

The bus dropped him at a tube station and just inside was a row of call-boxes. He telephoned the vaults and Trudy answered the call. 'They've just let me out of hospital.'

'I hope you're feeling better.'

There was no mistaking the coldness of her greeting, but he replied as if it had not been obvious. 'Nearly back to normal, or as normal as I've ever been. I'm ringing to find out what the drill is and how soon you want me back?'

'There's no need for you to bother.'

'I'm perfectly fit enough . . .'

'The vaults are being closed down as soon as all the clients have removed their deposits and that should be within the week. Until then, Mike and I can manage.'

'What's happened to Paul?'

'He's been very ill with asthma again, so ill that he's flown out to Mallorca to see if that'll get him better.'

'Then I must come along and spell you and give you a break.'

'That's not necessary.'

'For Pete's sake, why be so difficult? I told you, I'm perfectly fit enough to sit on my backside and watch the screens.'

'Don't you even begin to understand?'

'No, I don't.'

'How can you be so stupid? It's all happened because of what you did.'

'Remind me, exactly what did I do?'

She said angrily: 'You sold the murderers the details of the security system.'

'You sound very sure.'

'And you sound as if you just don't care that Dick got killed and . . . and everything . . .' Abruptly, she cut the connection.

He left the call-box and slowly walked over to the booking office. Trudy was normally one of the most level-headed of women and despite the obvious path of the police investigations had previously remained friendly, yet now she'd not hesitated to name him guilty . . .

'Where to, mate?' asked the booking clerk.

He jerked his mind back to the immediate present. 'Ealing Broadway, please.'

He collected his ticket and change and made his way down the steps to the platform which, since this part of the line was above ground, was partially in sun. How the hell, he wondered bitterly, was he ever going to prove his innocence to people who were convinced he was guilty?

Mrs Harbuckle asked him how he was feeling and then, before he had time to answer, told him about a friend of hers who'd gone to hospital because of a pain in her elbow and had ended up by having her womb removed. He finally escaped the detailed descriptions and made his way up to his room.

He stared round at the familiar setting; bed with its multi-coloured, crochet-squares bedspread, bookcase filled with textbooks and a few paperback novels, desk littered with files and papers, battered chair, worn carpet, and ancient cupboard. A familiar enough sight, yet now seen and appreciated with fresh eyes because there had been a time when it had seemed he would never see it again.

In his absence, Mrs Harbuckle had put his post on his desk. He opened the several envelopes. Access account, off-licence bill, advertising circular, bank statement, a set of corrected papers on Real Property with terse comments in red ink—'Check', 'Good', 'What about Act of 1953, sec. 45?', 'Ingenious but totally wrong' . . .

The law in the textbooks was always historically logical or in accordance with statute; but the law in the real world could be harsh, illogical, and very far from equitable . . . In the textbooks, innocence was one thing, guilt another; in the real world, one shaded into the other . . . In the textbooks, circumstantial and hearsay evidence were strictly bounded by checks and reservations, in the real world, they were free to roam . . .

He stood abruptly, left the room and went downstairs. Mrs Harbuckle was watching television. 'I'm going out for a bit,' he said. She nodded, but did not look up, loath to miss some vital moment of the soap opera.

He walked down to the station and went into one of the telephone kiosks. He dialled Susan's home.

'Three one three one two,' said a female voice.

He inserted the first of the coins. 'Is Susan at home?'

'Who's speaking?'

'Jim Thorpe.'

'Will you hold on, please.'

Like Pamela, Susan had known a conflict of loyalties. As Pamela had been, now Susan must be convinced that the conflict could be resolved on logical grounds, however hard this might prove to be . . .

'Mr Thorpe, this is Mary Reynolds, Susan's mother. I'm afraid she's not in at the moment.'

He was certain she was lying. 'When she returns, will you tell her I'm out of hospital now?'

'Yes, of course.' There was a brief pause. 'I hope you're very much better?'

He answered that he was, said goodbye, and rang off. He began to walk back to Ponds End Road. Obviously, Susan hadn't resolved her conflict of loyalties on hard, logical grounds, but solely on emotional ones. Accepting that her father's evidence was true, because he was her father, unhesitatingly believing the lies he'd told her . . . But then, what the hell did he expect? That, in the face of all her father had said, she'd accept his innocence, thereby ignoring all the evidence which had persuaded the police of his guilt? . . . Until he could prove his innocence, she must believe him guilty; and the only way in which he could do that was to show that her father had worked with murderers and

then done his damnedest to see an innocent man was
charged with his own crimes . . .

He was asked to call at the police station on Friday morning.
He didn't realize this at the time, but the fact that it was a
request and not an order was of considerable significance.

He spoke to Bell in an interview room, two along from
the previous one, but exactly similar in size and appearance.
With Bell was a uniform PC.

They sat at the table, Bell at the head, the PC at the foot,
Thorpe in the middle. Bell said: 'I asked you to drop in here
to find out if you can help us any further.'

'How can I do that when you refuse to believe a word I
say?'

'Not refuse. If we have been guilty of anything, I suggest
it is of adopting too cautious an attitude.'

'If there's a difference, it's too subtle for me.'

'I doubt that.'

'Look, what are you after now?'

'Some more answers.'

'They'll be the same as last time.'

'Even if the questions are different?'

'Why should they be?'

'For several reasons, the main one of which is that you
weren't murdered after they tortured you.'

'What difference does that make—except to my state of
health?'

'I think that for the moment you'll just have to accept
that the fact could be quite significant . . . And also accept
one thing more. If I'm to uncover the truth—and you know
whether or not that's in your interests—I must have your
full cooperation.'

Bell's manner was almost friendly, as if he could accept
that after all he might be innocent. But, continued Thorpe's
thoughts, was this a ploy, designed to soften him up and trap
him through sympathy? 'I've told you everything I can.'

'I rather doubt that.' Bell scratched the lobe of his right ear. 'You're an intelligent man, so you must have considered the question of who the traitor was, if not you?'

'Yes.'

'Who did you identify?'

He was back to the insoluble problem: how did he establish his innocence without establishing Fifield's guilt? 'I couldn't imagine who it was.'

'Sometimes life can present us with an impossible conflict of interests, can't it?'

If these words meant anything, they meant that Bell had identified Fifield.

'You can't give us any information that might help us?'

'No.'

Bell opened a folder on the table and read what was written on a single sheet of paper. 'An incident which occurred on Saturday, the seventh of this month, recently came to my notice. A man was injured in a traffic accident in Glastonbury Road. His name's George M. Smith and he works for a firm of private investigators; private detectives, if you like. The facts of the accident aren't in contention. Smith ran out into the road very suddenly and an oncoming car hit him and then a second car. The driver of the second car made an interesting statement. He said that he saw Smith come out from the pavement in such a way that it seemed he might have been pursued.'

There was a short silence, broken only by the PC's snorting through his nose as he tried to clear it.

'You remember the accident?'

'Why should I?'

'You went to the aid of the injured man. Prior to the accident, were you chasing him?'

'No.'

'He had had on him a wallet which contained twenty-three pounds in notes, a list of shopping, one bank and two credit cards, four business cards, and some personal papers.

One of the PC's at the scene of the accident searched him, seeking means of identification, but came across no wallet. It was assumed that one of the onlookers had stolen it. But several days later, the wallet was posted to the local police station and when the contents were checked it was discovered that only one item was missing, one of the business cards. Smith, a very precise man, is quite clear on that . . . Why should a business card and nothing else be taken?'

'I've no idea.'

'You realize that it might well make a difference if I knew the answer?'

'Maybe. But my answer remains the same.'

Bell closed the folder. 'Then we've covered everything I wanted to talk to you about.'

After a moment Thorpe stood and left.

CHAPTER 15

Pamela rang Thorpe that evening and said she had something to tell him; he arranged to meet her on Saturday morning at an Austrian café, just off Oxford Circus.

She finished the last mouthful of pastry. 'And now I'll suffer from a conscience for the rest of the day.'

'Why so?' he asked.

'That must have clocked up an astronomical number of calories and I'm meant to be on a diet.'

'You've no need to be.' The moment he'd spoken, he realized that his words were open to a derogatory interpretation. Ugly women did not need to bother about their figures since it wouldn't make much difference to their love-lives whether they were thin or fat . . .

'It's all right, Jim,' she said quietly.

He was startled.

'I know how you meant that, so I won't take it the wrong way.'

'I wasn't . . .'

'Before you perjure yourself too far, know that I can sometimes read other people's thoughts. It's the Irish blood in me.' She brought her cigarette case out of her handbag, lit a cigarette. 'And now you're asking yourself, why doesn't the fool woman tell me what I've come to hear?'

'Your Irish blood's betrayed you this time. I was thinking that you're one of the nicest persons I know.'

She coloured. Then she said: 'I've been looking through some personal papers . . .' She became silent.

'It's a filthy feeling, isn't it, if one has a conscience. But circumstances can alter things so much.'

'Do they really? Can they ever justify the means, if the means are so obviously wrong?' She drew on the cigarette, exhaled slowly. 'There's a small safe in his office in which he keeps personal papers and the more confidential office papers which he's immediately concerned with. In the normal course of events, I don't go to it, but there have been several occasions when he's been away and has needed information that's in it and he's telephoned and told me to open it, so I know the combination. He was in Germany on Thursday, so I . . . Well, I went through all the papers that were in the safe. I discovered he has a multi-currency account with a Swiss bank which I knew nothing about before. There's been very little movement in the account, but what there has been may be significant. I copied down the figures.' She put her cigarette on the ashtray, opened her handbag, and brought out a folded sheet of paper which she passed across.

The figures covered a period of just over two years. A hundred and fifty thousand pounds had been paid in, in three sums, and every three months sixty thousand Swiss francs had been withdrawn on cheques made out to cash. He looked up. 'Could these debits be easily explained?'

'All his personal expenses are carried by two accounts with Barclays, all business expenses are carried by several accounts with NatWest and Lloyds.'

'Was there any cash in the safe?'

'Perhaps a hundred pounds, but no more . . . Could this be what you said you were looking for?'

Regular withdrawals, on a Swiss account so that there was absolute banking secrecy, made by a man whose normal and known expenses were always met by domestic bank accounts . . . 'Yes, I think this could very well be what I wanted.' Evidence that Barnham had been blackmailed by Watson; that the vehicle for the blackmail had been the letter in box one-five-six in Fifield Vaults; that Fifield had identified Watson, had opened the box and stolen the letter, had set up the robbery to cover his theft.

'What are you going to do now?'

'I don't know.'

She stubbed out the cigarette. 'Please don't tell anyone I gave you the information. I'm . . . I'm a coward. I couldn't bear people knowing I'd betrayed his trust in me.'

Just as he couldn't face people knowing that he'd taken that wallet from the injured Smith. He also was a coward. 'No one will ever learn about it from me.'

Thorpe slowed as he approached the main door of the police station, a solid, chunky, ugly building dating from the Thirties. Then, mentally squaring his shoulders, he walked on and into the front room. He spoke to the duty sergeant and asked to see Detective-Superintendent Bell. After a quarter of an hour's wait Bell, looking tired, came through one of the doorways beyond the counter.

Bell shook hands, spoke with his usual courtesy. 'It's quite a coincidence, your coming here. I was on the point of getting in touch with you.'

'Come into my parlour, said the spider to the fly?'

Bell smiled. 'Shall we sit down over there?'

They settled at one of the two low tables, on which were several magazines, at the far end of the front room. Bell said: 'I don't know whether you've heard yet—perhaps it's what's brought you here?—but unfortunately Mr Fifield died last Thursday.'

Thorpe let the news wash through his mind.

'His asthma became acute and the doctor stepped up the drugs and put him on oxygen, but during the night his heart packed up.'

He wondered how Susan had reacted to the news.

'From your expression, I take it you hadn't heard?'

'No, I hadn't.'

'I'm sorry,' said Bell formally. He waited for a few seconds, then spoke again. 'Since obviously it wasn't news of his death which brought you here, would you tell me what did?'

'I came to tell you . . .'

'Well?'

'I don't know that it matters now.'

'I'd like to be the judge of that.'

'The letter was used for blackmailing Sir Thomas Barnham.'

'D'you mean the financier and MP?'

'Yes.'

Bell whistled. 'And just how in the hell have you discovered that?'

Thorpe had nerved himself to come to the station to confess to his taking of the wallet from the injured man, but now that it was time to put his confession into words he knew an almost overwhelming, cowardly urge to stay silent. But he forced himself to speak. 'I . . . I took that wallet.'

'I never doubted it. Why?'

'I'd seen Smith a couple of times and vaguely thought he might be following me and then I saw him a third time and became certain he was. I chased him, he ran like hell . . .

And there was the accident. I went to see if there was anything I could do and saw the wallet. I reckoned there might be something in it that would tell me why he'd been following me.'

Thorpe described the four sheets of paper on which had been figures and how these had led to his identifying the firm of Haysair and Waites Holdings. 'So I went to see Barnham in his office. His secretary told me he'd never see anyone without an appointment, but I told her to give him Smith's business card. He saw me immediately. That made it obvious he'd been employing the detective agency.'

'Did he admit this?'

'He admitted nothing. I told him my real name and he ordered me out.'

'Is that all?'

'Yes.'

Bell finished making notes. 'You surely won't need me to point out that in the legal sense there is no proof whatsoever that Sir Thomas was being blackmailed. I presume there's other evidence?'

He'd promised Pamela that her part in the matter would never be known. 'No.'

'You're relying solely on the assumptions you've drawn?'

'Facts.'

'Assumptions,' corrected Bell quietly. 'You've still not told me all you know, have you?'

'Yes.'

He sighed. 'More conflicting loyalties?'

After a while Thorpe said: 'What about the wallet?'

'Had you been caught in possession of it, I don't suppose you'd have escaped a charge of theft. However, since it was returned with all its contents, less one business card, it's obvious that your intention was not to keep it permanently. There might be grounds for a lesser charge, but I doubt one will be made. Frankly, I wouldn't be surprised if Smith would far rather the whole matter were dropped.'

Thorpe telephoned Susan's home, but once again her mother answered the call. 'I was very sorry to hear about Paul,' he said.

'Thank you,' she answered, not trying to make out that the news of the death had caused her much grief.

'May I speak to Susan?'

'She's abroad, in Mallorca. Naturally, there are certain matters which had to be dealt with.'

'When do you expect her back?'

'Fairly soon, unless something quite unexpected turns up.'

'I'll ring at the end of the week, then.'

'Mr Thorpe, let me be quite frank. It will be very much better if you do not try and get in touch with her again.'

'Why?'

'Surely that's obvious?'

'No, it isn't.'

'Then I will try to explain. Because of the robbery, and the murder of that poor guard, the vaults are being forced to close. The worry of this exacerbated Paul's asthma to such an extent that he died from it. Susan is not the only person to hold you directly responsible for his death.'

'That assumes that I was the traitor.'

'An assumption that is not difficult to make.'

He wanted to shout at her that under English law a person was innocent until found guilty, but instead he said goodbye, politely, and rang off.

Although unemployment was so serious and widespread, there were still jobs available for those who were prepared to undertake unsociable work or hours. On the following Friday, Thorpe obtained a job as night watchman in a garment factory in Battersea. It was a quiet, uneventful job, with little risk attached to it since it was very doubtful that anyone would ever consider it worthwhile to try to rob the factory—the clothes produced in it were of poor quality, designed to combat imports from the Far East rather than to be fashionable or of good quality.

He had a small office on the ground floor at the rear of the large, ungainly brick building and in this was a table with legs of unequal length, a chair that was worm-eaten, a gas-ring, a kettle, a telephone, and a copy of Ovid's *Amores* which was used to prop up the shortest leg of the table. He often wondered how such a book had ever come to be in the office.

The telephone rang on the Tuesday evening. 'It's Bell here. I've had quite a time getting hold of you. Your landlady seemed to think that your whereabouts was a state secret.'

'It's not that so much as she reckons I've gone down in the world and she doesn't want anyone else to know this. Alternatively, you may have interrupted one of her favourite TV programmes.'

'I thought you'd like to know that we've been checking up on the information you gave me.'

'With what result?' he asked, voice rising.

'None, I'm afraid.'

'Then you . . .'

'Sir Thomas Barnham states quite categorically—and I could add, with considerable vigour—that he has never been blackmailed and that he did not hire Harrison and Carmichael to have you investigated. Smith—who is now out of hospital—says that he wasn't following anyone and the only reason he was running was that he was late and was in a hurry to get home.'

'Pressure's been put on them to forget.'

'We've found no suggestion of that.'

'The evidence has to be around somewhere.'

'If so, it'll be buried under a lot of money; money can hide most things.'

'You don't sound concerned.'

'I'm afraid the years have forced me to become a realist and not to beat my brains out over something that can't be changed.'

'And to hell with the victim?'

'No,' said Bell sharply. 'Never that.'

'I'm the victim. So force them to tell the truth.'

'Used in that sense, "force" is a word we are not allowed to use.'

'Check them out again.'

'I've already allowed your part in this case to take up a disproportionate amount of the time available.'

'Disproportionate from whose point of view?'

'That is always a good question.'

'What's that supposed to mean?'

'Unfortunately, in practice justice can hurt a bystander almost as much as injustice can.'

'That's a hell of a thing for a policeman to say!'

'My excuse is, I'm nearing retirement.'

'All right, you're nearing retirement, but I'm not. Where am I left?'

'I suppose the truthful answer has to be, in mid-air.'

'Which isn't your concern?'

'I've done all I can on the information you've given me; to make any progress, I need to know more. Is there any other information which, for whatever reason, you've been holding back?'

'No.'

'You are quite certain?'

'Yes.'

'Then I'm afraid that there's virtually no chance of our taking the case further.'

'That's not fair.'

'Life seldom is.'

'Is that supposed to comfort me?'

'It depends on whether you're the kind of person who's comforted by knowing that things could be worse. You may be left in mid-air, but you are not under arrest, as at one time seemed inevitable.'

'I . . . Will you do something for me?'

Bell was quite some time in answering. Then he said, very carefully: 'That entirely depends on what it is you're asking.'

'When I give the word, to explain the facts as they concern me to Miss Fifield.'

'Explain what facts?'

'That I was not the traitor.'

'I cannot go that far.'

'Why not? What is it? You're like some bloody bureaucrat, frightened to do anything in case it might just conceivably come back on you?'

'I have learned to be careful.'

'All right, be careful. Just tell her that it's far from certain I am guilty.'

'Yes, I'll do that . . . Mr Thorpe, if you do have some further information which you haven't so far given me because it will inculpate someone closely connected with Miss Fifield . . .'

'I told you, I don't know anything more.'

'You do realize that in order to prove your innocence, you must be ready for the guilt of someone else to be established?'

'Of course I do.'

'Yes, of course . . . I'm sorry things are as they are.' There was sympathy in his voice.

CHAPTER 16

Thorpe drove up to Oxford in a turbocharged Saab which had been lent to him by a schooldays' friend. Alding House, some four miles out from the city, lay in its own park. It was a large, attractive, Queen Anne Cotswold house, so at one with the land that it might have grown rather than have been built, surrounded by immaculate lawns and large flowerbeds. To the south there was a kidney-shaped swimming-pool and, beyond, a hard tennis court. To the west there were half a dozen loose boxes and several paddocks, smartly set about with post-and-rail fencing. He had always appreciated that Susan's stepfather was wealthy, but had not understood that he was rich.

He parked in the turning-circle at the end of the drive beyond the central, raised flowerbed. He crossed to the columned portico, on either side of which were stone griffins, three feet high. The front door was of panelled wood and the cast-iron knocker was in the shape of a fox. The door was opened by a middle-aged, elegantly if simply dressed woman whose appearance was sufficiently like Susan's for him to be certain who she was. 'Mrs Reynolds, is Susan in?'

'Yes, she is. She's about to go riding . . .' She suddenly checked herself. 'I'm sorry, but do you mind telling me who you are?'

'Jim Thorpe.'

Her expression became sharp. 'Why are you here? I thought I made it quite clear when I spoke to you . . .'

'You made lots of things quite clear, Mrs Reynolds, one of which was that you've no idea what the facts are.'

She was obviously surprised by his aggressiveness. 'I am perfectly well aware of them. Now will you please leave . . .'

'You are not, and I'm not going anywhere until I've spoken to Susan.'

'Really, I . . .' She stopped as she heard footsteps in the hall behind her.

'Who is it?' Susan asked, just before she walked into sight of the doorway. She was dressed in beautifully cut riding clothes and, with her hair swept back, she looked smartly beautiful, a touch supercilious, and rather haughty.

'I've asked him to go, but he won't,' her mother said angrily. 'He's been quite rude.'

'Refused to do as you said; rude—how very out of character!' Her voice was laced with county tones and she might have been discussing an errant groom. She said to Thorpe: 'Were you rude to my mother?'

'Only if telling the truth is rude.'

'The truth? What is truth?'

'Said jesting Pilate . . . Only there's not much jesting at the moment, is there?'

Her expression of surprise deepened.

'Shall I get Alfred?' asked Mrs Reynolds.

'Good heavens, Mother, there's no need to blow this up into a melodrama. I'm sure Mr Thorpe will manage to summon up sufficient manners to leave now he realizes just how unwelcome he is.'

'Unwelcome, or not, you're going to listen,' he said roughly.

'You have changed! But not for the better. You've become boorish.'

'It's the peasant blood coming out in me.'

'Really, Susan . . .' began Mrs Reynolds.

'It's all right.'

She showed her annoyance, turned, and walked quickly across the hall, her shoes clacking on the parquet flooring.

'Now that your peasant's blood is in full flow,' said Susan, 'am I in physical danger? Are you likely to start hitting me?'

He stepped into the hall. 'If that'll bring an end to the bitch act.'

Her supercilious attitude gave way to sharp anger. 'My God, you've got a nerve! Coming here after all that's happened and acting . . .'

'According to you, what has happened?'

She said contemptuously: 'You're the traitor. You ruined my father and drove him to his death.'

'I did not betray him and I had nothing to do with the robbery.'

'D'you really imagine I'm going to begin to believe you? After his telling me everything that was going on? After seeing him struggle to breathe because his asthma was terrifyingly bad because he was so upset mentally? After going out to Mallorca and trying to settle up his estate out there . . .' Tears welled from her eyes and with an angry gesture she brushed them off her cheeks with the back of her hand. 'You wouldn't care what it was like, would you? Being in a foreign country and trying to cope—paying the undertakers, finding out how to get the death certificate, what I had to do legally, even discovering where his grave was so I could put flowers by it . . . And all the time knowing that if it hadn't been for you, he'd still have been alive.'

'I wasn't responsible for his death.'

'What you mean is, you haven't the courage to admit it.'

'Have you the courage to face up to the fact you could be wrong?'

They stared at each other, remembering bittersweet memories.

He spoke in a quieter voice. 'Did you read in any of the papers what happened to me?'

'No.'

'I was roughed up by the gang who committed the robbery.'

'Then there is some justice in the world.'

'They tortured me.'

'All the time Father was trying to breathe, he was tortured.'

'But although I couldn't tell them anything, they didn't finally murder me. And because they didn't, and because of a few other facts, the detective-superintendent is convinced, even though he hasn't the proof yet, that I've been telling the truth right along.'

'Then he can't be much of a detective.'

'On the contrary, he's a very good one.'

'I know what happened, even if he doesn't.'

'You only know what your father told you.'

'I suppose you think it's safe to call him a liar now he can't do anything about it?'

'He got things wrong. Susan, listen to the detective-superintendent. He'll explain that now there's absolutely no certainty that I had anything to do with the robbery. You've got to listen to him.'

'Got to? Who the hell says so?'

'For my sake.'

'Don't you still understand one simple thing? I hate and despise you for what you did to Father and I wouldn't lift a finger to help you.'

'You don't think you owe it to me from a sense of justice?'

'You bloody hypocrite,' she shouted.

A man dressed in a country suit entered the hall. He said in measured tones: 'Would you mind leaving.'

Susan turned and ran across the hall, past her stepfather, and through an open doorway.

Thorpe spoke to Reynolds. 'All I'm asking is that she should listen.'

'Please go.'

Thorpe left.

The good weather lasted until late August before it broke and there was a succession of gales, interspersed by days of grey clouds and drizzle; people began to dress in winter clothes. Then there was another change and the second week in September brought an Indian summer which, with two very short breaks, lasted through to October.

Thorpe met Pamela at the Austrian café. She looked across the table. 'I suggested meeting here because I thought it was better than talking over the phone; these days one never knows who may be listening in.'

'I'm very glad you thought like that.'

'You really don't mind coming here?'

'I've been looking forward to seeing you again ever since you phoned. Cut my throat and hope to die.'

She smiled. 'You often say that. You make it sound as if you suffer from a death wish.'

'Only after a heavy night on the tiles.'

She reached across and briefly touched his wrist with her fingers. 'You're a wonderfully kind person, Jim.' She flushed, as if suddenly self-conscious about, and regretting, her words.

What a pity Susan couldn't hear her say that! But then even if she could, she wouldn't accept it was in any way true, having made up her mind . . .

'Will you accept a penny?'

He started.

'For your thoughts.'

'I don't think so, no.'

'I'm not surprised. They looked expensive thoughts.'

He made no comment.

She used her fork to cut off a piece of the apple cinnamon tart she'd chosen. 'I suggested meeting because . . .' She ate. When she next spoke, the words were delivered in a rush. 'Because I've been through the papers in his safe whenever I've had the chance. It's a strange thing. The first time I did that, I felt absolutely despicable. But the next time it wasn't nearly so bad and soon it became . . . I felt more excited than ashamed.'

'They say the devil has all the heavy ammunition.'

'Maybe . . . Anyway, on Thursday afternoon I found a fresh bank statement from his Swiss bank and that shows that half a million pounds were paid into the account on the fourth of July and four hundred thousand Swiss francs were drawn on it on the third of August and again on the third of September. If you were right and he was being blackmailed, the blackmail money's been considerably increased.'

'But that's impossible.'

'Why?'

Fifield had stolen the letter from Watson with the intention of continuing the blackmail, but Fifield was dead. Could he have lost the letter before he died? Hardly likely, since he'd have been guarding it closer than he'd have guarded the Crown Jewels. Could it have been stolen from him? But that presupposed someone who knew it was he who'd engineered the vault robbery after taking the letter from the strong-box, and at the beginning of July when the half million had been paid into the Swiss account by Barnham, both the police and the mob who'd carried out the robbery had been convinced that he, Thorpe, was the guilty traitor. There had never been the slightest suggestion that anyone else had known about the letter . . . 'How was the money paid out?'

'Each time by a bank draft.'

'Was there any indication to whom the drafts were made out?'

'No, none. The statement just identified them as sent to a branch of the Banque du Languedoc in Carcassonne . . . Why did you say it's impossible the blackmail is still going on?'

'Because the blackmailer is dead.'

'Then you know who he is?'

'I know who he is.'

'Have you told the police?'

He shook his head.

'Why not?'

He didn't answer. After a while she used her fork to cut off another piece of tart. 'There's something in this that hurts you a lot, isn't there?'

'Yes.'

'Then I wish I'd stopped looking through his private papers.'

He wished she had, too.

CHAPTER 17

Thorpe stepped on to the after gangway which had been lowered in the tail of the 727 and went down to the tarmac. Clear of the aircraft's shadow, the sun was sharp and hot. He stared across at the distant terminal which was fronted by brightly coloured flowers and the tortured shapes of cacti. Although this scene bore very little direct relationship to any he had faced in Africa, nevertheless his mind was pulled back to there.

He walked, along with the other passengers, to the bus. After a long wait, for no discernible reason other than that the driver was talking to one of the baggage handlers, they drove to the main entrance of A Terminal.

Their immigration cards, carefully made out on the flight, were collected with a carelessness which suggested that no one was interested in who was entering the island; the Customs officers waved everyone through with a lordly disregard of possible smuggling. Beyond the doors of the arrival area there was a crowd of friends and relations of travellers and couriers who directed the incoming holiday-makers to the buses which were parked immediately outside.

During the hour-long drive across the central plain, which had as a dramatic backdrop the mountain range which formed the spine of the island, he wondered how much of a fool he was being? The police had obviously satisfied themselves that Fifield really had died, Susan had dealt with undertakers and solicitor, so surely it had to be an act of lunacy to come out to check whether he really had died?

At Puerto Fortaix the bus drove along the front, stopping in turn at three hotels to let off passengers. Then it reached the end of its drive at Hotel Fortaix. In company with the last fifteen passengers, Thorpe disembarked. Passports were collected by the receptionist, luggage was sorted out, and he was shown up to his room by a young man who accepted fifty pesetas with a quiet dignity which turned the tip into a friendly expression of gratitude.

He went past the two single beds, opened the french windows, and stepped out on to the small balcony. Being three floors up, he could look over the tops of the trees which grew immediately in front of the hotel, at the bay, flat calm, travel-poster blue, enclosed by mountains. He remembered Fifield telling him that this was one of the most beautiful parts of a beautiful island. He'd imagined himself here, with Susan . . . He looked down and to the side of the trees, past the outside bar, at the sand—in view were two young and shapely women, stretched out on towels, topless . . .

He spoke to the concierge who proved to be a man who never used two words where four could fit. There were, the concierge said, two doctors who practised in the port. Dr Salas had been working there for many, many years and was preparing to retire; his English was so poor that it would be almost impossible for an Englishman who did not speak some Spanish to communicate with him. Dr Buades was young and very up to date, had trained in Barcelona, had worked for two years in West Germany, and spoke English nearly as well as he did himself . . . With the smooth air of respectful confidentiality, which was the mark of his profession, he made it clear that Thorpe really had no choice.

Thorpe left the hotel by the sea front entrance and walked along the side pedestrian track. If he had been ill, he undoubtedly would have consulted Dr Buades. But if his theory was right, it was the much older man, abandoned by patients who favoured his far more modern and energetic colleague, suffering a heavily reduced income, to whom he needed to talk.

The port was just over a kilometre from the Hotel Fortaix

and his walk took him past many new blocks of flats and the few remaining old and luxuriously large houses in which the wealthy of Palma had once spent their summers, but which were now let at exorbitant rents to foreigners. Once a small fishing village, Puerto Fortaix had developed with the growth of the tourist trade but, thanks to the fact that successive mayors and councils of Fortaix had always been prepared to consider both God and Mammon, the development had never become destructive and the port still preserved a lazy charm.

When he reached the older part, the houses and flats gave way to restaurants, cafés, memento and leather shops, food and drink stores, in all of which the prices were considerably higher than in corresponding places one road back from the front; when level with the western arm of the harbour, he turned right into a side street. The doctor's house was in a terrace row. A notice, which set out surgery hours, was stuck to the glass of the front door. He entered.

The waiting-room was the short passage immediately inside and on the left-hand side four chairs had been set out against the wall; beyond them was a bamboo table on which were a number of dog-eared magazines. Waiting was a woman, stout, with her two children, thin to the point of beanpoles. Conversation between them consisted of a series of shouts.

An elderly man, right hand bandaged, came out of the room on the right-hand side of the passage. He left. An elderly woman in a white nurse's apron called the woman and children into the surgery and for the next ten minutes Thorpe could clearly hear her as she shouted, pausing only briefly when, presumably, the doctor was allowed a few words. When she came out, followed by her children, she looked highly satisfied with herself, as if she had just successfully proved some point against strong opposition. She was audible for quite a long time after she had left the house . . .

The nurse indicated that he was to go in to see the doctor.

The surgery was like any other; desk, chairs set out in front of this, cupboards with textbooks and instruments, washbasin, examination couch and screen, a powerful standard lamp and, hanging on the walls, framed certificates.

'Please to sit,' said Salas, correctly identifying Thorpe's nationality. 'You are wrong? Where?' His white hair was wispy, his face was heavily lined, with roughened skin; there was a tired look in his eyes. His white linen jacket had clearly not been freshly laundered when put on that morning. The fingers of his right hand were heavily stained with nicotine.

'I'm not ill,' Thorpe said. I have come to ask you about a friend of mine. Paul Fifield.' The doctor's consternation was obvious. 'Do you remember him?'

'I not understand.'

'It is only three months since you treated him.'

Salas began to fidget with a sheet of paper on his desk.

'What was wrong with him?'

'Please?'

'What illness was he suffering from?'

He shook his head.

'Where did he die?'

'Please?'

'Did he die in his flat?'

'I not know.'

'You signed the death certificate.'

'No.'

'What was the cause of death?'

Salas stood, hurried round the desk, and crossed to the second door which he opened. He shouted and when the nurse appeared he spoke excitedly in Mallorquin, then pushed past her and disappeared.

'The doctor is not well,' she said, in reasonably easy English. 'Please go.'

'Do you remember Paul Fifield?'

She was a large woman, tall for a Mallorquin; her face was

chunky and her mouth was set in hard, perhaps bitter, lines.
She looked at him with angry dislike. 'He die.'

'You are quite sure of that?'

'He die.'

'Where was he buried?'

'In cemetery.'

'Which cemetery?'

'Fortaix. Now you go.'

Fortaix, six kilometres from the port, had originally been
built round a hill, as so many of the towns on the island
were, for defensive reasons. Since the days of marauding
Moors had gone, it now spread out from the hill as far as
the main Fortaix/Palma road. The cemetery lay three-
quarters of a kilometre on the opposite side of the main
road.

A high sandstone wall surrounded the hundreds of family
tombs, some marked by simple stone slabs and headstones,
others by sizeable and even grandiose structures, the largest
of which contained small chapels. On many of the headstones there were photographs of the deceased and on more
than half the tombs there were fresh flowers. As he walked
down one row, Thorpe came to a tomb under construction
and he looked down it; there was a five-metre shaft on one
side of which, at approximately one metre intervals, were
concrete shelves.

It took him over half an hour to be certain that none of
the headstones bore Fifield's name. How significant was
this? As a foreigner, would he ... Thorpe saw a man,
carrying a mattock and a senalla—the two-handled rubber
basket used for a multitude of jobs—enter the cemetery. He
hurried down the row he was in and met the man half way
along another row. He asked if he spoke English. The man
shook his head.

'Fifield. Paul Fifield.' Thorpe pointed at the nearest tomb,
then at the next one to it.

The man dropped the mattock and the senalla on to the ground, spoke rapidly first in Mallorquin, then in Castilian, shrugged his shoulders when it became obvious he'd not been understood. Thorpe, because it was so warm, had been carrying his coat over his arm and now he searched the pockets and brought out an old letter. On the back of the envelope, he wrote 'Paul Fifield'. He pointed once again to the nearest headstone and showed the envelope.

The man suddenly nodded vigorously and indicated a wrought-iron gate at the far end of the cemetery. He spoke two words several times, one of which was obviously 'English'. For a moment, Thorpe was nonplussed, then he remembered something which should have occurred to him before; Spain was a Catholic country and only Catholics were allowed to be buried within consecrated cemeteries. He thanked the man, who was plainly delighted that in the end he'd been able to help, and walked over to the gateway, opened the gate, and went through.

Ten metres beyond the wall, resembling in form a large concrete travelling trunk of the kind used in the days of steamship travel, was a tomb along the sides of which were rows of small plaques bearing English, German, French, and a few Scandinavian names. Three of the plaques were dated the present year and one of these bore the inscription, *'In memory of Paul Mark Fifield, Requiescat in Pace '*

The building was in a road which ran down to, and was sideways on to, the front. On one of the balconies of Fifield's flat was a 'For Sale' notice and this gave the name and address of the estate agents.

As he stared up at the flat he wondered, almost with exasperation, why he was still refusing to accept the obvious? He'd seen Fifield's grave, so why wouldn't he believe Fifield was dead? On what was he basing his disbelief? The fact that it seemed Sir Thomas Barnham was still being blackmailed. But was he? There'd never been any certainty that

152 AN IDEAL CRIME

the money paid out of the Swiss account had gone to a blackmailer. Or someone else might have 'bought' the letter . . . Yet the streak of stubbornness in him—the streak that his mother had once said would shame any mule ever born —insisted he went on searching, asking questions . . .

The estate agent's office was two roads away, in a building on a corner site. The show windows contained photographs of properties for sale or to let, each one apparently more desirable than the last, and set inside on stands were poster-sized plans of two new urbanizaciós, offering paradise on earth for one million pesetas down and the rest in monthly instalments. A young woman, very casually dressed, was behind the counter, typing. He spoke to her and she replied in English. He smiled. 'Thank goodness you speak the language!'

'I should do, coming from Norwich.'

They chatted for a while then he said he was interested in the flat for sale in Calle Bahía.

'It's only come on the market recently. I'll get you the details.' She searched among a pile of papers, handed him a sheet. He read. Three bedrooms, one bathroom, one shower-room, dining/sitting-room, kitchen, utility room, and view of the sea. Furnished. Six and a half million pesetas.

'Could I have a look at it?' he asked.

'Sure. When would suit you?'

'I'm a bit pushed for time, so how about now?'

She frowned. 'Jaime's out and I don't know when he'll be back and I can't leave the place right now with a phone call due from Palma . . . Look, if I give you the key, bring it back when you've finished with it, will you?'

He said curiously: 'Aren't you afraid I might pinch something?'

'Not really. There's only basic holiday furniture and all that's pretty hefty. I guess you'd have a job to carry it away.'

As he waited for the key, he remembered Fifield telling

him that half the charm of Puerto Fortaix was the inhabitants' casual attitude towards life; Fifield had once gone into one of the banks and found it quite empty. True, times were unfortunately changing and democracy had, so Fifield had added, brought in its wake pornography, drugs, and a very greatly increased crime rate, but clearly people's attitudes had to some extent remained old-fashioned.

He returned to Calle Bahía. The entrance to the flats was between two shops and just inside, set in the wall, were a number of mail boxes. There was no lift and he climbed the several flights of stairs up to the fourth floor and flat 4b, on the right-hand side of the small landing. He inserted the key, turned the lock, opened the door and went inside.

He was in a very small hall, furnished only with a mirror and, under this, a square table. To his right was a corridor and immediately opposite, seen through an open doorway, was the sitting/dining-room. He crossed to the sitting-room.

As the assistant in the estate agent had said, the flat was only furnished for holidays, or lettings, but even so the overall impression was, thanks to the Spanish furniture, attractive. He crossed the tiled floor to the windows, opened them, and stepped out on to the small balcony. The For Sale leaflet had said the flat had a sea view; by leaning out from the balcony—ignoring the risk of toppling over the wrought-iron railings—it was just possible to see a small segment of the bay.

'For God's sake!' said a woman.

Startled, he swung round. Standing in the doorway of the sitting-room was a young woman. She wore a blue towel wrapped round her hair like a turban and red plimsolls.

'So what's so interesting?' she demanded aggressively. 'Haven't you ever seen anyone skinny before?'

'Not wearing red plimsolls.'

'What's your bent—a shoe fetishism?' She unwound the towel from about her head and wrapped it about her waist. 'Does that make you feel happier?'

'I'd substitute the word, calmer.'

'So now you've stopped trembling. Then let's hear who in the hell you are.' She was tall and fashionably thin except for her generous, shapely breasts. Her oval face was regularly featured, with a cheerfully shaped, full mouth, a straight nose, light blue eyes, and curly black hair which, now damp, flopped. Obviously only in her early twenties, from time to time an expression in her eyes suggested that some of her years had been filled with hard experience. 'Well?'

'I suppose I could ask you the same question.'

'Look, mister, you'd better give me a good answer or I'll be out on that balcony, screaming rape; the locals'll be up in a second.'

'I don't blame them, if you step outside as you are now.'

'What are you doing in this flat?'

'Looking round to see if I want to buy it.'

The answer disconcerted her. 'Buy it? . . . How d'you get in?'

'With the key the estate agent gave me.'

'Shit!' She walked over to one of the chairs and sat. 'Two thousand villas and flats in the port for sale and you have to pick on this one, just when I'm having a shower and doing my hair.'

'If they'd told me you might be in, I'd have rung first.'

'If they . . .' She stopped.

'If they'd known you were here, they'd be surprised?'

Her tone became defensive. 'All I've done is take a shower.'

'No showers where you live?'

'I haven't even got running water. There's a well and sometimes a couple of feet of muddy water at the bottom of it. The weather's still warm enough to swim every day, but salt water never makes you feel clean . . . Goddamn it, what's it matter to you why I took a shower?'

'It doesn't. But purely as a matter of interest, how did you get into the flat?'

'With a key, same as you.'

'But not one provided by the estate agent?'

'Polly gave it to me, if it's any of your bloody business.'

'And where did she get it from?'

'From Paul.'

'Who's Polly?'

'She was my best friend, until she cleared off and left me on my own, skint. How the hell could she do a thing like that?' She thumped the arm of the chair with a clenched fist. 'She knew I couldn't work the unemployment racket like she did and get the money sent out from home.' She stared into the distance, her expression resentful. Then she turned her head and faced him. 'So who are you?'

'A night watchman on a week's holiday.'

'Thinking of buying this flat? . . . . You don't sound like no night watchman, either.'

'How d'you expect me to sound?'

'I'm going to get dressed.' She stood, began to say something but stopped, then left. When she returned, she was wearing a T-shirt and jeans.

'D'you feel like a drink?' he asked.

'Might do,' she replied, with little apparent enthusiasm.

CHAPTER 18

The front cafés had tables set out on the pavement on the far, or sea, side of the road and they sat at one of these. Beyond the pavement was the sand and beyond that the intensely blue waters of the bay. To their right was the eastern arm of the harbour, to their left at a distance of a kilometre and a half the naval base which was backed by the hills which reached down to form the eastern shore of the bay; a number of windsurfers, with multi-coloured sails, were inshore while further out were a couple of fair-sized yachts under way; on the beach, people sunbathed, read, slept, made sand castles, ate ice-creams or, if French, played boule with ill-tempered intensity.

The waiter brought them their drinks. Fenella used her finger to draw a meaningless pattern in the frosting on her glass.

'You were going to say where and how you first met Paul,' Thorpe prompted.

'Polly introduced us.'

'Where did she meet him?'

'How the hell do I know? How does anyone meet anyone in this place? It just happens.'

'Had she known him long?'

'She'd been out here for a couple of years or so and she used to see him every time he came over. God knows why; he was old enough to be her grandfather. But then she seemed to go for old men. Or their money,' she added cattily.

'And how long have you been living here?'

'Since May. Came out on a fortnight's package.'

'And never returned?'

'Having seen it here there was no way I was going back to that grotty little dump in Armadale Road. Or that job, with the smarmy little sod of a manager trying to get his hands up my skirt . . . I came with Mary. It was raining buckets when we left and it was hot and sunny when we reached here and there was sun every day but one. So when it was time to fly back, I didn't.' She stared out at the bay, her expression relaxed so that suddenly she looked slightly vulnerable. 'When I told Mary I was staying, she thought I'd gone round the twist. Couldn't understand what I was on about; but then she's always been for a steady life, doesn't matter how boring.'

'So you stayed on and met Polly and through her, Paul?'

'I couldn't work the unemployment racket back home like her, so I was always short. It's not easy to earn out here, not with the police waiting to catch you working without a permit and throwing you off the island . . . Answered an advert once, for serving drinks in a bar. Turned out to be topless. Two thousand pesetas a day, and tips. They didn't have to spell out what the tips would be for. I told 'em where to put their job.'

'Did you like Paul?'

'If you mean, did I make it a threesome in bed, I bloody didn't.'

'I wasn't thinking of bed.'

'Then you're the first man I've met who isn't.'

'How did you get on with Paul, forgetting the bedroom?'

'All right. He took me out to meals with Polly. She could be a real friend like that, making certain I got a decent meal. But she wasn't a friend when she bloody cleared off without a word, leaving me skint.'

'When did that happen?'

'What's it matter?'

'I'm interested.'

'You ask too many bloody questions.' She picked up her glass and drained it.

'Would you like another drink?'

She didn't say no.

He signalled to the nearest waiter, who dodged between the tables, each one shaded by a sun umbrella, took their order, and collected up the dirty glasses.

'Here,' she said, 'give me a fag.'

'I'm sorry, but I don't smoke.'

'You wouldn't, would you!'

'Ask the waiter to bring you a pack.'

She spoke to the waiter in a Spanish that was easy but incorrect; he answered her in an English that was nearly perfect. 'Up yours,' she said, as he walked away.

Thorpe laughed.

'He was trying to take the mickey out of me, answering like that.'

'I doubt it. Just trying to be helpful. You'll probably find he's a graduate of Jesus.'

'Christ! you can pack that in for a start. I can't stand hearing blasphemy.'

'Jesus is a name of a college in both Oxford and Cambridge.'

She was annoyed. 'I know that. You're not the only one who's smart.'

'Of course not . . . You were going to say why Polly left here?'

'No, I wasn't . . . And what's it to you why she left?' A sudden thought occurred to her. 'Here—are you from the unemployment people back home?'

'Do I look the type?'

'There's no telling these days,' she muttered. 'Where's that smart-arsed waiter with my fags?'

She knew facts about Fifield which might be important, but it was clear that for the moment she was not prepared to give them. 'I've been thinking it would be fun to have a meal together later on.'

'Would it?' But she could not quite hide her eagerness.

The restaurant was small and, as far as any restaurant could be in so touristy an area, genuine; prices were reasonable and the menu did not try to be all things to all nations.

The waiter cleared away the sweet plates and spoke to Thorpe, who looked inquiringly at Fenella. 'He's asking if we want coffee and a brandy?'

'How about you?'

'I wouldn't say no.'

'Then it's two coffees and two brandies.' As she spoke to the waiter, Thorpe reflected that the drinks and the meal had mellowed her, smoothing out the rough edges so that she had become an amusing, and often unexpectedly interesting, companion.

She lit a cigarette. 'God, if only I could eat like that every day!'

'I'll tell you one thing—if you did, you'd need a bigger towel when visitors called.'

She giggled. 'I bet you never thought you'd be getting an eyeful like that when you unlocked the front door?'

'Dead right, I didn't.'

'D'you know what you looked like, when you spun round, eyes on stalks?'

'No. But I know who you reminded me of.'

'Who?'

'Venus at her birth.'

'A baby? You must need your bloody eyes tested.'

'According to Botticelli, she was born fully formed, hands delicately concealing certain vital parts of her anatomy.'

She giggled again. 'My hands weren't concealing anything.'

'So I gratefully observed.'

'Polly always told me I shouldn't walk around so much in the starkers. But as I said, what's so different about me from anyone else so where's the panic?'

The mention of Polly had given him the lead he'd wanted. 'Was Polly the same age as you?'

'She tried to make out she was, but I knew she was a good bit more; saw her passport one day.'

'Is she very beautiful?'

'Depends what grabs you, doesn't it? She'd do if you don't mind someone who has to tart herself up five times a day to keep looking good.'

'But Paul thought she was all right?'

'He would, wouldn't he?'

'Why?'

Her mood changed abruptly. 'Why do we have to keep talking about him?' She stubbed out her cigarette. 'He

wasn't bad for someone so old, but he didn't get me moving.'
She lit another cigarette.

The waiter brought the coffees and brandies. She picked
up a glass and sipped the brandy. 'You know something?
My old man used to say that drinking was worse than lying
with the devil. So how did he know what that was like? Silly
old bastard never knew what he was missing.'

'Did Polly and Paul go out together a lot?'

She said, carefully: 'If you ask one more question about
either of 'em, I'll sling the bloody coffee all over you.'

Since it was late in the year, the number of tourists was not
large, but the unusually fine weather had resulted in there
being more than was normal in October; as a result, most
of the restaurants and front cafés were still open and doing
a good trade. In the bay, several hardy Norwegians were
swimming, their bodies marked by quick flashes of phos-
phorescence.

Fenella and Thorpe came to a halt at the junction of the
front and the Fortaix/Palma roads. 'Which way do you go
now to get to your place?' he asked.

'Up the main road for a couple of kilometres and then
down a dirt track. Only I've not been living there for a bit.'

'Where are you staying, then?'

She said sarcastically: 'Are you thick or just slow?'

He laughed. 'Thick and slow.' It would never have occurred to him to take up residence in someone else's flat.

'Why shouldn't I use the place when no one else is? I'm
not doing any harm.'

'It's difficult to put forward a logical objection.'

'Sometimes I could kick you where it really hurts.'

'Why the vicious streak?'

'Because you sound as if you're laughing at me.'

'If I am laughing, it's not at you, it's at life.'

'Don't talk so daft . . . Come on, let's get moving.' She
linked her arm with his and led the way across the road.

Three minutes' walk brought them to the block of flats in Calle Bahía and they went up the stairs to the fourth floor. She opened her handbag and brought out a key, unlocked the front door. She stepped inside and then looked round to find him still standing outside. She said pugnaciously: 'What's the matter? Are you gay?'

'Only in the old-fashioned sense.'

'Then what are you waiting for? A gold-printed invitation?'

He hesitated.

She put her hands on her hips so that her handbag dangled against her thigh. 'You want to know something about Paul, right? So bloody inquisitive you can't find time to talk about anything else. But if you reckon to hear anything more, you bloody come on in and stop standing there as if you're wondering if I'm clean.'

He entered the flat.

She giggled. 'And I really was wondering if you were a queer!' She moved until she could rest her breasts on his chest.

'Have you no residual doubts?'

She kissed him. 'All right, I was being daft. But it was the way you talked sometimes and because you weren't all macho and wondering how soon you could make me.' She ran her hands over her stomach. 'Jim . . .' Unusually, there was a note of uncertainty in her voice. 'Suppose I hadn't said I wouldn't tell you anything more about Paul unless you came in?'

'I'd have found some other reason for making the first move.'

'You just use a different technique to get a girl into bed?'

'Apparent reluctance—works wonders. But I keep it for very special occasions.'

She kissed him again. 'You know, sometimes you make me feel like I'm someone who . . . Jeeze, I can be bloody

stupid. Polly always said I was real soft because I believed
not everyone was always on the make.' She was silent for a
while, then she asked: 'Why are you so interested in Paul?'

'Because of something that happened back in England.'

'What kind of something?'

'There was a problem with money,' he answered vaguely.

'He didn't have much of a problem last time he was here.
Took Polly to the Casino and she told me she lost over a
hundred thousand pesetas on roulette and he didn't turn a
hair. I asked her, how could she be so bloody daft? That
sort of money could've kept her going for weeks.'

'How did she reply?'

'Just laughed. Then when I told her to remember money
doesn't grow on trees, she said but it grew in fields.'

'What did she mean by that?'

'And you're supposed to be sharp? His name was Fifield,
wasn't it?'

'She reckoned he'd plenty more to give her?'

'She was certain. She showed me a load of frog money
he'd given her, just to show how rich she was. Crowing
about it. She could be a right bitch without going to any
bother.'

'Did you know she was going to leave?'

'I told you before, I didn't. She never said a bloody thing
to me. One day she was here, the next she'd vanished and
even her landlady didn't know anything. I couldn't make it
out, not with Paul still around.'

'Then she vanished before he died?'

'Yeah. I suppose in a way that was a good thing for her.
Not that she'd have drowned in her own tears. Underneath
that little girl act, she's as tough as they come.'

'Was he very upset when he discovered she'd vanished?'

'There's a funny thing. I asked him where she'd gone to
and he said he hadn't a clue, but he just wasn't worried.'

'Then perhaps he wasn't really fond of her?'

'For Christ's sake, don't you know what an old man gets

like with a woman half his age? If she'd told him to go down
on hands and knees and lick her shoes, he'd have rushed to
do it.'

'Unless he'd found someone else, maybe even younger?'

'Up until she went missing, she made certain he didn't
look anywhere but at her; not that he ever wanted to. I tell
you, he was gone to hell and back over her.'

Fifield had been infatuated with Polly. So when she had
suddenly disappeared it was to have been expected that he'd
have been very concerned. But he hadn't been. Then surely
he must have known she was going to disappear because
he'd arranged she should? And his only logical reason for
doing that was that he would very soon be joining her . . .

'Here, where have you got to?' she demanded.

'How d'you mean?'

'Not a word in five minutes. You clean forgot I was here.'

'That would be very difficult in the circumstances.'

'Then let's make the circumstances still more difficult,'
she said, just before she kissed him with fresh urgency.

As they walked down the short street of terrace houses made
gay by window-boxes, bougainvillæa, and brightly coloured
shutters, she said: 'Why the hell d'you want to see an
undertaker?'

'Just to ask him a couple of questions.'

'But I mean, why an undertaker?'

He didn't answer and her expression became sulky. She
was, he had quickly discovered a woman of rapidly changing
moods; also, she feared what she didn't understand.

They stopped at No. 7 and he knocked on the front door.
Nothing happened and after a while he knocked again.

'Out here, you don't do it like that,' she said, in tones of
contempt for such ignorance. 'You go straight inside and
shout your head off.' She pushed past him, opened the door,
went inside, and shouted.

Because the house was one in a terrace and from the

outside rather mean despite all the colour, he had expected a mean interior—but the room they'd stepped into, though dark because of the closed shutters, was quite large and it was attractively furnished and immaculately clean and tidy. An archway, across which a curtain could be drawn, separated that room from the next, and a woman came through. She was short, stocky, and dark-skinned, and dressed in a jumper and skirt. Fenella spoke to her in Spanish and she replied. Fenella turned to Thorpe. 'She's the niece of the undertaker and she says that he doesn't live here any more. He's with his daughter in Barcelona.'

'When did he leave?'

Fenella put the question, translated the answer. 'Several weeks ago. She can't say how many. They never can.'

'See if there's some date that'll fix it. Was it soon after her uncle buried a foreigner?'

The woman thought for a while and then said that her uncle had buried a foreigner and perhaps it was not long after that that he had left.

'Was her uncle's move unexpected?'

'How the hell can I ask a question like that?'

'Try.'

Sullenly, she put the question. 'She says her uncle's been a widower for years and he'd wanted to live with his daughter ever since she left the island to get married, but the daughter's husband hasn't much of a job and they couldn't have him unless he paid for making the house bigger. But he was getting old and hardly anyone was coming to him for funerals because he couldn't do things in much style and nowadays people want smart funerals and so he didn't have the money to help enlarge the house.'

'But he went to Barcelona so presumably the money turned up—where did he get it from?'

The woman shrugged her shoulders.

'She must have some idea,' he persisted.

'Why must she?' demanded Fenella. 'Don't you understand? These people aren't like you. If something happens, it happens, and that's all right by them and they aren't so bloody stupid as to beat out their brains wondering why. If her uncle suddenly had money, she's happy for him and that's the end of it as far as she's concerned.'

'Does she think a foreigner gave her uncle money?'

The woman's expression became uneasy.

'She doesn't know where it came from and she doesn't care since it helped her uncle go and live with his daughter and that meant the niece and her husband could rent this place from him.'

'What's his address?'

She denied knowing her uncle's address and her manner was now openly antagonistic. It was clear she would not help them further.

Outside in the street, as they began to walk along the pavement, skirting a band of children who were playing a local version of hopscotch, Fenella said: 'So what was all that about?'

'I'm not quite certain.'

She came to an abrupt stop. 'Just who are you really, asking questions about an undertaker?'

'Someone trying to prove he didn't help commit murder.'

'All right, if you won't tell me, bloody don't.'

As she slept soundly, her breathing becoming audible from time to time, he lay on his back and stared up at the ceiling of the bedroom, vaguely outlined by such light as came up through the slats of the closed shutters.

Fifield had been the traitor. Since a successful raid on the vaults must almost inevitably lead to the ruin of his business, there had had to be some very good reason for this act of financial suicide. That reason was the extremely valuable letter used to blackmail Sir Thomas Barnham. Fifield had come out to the island, ostensibly because of his health. He had resumed his infatuated relationship with Polly and she had suddenly had money to burn. She had unexpectedly disappeared, but he had been unworried and unmoved. He had died and had been buried, which apparently brought everything to an end . . . Both the doctor and the undertaker were old men whose careers were either failing or had failed and who, therefore, were likely to be open to bribes . . .

He was left with only one way of proving the truth.

CHAPTER 19

They lay on towels on the sand, drying themselves after a swim which, despite the time of year, had been warm. She was on her back, eyes closed, topless, her body a uniform shade of bronze. Would she ever summon up the courage to realize that she ought to return to Armadale Road? he wondered. To find that courage she would need to recognize that this was the land of the lotus, that dangerous fruit which turned a mind away from life . . .

'If you got paid for talking,' she said, 'you'd starve.'

'I was thinking.'

'My dad used to say that all the troubles in the world came from people who are so bloody stupid, they think.'

'He was probably right.'

'So what are you thinking about?'

'I was wondering how they go about a burial in this country.'

'You what?' She propped herself up on one elbow and stared at him. 'Sometimes you make me feel . . . What's it matter how they do that out here?'

'I had a wander around the local cemetery.'

'Did you? Look, when I'm asleep do you start biting my neck?'

'I can't see any fang marks, so I don't think so.'

'You're not sure what you get up to? . . . Why walk round a cemetery before they carry you into it?'

'The burial customs of a country can tell you quite a lot about the people ... I noticed one tomb that had just been built and it struck me as a bit odd, with the rows of shelves. Reminded me of a railway left-luggage store.'

'What d'you expect, when so much of the ground is solid rock? They're not going to blast out dozens and dozens of graves, like we have back home.'

'Surely over the years the tombs get rather crowded?'

'Not according to what I was told.'

'What was that?'

'Forget it. I don't like talking about burials.' She lay back once more and closed her eyes.

He put his mouth against her neck and nibbled.

'Christ!' She jerked her head away. 'What are you doing?'

'I'm hungry ... Shall we move and find somewhere to eat?'

'I've a mind to tell you to eat on your own ...' She picked up the top of her bikini and clipped it around herself.

They ate at a restaurant which lay up a valley that reached into the mountain range which stretched the length of the island; the old house had once possessed an olive press and some of the equipment—the wood worm-eaten, but the stones apparently good for another century of work—remained. Outside there was a large mulberry tree and they sat in the shade of this, looking out over a mosaic of small fields, most of them intensively cultivated since there was plenty of water for irrigation, at the starkly crested mountains.

She ate the last piece of lechona, suckling pig cooked with spices and brandy, and then regretfully put down fork and knife. 'You're thinking again!'

He smiled briefly. 'I plead guilty.'

'What's it this time?'

'I was wondering how it is that the tombs don't get overcrowded.'

She swore, with remarkable fluency. 'You couldn't wait until I've finished eating, could you?'

'You have.'

'I still want some pud.' She refilled their glasses from the earthenware carafe of wine, drank.

'What was it you were told?'

'What the goddamn hell are you reckoning on doing?'

'Who said I was going to do anything?'

'You want to know how Paul died, when, what exactly happened; you try to talk to the undertaker, but he's not around so you ask the niece a whole raft of questions; you stroll round the cemetery and now you're on about burials . . . So for God's sake, what's it all about?'

'Just vague interest.'

'You're a bloody liar.' She was silent for several seconds, then she said: 'Jim, whatever you're thinking of doing, please don't do it if it means trouble.'

'There's no need to worry. You know me—anything for a quiet life.'

She finished the wine in her glass, picked up the carafe but found it was now empty, lit a cigarette.

'What were you told?' he asked.

For a while it seemed she was going to refuse to answer, but then she said angrily: 'The coffins are made to let the air in so the body rots away. After seven years they take the bones out and store 'em and that way there's always some empty shelves . . . And now for God's sake talk about something else or I won't be able to eat any pud. And let's have another jug of vino.'

'" . . . for wine inspires us, And fires us With courage, love and joy."'

She reached across the table and gripped his hand. It was as if after so much talk of death she needed to reassure herself that they were both alive.

*

He left the flat as soon as he was certain she was asleep. He carried the large holdall and four-foot-long crowbar to the Seat Panda, rented that evening, which was parked in the first side street. He unlocked the driving door and put the holdall on the front passenger seat.

He sat behind the wheel and started the engine, but did not immediately drive off. He had the strange feeling that he was both sitting there and also was some way apart, looking at himself and able to judge how extraordinary it was that he—brought up to honour and respect goodness —was about to set off to commit one of the most despicable of all acts, desecration of the dead. His father had always claimed that man made the circumstances. His father was being proved wrong. Circumstances made the man. He drove off.

Turning off the main road, when level with Fortaix, he went up the narrow lane that was bordered on each side by a drystone wall; half way along, the headlights shone over the low wall to be reflected by the eyes of several hobbled sheep. The lane broadened out and he was at the cemetery.

There was no moon and the night was dark with the sky cloudless and alive with stars. He stepped out of the car and shut the door, waited, listening for any sounds which might suggest his arrival had been noted. There was the intermittent, wavy buzz of traffic—surprising how many cars were on the road at such a time—the barking of several dogs chained at the entrances to fields, the belling of a Scops owl, and the nearby rustling of something small which made its way through the undergrowth, but nothing to cause alarm.

He walked along the stone-chip path, past the high wall which enclosed the faithful to the large and ungainly tomb of the heretics. He put the crowbar and holdall down and from the latter brought out a torch whose beam he had restricted with a circle of cardboard. He switched the torch on, satisfied from his previous visit that since in the fields around there were the usual concentration of fig, almond, and citrus trees, all in leaf, and since no house directly overlooked where he now stood, it was safe to show a light.

The door was made of sandstone, as was the rest of the tomb, and it slotted into two metal brackets which, in conjunction with a bolt at the top, held it in place. He gripped the metal handle set in the stone, withdrew the bolt, let the door fall out as far as the brackets allowed, and then lifted. It was heavy and by the time he'd laid it on the ground he was beginning to sweat.

The torchlight showed him that the space inside was empty except for a crushed pack of cigarettes; in the centre of the floor was a sandstone trapdoor, with two lifting handles. He put the holdall and crowbar inside, climbed in and, bent over because the ceiling was little over four feet high, examined the trapdoor. As far as he could judge, it just lifted out. He set the torch down to one side, took a grip on each of the handles, and pulled. It was heavier than the door had been and he'd raised it only a couple of inches before he had to let go. It was a problem for which he had prepared. He positioned the crowbar so that he'd be able to nudge it forward with his foot, then gripped one handle with both hands and lifted up that end of the trapdoor high enough for him to be able to nudge the crowbar under it. Then, by dragging the trapdoor across the crowbar with a series of hard jerks, lifting up as he jerked, he was able to pull it back until over half the entrance of the square was exposed.

He picked up the torch and shone it below. This shaft was no larger than the one he had seen before, but there were shelves on either side of it and each shelf was large enough to take three coffins. Resting on the bottom of the shaft were the legs of an adjustable platform, made from tubular scaffolding, which could be set at each level of shelves, facilitating the storing of coffins. The first three levels on either side were full, the fourth contained three coffins and the platform was set to this height.

From the shaft came a smell which made him swallow repeatedly. He worked quickly, not daring to think about what he was going to have to do. From the holdall he brought a length of rope, knotted at foot intervals, and he secured one end of this to the crowbar, dropped the other down the shaft.

He'd previously secured a long loop of string to the handle of the torch and now he slipped this over his neck. He sat on the edge of the shaft, took hold of the rope, reached out with his feet until they were gripping the rope immediately above a knot, eased himself off the edge. Because the rope was away from the edge of the shaft he hung free and momentum slowly spun him round until his shoulder hit one wall; the beam of the torch followed him round, illuminating some of the coffins on the top shelf. The moment his feet reached the platform he released his hold on the rope and brought a handkerchief out of his trouser pocket and tied it round his nose, wishing as he did so that he'd had the forethought to bring some scent.

Above him the shelves were filled, on the level on which he now stood there were three coffins, all to his right. Since it seemed logical to suppose that the coffins were placed on the shelves in chronological order, the three on his present level should be the last to be entombed. The plaques outside had detailed three burials in the present year, a Frenchman's, a Dutch woman's, and Fifield's. Fifield's coffin, then, should be one of these three.

He lifted the torch from about his neck and set it down on the platform. He knelt in front of the left-hand coffin, took hold of the two ornate brass handles, and pulled, jerking the coffin from side to side as he did so, gaining extra purchase with his feet. He brought it clear of the shelf.

The middle-sized screwdriver fitted the screw heads on the lid of the coffin. He undid the fourteen screws, carefully putting them down by the side of the coffin, tapped the lid free, lifted it up. Tissues of the corpse had softened and disrupted, the eyes were bulging, liquefaction had started; it was a mask of corruption and not a face and as such was unidentifiable, but the matted hair was long and grey and had once belonged to a woman. He replaced the lid and had tightened the first of the screws when his stomach finally revolted and he was violently sick.

There seemed to be little room in his mind for anything but the screaming urge to escape this hell, but somehow he found the strength of self-control to continue. He secured the lid and inched the coffin back into the shelf.

He moved until he could work on the middle coffin. He pulled this out, unscrewed the lid and lifted it . . . Inside was no corpse, but only a number of small, filled sandbags, wedged into place with loose polystyrene.

He soaped himself from head to foot for the third time, washed off the soap, and stepped out of the shower. As he began to dry himself, the door of the bathroom opened and Fenella, naked because that was how she slept, stepped inside. 'What the hell are you doing?' she asked, her voice still thick from sleep.

'Taking a shower.'

'Not being struck blind, I can see that, can't I? Why?'

'Why not?'

'At four in the morning? . . . What's that stink? The drains again?' She sniffed the air. 'It's not drains. It's like something I once smelled . . .' She went forward towards his clothes, which were in a pile on the floor, and was about to pick them up when his harsh command to leave them alone stopped her. Bewildered, she said: 'Where . . . where have you been?'

He did not answer.

'Now I remember where that smell came from. When I was a kid a friend and me were playing in a tumbledown house and we found an old tramp who'd died and was

stinking . . . Oh God!' she exclaimed, shocked and frightened.

He stepped forward and put his arms round her and held
her tightly to himself.

CHAPTER 20

Fenella's eyes were over-bright and her voice was high. 'It's
been real fun, Jim.' She reached out and touched him
quickly. 'Except when you came back stinking of . . . Christ,
I hope I never know for certain what you were doing.'

'I don't expect you will,' he replied.

'I . . . I wish you weren't going.'

'I wish I were staying.'

'Then why the goddamn hell don't you? Look, you and
me could . . .' Her expression became bitter. 'There's got
to be an end, hasn't there? There always is in real life. It's
only in women's dreams that there's golden sunshine all the
way. So for God's sake go before—before I make a bloody
fool of myself.'

He kissed her and felt the damp of her tears. Then she
pulled free of him, ran across the hall to the corridor and
disappeared down that. He heard the bedroom door slam
shut. Never hurt anyone, his parents had taught him. He'd
hurt her. Unwittingly, but what consolation was that to her?

He left the flat, carrying his small suitcase, and once
outside made his way to the square where he sat down on
one of the garden seats, flanked by yuccas and a century
plant. Ten minutes before the bus was due to leave; perhaps
half an hour before it actually did leave because in Spain
the only thing that ran to time was a bullfight.

He pondered his next move. Fifield was alive, almost
certainly living with Polly, financed by the blackmail money.
But living where? On the face of things, anywhere in the

world: Bermuda, Australia, Tahiti . . . But there were certain hints as to where it was more probable he had settled. He'd always talked about his love for France and said that if ever he won the pools he'd retire there and buy a property with its own vineyard. The blackmail money had been sent to the Banque du Languedoc in Carcassonne. Fenella had seen Polly with a fistful of French money shortly before she vanished. So it seemed he might be living in France, within reach of Carcassonne. But he'd have assumed a new name, it was ridiculous to suppose anyone in the bank would discuss the money, and 'within reach of Carcassonne' could be a vast area. So even supposing so much, what chance was there of finding him? . . . Thorpe's mind flicked back to the night of Susan's birthday party. Above the mantelpiece in the sitting-room there had been hung a new painting, one which had seemed to possess a quality which Fifield's previous paintings had lacked. It had depicted a time-mellowed house, set above a vineyard, with in the background an unusual hill which looked like a rough pillar. Fifield had told him that the scene was imaginary, so it had seemed that perhaps the new quality was a more vibrant imagination, fuelled by a pipe dream. But what if the house existed, in that setting, and at the time it had already belonged to Fifield? Then the extra quality could have been proud satisfaction and the excitement which came from the secret knowledge that he had been so much cleverer than anybody else would ever guess . . .

There was the throb of a heavy diesel and Thorpe looked up to see a trailer bus draw up at the stop. He stood and walked across.

Five days of searching by car; five days of showing his crude sketch of the pillar-like hill to people who examined it and said that they'd never seen anything like it or shrugged their shoulders because they did not believe that such a hill could exist outside a child's drawing-book . . .

The Auberge du Forteil was owned and run by a married couple and their daughter; the wife and daughter worked like galley slaves and the husband chatted amiably with customers and accepted his wife's frequent remonstrances with a calm and dignified composure. The food was excellent, especially the trout which were caught locally and did not come from a farm, and the beds were comfortable despite feather mattresses which had become rather lumpy. The breakfast croissants were so light that one ate them quickly for fear they'd float away.

In the dining-room—small, with heavily beamed ceiling —Thorpe moved his cup to one side of the table and spread out the road map. Maps made it all look so easy, he thought gloomily; mountains were flattened, roads were straightened, towns were cleared of traffic, and kilometres became centimetres, traversed in the flick of an eyelid . . .

'Monsieur is wondering where to go today?'

He looked up to see the husband, in shirtsleeves and blue apron, a bottle of wine in his right hand. 'That's right,' he said, his French rusty but, in spite of having learned it at school, adequate for elementary conversations.

'A lot of foreigners come to tour our beautiful countryside,' said the husband with pride. He put the bottle of wine down on the table. 'Have you been to the mountains?'

'Not yet, no.'

'You must go, monsieur. They are the most dramatic mountains in the world; I was born in Font Romeu, so I know . . . Do you like wine?'

'Yes, very much.'

'Good. You will join me in drinking a little of the wine my cousin makes?'

'I'd like to, but it is a bit early in the day . . .'

'It is never too early to drink wine . . . I promise you, monsieur, that you will agree that all the barons of Bordeaux cannot produce anything finer.' He produced a corkscrew from one of the large pockets of the apron and with practised skill extracted the cork. There were clean glasses on the dresser against the far wall and he brought two of these over. He filled them with wine, passed one to Thorpe, raised his own and drank deeply.

There was a call of 'Henri' from the kitchen. He ignored it. 'My cousin, by marriage and not by blood, has a large vineyard and he looks after it as a rich man looks after the centimes. And when the harvest is in, he invites his friends to taste the new vintage and to drink the old . . .'

'Henri!' His wife appeared in the doorway of the kitchen. She was small and thin and her face was notable for the strength of her mouth. 'What are you doing?'

'Talking to monsieur, the Englishman.'

'You are not talking, you are drinking.'

'Being a man of great discernment, monsieur expressed a wish to taste our cousin's wine.'

'Where are the lamb and beans?'

'In the van, my love.'

'How can I begin to prepare lunch when there is nothing to prepare. Get them.'

'Immediately.' She withdrew and the door swung shut. 'My wife is a brilliant cook.' He patted his generous stomach. 'She prepares a leg of lamb that the gods themselves would fight over . . . You are staying to lunch, of course?'

'I'm afraid I haven't the time.'

'That is a tragedy.' He pulled a chair out from under the table and sat, refilled his glass and topped up Thorpe's. 'People come from dozens of kilometres away to savour my wife's lamb, cooked to perfection with garlic and a sauce which is a family secret. You should stay . . . But I forget, you are looking for a hill which resembles . . . A man of breeding hesitates to say exactly what it does resemble. I was born in the mountains, monsieur, but as I told you last night, I never saw a hill which looked like the drawing you showed me.'

Perhaps it didn't exist, thought Thorpe. Perhaps all his

conclusions had been based on fallacious reasoning.

The husband drained his glass for the second time, saw Thorpe's glass was still full, once again refilled his own.

'Henri!'

He turned and smiled at his wife. 'My love, I was this very second about to go out to get the lamb and the beans.'

'Did you remember to buy the lettuces as well?'

He thumped the table with a clenched fist. 'Damnation!'

'You can't be trusted to do the simplest thing. Bring me the lamb and the beans and then go to the market and buy a dozen lettuces and make certain this time that they've got decent hearts. And if there are any young artichokes, I'll have five kilos of them.'

'Immediately, my love.'

She disappeared. Thorpe was reminded of the weather-forecasting Swiss cottage he'd had when young; the cottage had had two doorways and when it was going to rain a man dressed in Alpine costume had appeared in one, when it was going to be fine he'd retired and a shepherdess in a highly impractical frilly skirt had appeared in the other.

The husband finished his third glass of wine with as much enthusiasm as he had the first. From behind the doorway into the kitchen came a shout. He stood. 'My wife, as befits a genius of the oven, is a woman of considerable temperament. I think I will fetch the things she wants and then continue to the market.' He regarded the bottle with a measure of sadness—it was still a quarter full—and re-corked it.

'Can you suggest anyone else I might ask about the hill before I leave?'

'No one knows the district better than I do, monsieur,' he said gravely, before crossing to the outside door and leaving.

Thorpe folded up the map. He was travelling as cheaply as possible, but even so his money couldn't last all that much longer. Then what? Return? But return to what?

The husband, bottle still in his hand, opened the outside door and looked in. 'I have just remembered Philippe. He is old and sometimes speaks stupidly, but he's been around for so long that he knows the countryside like the back of his hand. But not the mountains, mark you; only a mountain man can ever truly know them. I remember a time when the densest fog you ever saw came down . . .'

Thorpe interrupted these reminiscences. 'Where can I find Philippe?'

'Down at the forge, of course.'

'Henri!'

He disappeared and the outside door clicked shut seconds before his wife appeared in the doorway of the kitchen. She looked as if her temperament was rapidly coming to the boil.

The forge stood just below the crown of the shallow hill which divided the small town in two and outside it were ranged several pieces of wrought-iron work, including a very intricately designed and executed pair of gates. Philippe was a large man who had begun to shrink from age with a head of unruly white hair which at times looked rather like a halo. His long, jutting nose, fierce blue eyes, wide-spaced cheekbones, and cruelly shaped mouth, suggested a man who had once lived life to the full.

He proved to be a man of few words. He listened in complete silence to Thorpe and then stared at the rough drawing. After a while, he hawked and spat. 'Raunchville,' he finally said.

South of Raunchville, a hamlet astride a D road, there were a number of solitary hills which stretched for several kilometres and looked as if they had been set there in some past age by giants, for a game of Brobdingnagian skittles. They were rough, uncompromising, sharply shaped hills, their contours only occasionally relieved and softened by trees. One of them was unmistakably the pillar hill in Fifield's painting.

Thorpe stared at the hill through the windscreen of the parked Talbot. Seen in the dull light of an overcast, rain-promising day, it had an ominous character; a magnet for primitive rites and sacrifices. In the painting the day had been sunny and the shadows had stretched upwards, which meant the house was to the south. The hill had not appeared much higher than the house so if the perspective had been true, the house was some distance away. On the right-hand side of the hill there had been a ledge, seen in sharp outline. So now he needed to drive along the lanes to the south of the hill until that ledge showed in sharp outline. Then the house should not be far away.

Twenty-five minutes later he braked to a halt, certain he must be very near the house yet conscious of the fact that because the gently sloping land lay in folds he could easily miss it. He must, he thought, find someone whom he could ask about foreigners newly come to live in the area . . . He reached a village which looked deserted because all the shutters facing the road were closed, but half way along the street he found a baker. The shop was filled with the mouth-watering smell of newly baked bread. The woman behind the counter looked to be a battle-axe, but she proved to be pleasant and helpful. After a moment's thought she said yes, an English couple had recently come to live nearby. She wasn't sure of the name of the property, but it was on the Retagne road and he would know the house as soon as he saw it because in front was a vineyard and to the left—when seen from the road—were two barns which Jules, the old fool who'd sold the house to the foreigner, had allowed to fall into complete disrepair because he was a miser and wouldn't spend a franc until he was forced to, even if that meant losing ten francs later on.

He left the village heading south and at the first cross-roads turned right into a narrow lane that wound its way between fields and, for half a kilometre, alongside a stream whose waters bubbled over rocks. Then, rounding a left-hand corner, he came in sight first of the two tumbledown barns, then of the vineyard and the stone-walled house with Roman roof tiles, small windows, and off-set front door, which he had last seen in the painting. He experienced no sense of excited triumph, only one of weariness and regret.

He drove up the dirt track past the vines whose leaves were just beginning to be touched with brown and he wondered if Fifield had harvested the grapes and trodden them in traditional style, ignoring modern progress in order to fulfil an ambition which had been with him for so many years? Now, that ambition was about to turn to dust.

In front of the house was a new Renault 25. He parked alongside it and crossed to the wooden front door. He knocked.

A woman opened the door. "Morning. What can I do for you, then?' she asked in English, her tone aggressive because she was so certain she wouldn't be understood.

She closely resembled the mental image he had painted. Beginning not to be young any more and making the mistake of trying hard to conceal that fact. Hair too blonde and curly, make-up too noticeable, clothes too tight 'Polly Cathlan?'

'That's right, but how did you know . . .' Surprise gave way to dismay.

There was a call from inside and Thorpe recognized Fifield's voice. 'Who is it, Poll?'

'Paul,' she said shrilly, 'you'd better get out here.'

They heard footsteps crossing a tiled floor. 'Someone selling junk? Tell him we're not buying . . .'

Fifield stopped as he saw Thorpe. He was dressed casually, but in clothes whose quality was unmistakable; in England there had always been a greyness to his appearance, here he had captured both colour and style.

They stared at each other. Polly, now very uneasy, said: 'D'you know him, then?'

Thorpe spoke before Fifield could. 'We're old friends,' he said ironically.

She saw the look on Fifield's face. 'Here, Paul, what's going on? Who is this?'

'What d'you want?' Fifield asked Thorpe.

'A drink and then a chat.'

'Paul, you've got to tell me—what's happening?' She gripped Fifield's hand.

'How did you find me?' Fifield demanded.

'It's a long story.'

'Who else knows I'm here?'

'No one. Yet.'

'Yet?'

The reply, 'That's right,' seemed to afford Fifield some confidence. 'Let's get that drink . . . Poll, suppose you go out and find something, to do.'

'Why can't I stay?'

'Confidential business.'

'I don't want to . . .'

'D'you remember that brooch we saw the other day?'

'What about it?'

'When we're next in town, I'll buy it for you.'

She was pleased, but still uneasy. 'You told me there wasn't anyone who could ever know we were here.'

'I said, no one who shouldn't know.'

'I don't understand what you mean.'

'I'll explain later. Now go on out.'

When she still didn't move, he released her hand and gave her a push. She crossed to the outside door, stared at Thorpe with dislike and fear, opened the door and went out.

Fifield led the way into the sitting-room, large and elegantly furnished except—as had been the case in the hall—for the paintings which included one of a goose in a farmyard which totally lacked any sense of composition or skill of execution. There was a mobile cocktail cabinet beyond the fireplace and Fifield opened out the split top, the two halves of which set down on either side to form shelves. 'What d'you want, Jim?'

'Gin and tonic.'

He poured out two drinks and handed one glass to Thorpe. He drank heavily, then said in a strained voice: 'How the hell d'you find me?'

Thorpe explained.

'Bloody hell! I spend months planning it all and then a primitive mug like you trees me!' He finished his drink, returned to the cocktail cabinet and poured himself another. 'All those years in the Force so I know every dodge and turn; work it as neat as a fiddler's bow . . . And you just stroll along and find me . . .'

'You seem more concerned about that than anything else.'

'What d'you bloody expect?'

'Some regret at Dick's death.'

'D'you think that didn't carve me up? It tore me apart. But how was I to know he'd got a thin skull and they'd crack him so hard?'

'Is that an excuse or an explanation?'

'Dick was an ex-copper and I liked him. If I'd realized . . . Look, it was me who had to tell Vera he'd died. Me who had to try and comfort her—only you can't comfort someone when her man's just croaked.'

'You must have known from experience that that sort of tragedy might happen.'

'If I had, I'd never have gone through with it.'

'And Watson?'

'What about him?'

'He was tortured and murdered.'

'He was a small-time villain.'

'So it doesn't matter what happened to him?'

'No.'

'He was still a human being.'

'You goddamn lily liberal! Why won't you open your eyes

and see what kind of a man you're talking about? His speciality was country houses. Break into 'em and nick whatever's around. Ever stopped to think what it's like for a woman to know that someone's been through her clothes, handling her pants, maybe even gloating over 'em; ever stopped to think what it's like to have something of sentimental value and irreplaceable nicked and to know the nicker'll only get peanuts for it? Of course you haven't. Your kind never does. The victim doesn't count, it's the criminal you agonize over. If a man rapes a woman, she must have led him on, even if he had a knife at her throat; if a terrorist murders half a dozen hostages, his motives were patriotic . . . Why don't you and the rest of your kind get out there and find out what it's like in the real world?'

'The old arguments.'

'Because they never change and your kind won't learn.'

'Does yours? Did it ever concern you that for your plan to succeed, I had to be falsely accused of robbery and murder?'

'I reckoned it'd maybe teach you the world's not all comfortable, it's a jungle where if you don't strike first, you get struck.'

'You didn't think of asking me whether I'd welcome the lesson? And what about Susan? You didn't worry about her believing you were dead and mourning you?'

'Mourning me? You're even softer than I thought . . . I'll tell you something I've never told another person. Mary meant everything to me. Even when she was so unthinkingly extravagant and I didn't know how in the hell I was going to pay the bills. Even then, I worshipped her. But she took off with someone else. Never mind how much I'd sacrificed for her. I begged Sue not to go with her. Sue wouldn't listen . . . One day I went up to Oxford to see where they were living; I was trying to find out what both of 'em found so much more attractive. I found out, didn't I? He's so rich he could spend my income and just wonder where his loose change has gone to. He'd bought 'em; both of 'em. I swore then I'd get my own back on 'em for letting themselves be bought.' Fifield emptied his glass. 'All right, let's get it settled. How much?'

'How much what?'

'How much are you asking?'

'You imagine I've come here to blackmail you?'

'Why else?'

'To be able to prove my innocence to Susan and the police.'

'Ten thousand now and ten thousand every year.'

'Can't you understand what I've been saying?'

'Make it fifteen thousand, then. Find yourself a woman. Start living.' Fifield went over and poured himself a third drink.

'You're not very smart, Paul. You don't understand people.'

'I don't understand bloody idiots.'

They heard the slam of car doors and both turned towards the window. A man came into view and then, as he neared the front door, went out of view. 'D'you know him?' Fifield demanded.

'No. Why should I?'

Fifield put down his glass and left the room.

Thorpe crossed to the nearest chair and sat. He and Fifield had been talking different languages. He ought to have realized that that had been inevitable . . .

The murmur of voices from the hall rose in volume and for the first time he could clearly hear the newcomer's voice. And with a sense of shock and fear, he identified the speaker as the man who had ordered his torture back in London.

CHAPTER 21

There was a king-size double bed in the main bedroom and after the three men had searched the house and failed to find the letter, they'd ordered Polly and Thorpe to lie down on it. Now the two of them were guarded by one man who sat near the door, a heavy automatic to hand.

Thorpe stared up at the ceiling, inconsequentially noting a point where a hairline crack had formed the shape of India. When they'd tortured him, the men had worn ski-masks so that there could be no fear he would ever be able to identify them; now, they were bare-faced. The significance of this was obvious.

There was a sudden scream from the ground floor, heard clearly through the closed door; it rose in volume and intensity of agony, then died away.

'Oh my God! What was that?' she said shrilly.

'I'm afraid it was Paul.'

'But . . . but what are they doing to him?'

'Forcing him to tell them where he's hidden the letter.'

There was another scream. She reached out and gripped his arm.

He remembered how the pain grew, even though only seconds before one had been so certain that it had already reached a peak impossible to be surpassed; the way in which the electric shocks sought out and tore at every muscle in the body . . .

The man on the chair lit a cigarette. He didn't look a thug. He had an open face and a humorous mouth. Met casually, he would seem an ordinary, pleasant person.

Another scream. Polly let go of his arm, turned over, and pulled one of the pillows over her head, like a child believing she could banish the world by hiding her eyes from it.

Even as he recognized the irrationality of the emotion, Thorpe felt sickeningly responsible for Fifield's suffering. He should have realized why they'd not killed him originally; he should have discovered that over the days and the weeks they'd been watching him, hoping he'd find Fifield . . .

Careful to make no sudden movement that would draw the attention of the man on the chair, he looked round the bedroom yet again, seeking anything that could offer hope. The distance from the foot of the bed to the man was roughly ten feet. At school, one of his sports had been shooting and he had been of above average skill with both rifle and revolver; he knew that although at a distance of fifty yards even a target the size of a man could prove extraordinarily difficult to hit with a handgun, at ten feet it was not easy to miss altogether. And the automatic looked to be of a sufficiently large calibre that to be hit anywhere would be to be immobilized . . . He looked to his immediate left. There was a table, part of the elaborate, padded headboard, and it was obvious that he occupied the side of the bed on which Polly normally slept. On the table were a number of bottles, lipstick, nail varnish, and other feminine mysteries. Beyond, beside the window, was a dressing-table on top of which was a set of silver-backed brushes. Either of them would make a reasonable cosh. But the table was some twelve feet away . . . On the wall opposite the bed hung two more of Fifield's paintings. It occurred to Thorpe, in the absurd way in which one's mind could work at times of stress, that judging by the profligacy with which Fifield hung his paintings in full view, he must consider himself a good, perhaps even a great, artist . . . The fourth wall consisted of built-in cupboards which stretched from floor to ceiling. Much of the contents of these had been thrown out on to the floor into untidy heaps and although it was possible that somewhere among the jumble there was something which would make a weapon, he'd be dead before he had the chance to make certain . . .

The man on the chair looked around, then dropped his cigarette on to the floor and ground it out with his heel. A small, brief wisp of smoke rose from the pale lilac coloured carpet.

There was another scream and Thorpe raised himself on one elbow. The man watched him, waiting for any further move. Thorpe lay back. Logically, it was hopeless. Yet that stubborn streak in him refused to accept this judgement and he visually examined the bedroom again. The windows? Too far away. In any case, the shutters had been closed and fastened. Even if he reached the window, opened it and the shutters, what then? There was not another house in sight. Ask to go to the lavatory and hope to find the chance to make a break? Almost certainly, the request would be refused . . . His attention returned to the bedside table. Among the feminine articles was a scent bottle in the shape of, and about the same size as, a cricket ball. He'd been a mediocre bowler, a very modest batsman, but a near brilliant fielder, chosen for the school's first eleven because of his ability to pick up a catch from the ground or shatter the stumps from thirty yards out when the batsman reckoned he'd all the time in the world to make his crease. Thrown with an accurate aim, that bottle could become a weapon. But when he reached for it he would come under suspicion, when his hand closed round it he would be shot . . . Unless the man's attention could somehow be distracted for long enough . . .

He turned on to his side so that he faced Polly. She'd withdrawn her head from under the pillow and was now lying on her back, staring blankly up at the ceiling. He waited until Fifield screamed again and then under cover of the agonized sound, whispered: 'You've got to help.'

She turned her head towards him. Her eyes were bloodshot, her cheeks wet from tears, her face slack with terror. She shivered repeatedly, as if suffering from a rigor.

He repeated his words, willing her to overcome her terror sufficiently to understand that he was offering her their only chance to continue living. This time, she understood what he'd said. She meant to whisper in return, but first she could find no voice, then she spoke far louder than she'd intended. 'I don't . . .' Terrified, she became silent.

The man looked curiously at her, but when neither of them made a move, he lost interest.

Thorpe whispered: 'You've got to distract his attention.'

Her lips formed the question, How?

'Let your skirt ride right up your legs.'

She looked at him blankly for a moment, then she suddenly realized what he meant. She raised her knees up so that her legs formed a V.

The man's gaze concentrated on her legs.

She let her knees fall further apart. The man's expression thickened and he leaned slightly to his right to gain a more uninterrupted view.

Thorpe moved with a speed that left no time for the fear of what would happen if he failed. He rolled off the bed and as he stood he reached out and grabbed the scent bottle. The man had been caught off guard and only now was beginning to come to his feet, bringing up the automatic as he did so. Thorpe threw. The bottle hit the man on his right eye and he dropped the automatic and put both hands to his eye as, doubling up, he fell back on to the chair.

Thorpe raced forward and kicked out and just reached the side of the man's head. The man toppled sideways off the chair. As he hit the floor he desperately reached out for the automatic which had landed a couple of feet away, but Thorpe stamped down on his outstretched fingers and he squealed from the pain. Thorpe picked up the automatic and slashed it down sideways, across the man's neck.

Polly was still lying on the bed, her legs up and wide apart, too shocked to move. Thorpe went out on to the carpeted landing; the sounds from below were sharper. Now, he could hear that Fifield was whimpering in between screams. One of the men said in a persuasive voice that all Fifield had to do to escape the pain was to tell them where the letter was hidden. For a while there was just the sound of whimpering, then the command was given to use the machine again. Fifield screamed once more.

Thorpe checked the automatic and made certain there was a round up the spout and the safety-catch was off. He crossed the landing to the head of the stairs. From the sounds, they had Fifield in the sitting-room—even if the door was open, unless one of them was standing in the doorway he was reasonably certain that he'd be out of sight up until the moment he stepped down into the hall. He went down the stairs. The hall was empty and the door was only partially open.

'Beef it up some more,' said one man.

'It's nearly on full strength now,' said the other.

'Keep it on longer, shove it up further.'

Thorpe approached the door, his passage silent thanks to the thick carpet. As he reached the doorway, Fifield screamed several times, each scream barely having time to die away before the next one started. The gun held ready, Thorpe kicked open the door.

They had stripped Fifield, then stretched him out and tied his hands and feet to armchairs. A black box, no larger than four inches by three, was on the ground at his side; from the box stretched two sets of leads, one of which was plugged into a wall socket, the other inserted in his body. One man knelt by the black box, adjusting the controls, the other stood by his head. As the door crashed back, they looked round. Their shock gave way to amazement, then to calculation.

Thorpe remembered the murdered Dick Vinay and the tragedy his death had brought to Vera. He remembered all he'd suffered when they'd tortured him and the humiliation he'd known because they'd broken his will to resist. He imagined the body-contorting agony which they'd been inflicting on Fifield . . . And he knew that for men who could willingly injure others like this, only death was fit. His first bullet struck the standing man in the chest and hurled him backwards, the second tore away part of his skull. The kneeling man, face twisted with terror, began to hold out both hands, either in a gesture of appeal or of surrender. Thorpe shot him twice in the head and he collapsed into a jerking heap.

Thorpe crossed to the wall socket and jerked out the plug, then removed the probe from Fifield's body. Fifield stared up at him, his gaze unfocused, whimpering continually as he waited for the next blast of pain, as yet unable to comprehend what had happened.

He returned upstairs to the bedroom. The man still lay unconscious by the side of the chair, Polly had moved and was sitting on the edge of the bed. 'What's happened?' she demanded wildly.

'There's no need to be frightened any more.'

'But the other two men . . .'

'I've shot them.'

She knew fresh horror.

'Is there a safe in the house?'

She appeared not to have heard.

He went up to the bed and shook her shoulders. 'Is there a safe in the house?'

She recoiled from him, as if his hands had been wet from blood. 'No. No. There's no safe.'

After all that had happened in London, Fifield would surely never have tempted fate by keeping the letter in a safe deposit or a bank? In any case, he was an unusually secretive man who must feel the need to make certain that the letter was safe; again and again, like a miser counting and recounting his hoard of gold, he must have looked at it. But before they'd tortured him, the men had searched the house from top to bottom and had failed to find it . . .

Thorpe returned to the sitting-room. Fifield, still stripped, was slumped in one of the armchairs. Thorpe stood in front of him. 'Where's the letter?'

Fifield shook his head.

'It's somewhere in the house.'

'No.'

'Where is it?'

'I swear it's not here.'

Thorpe raised his hand and Fifield flinched. Just for a second, Thorpe thought with self-contempt, he'd wanted to hit Fifield, to force him to reveal where the letter was hidden . . . His gaze passed, then returned to, the painting of the goose in a farmyard. Every other painting of Fifield's he'd ever seen had been a landscape and the longer one studied the goose, the more one realized why. Even allowing for the blindness of an artist's ego, Fifield must surely have realized that the painting was so crude it could only earn scorn and derision. But there was the story of the goose that laid the golden egg . . .

As he went over and lifted the painting off the wall, Fifield cried out, his words incoherent. Thorpe turned the painting over and pulled off the brown paper which backed it. The letter, stained on one corner, was in handwriting and signed Thomas Gerald Barnham.

CHAPTER 22

London was at its dreariest. Rain was falling from a leaden sky, pavements and roads were waterlogged, passing traffic splattered pedestrians with filth. The taxi drew up and Thorpe paid the driver the fare and added a generous tip, but this failed to earn him any words of thanks. He went into the slab-shaped building and took a lift up to the eleventh floor. The receptionist spoke over the internal telephone and then said that Miss Ewing would be down as soon as possible.

'That's all right, I'll go on up.' Thorpe walked past the desk.

'But you can't . . .' began the receptionist. She shrugged her shoulders. Let someone else do the worrying.

As Thorpe reached the head of the stairs on the twelfth floor, Pamela came hurrying along the corridor. 'What are you doing? You shouldn't have come up here,' she said breathlessly.

'I need a word with the boss.'

'For heaven's sake, Jim! He's in a difficult mood today because of work and if you try to interrupt him . . . Look, go on back down and if there's something you want I'll see if I can help you. Let's meet later on . . .'

He took an envelope out of his pocket. 'Give him this. Tell him I want to speak to him now.'

She looked at the blank envelope, then up at him, her beautiful eyes troubled.

'I promise you that it won't affect you in any way.'

'But . . .'

'No buts.'

She hesitated, finally took the envelope from him. She said, in a low voice: 'You'd better come and wait in my room.'

He followed her along the corridor to her office. She went over to the second door, knocked, went inside and closed the door. When she returned, she said that he was to go through.

Sir Thomas Barnham continued to read the single sheet of paper that had been in the envelope and he did not look up until Thorpe was standing in front of the desk. 'I presume you have the original?' he asked, his voice quiet and controlled.

'Yes.'

'Do you intend to try to blackmail me with it?'

'No.'

'Then why have you come here?'

'To warn you that I'm going to make certain the letter's published so that everyone will know that when you stood up in the House and said you'd never had any business dealings with Barber, you were lying; to prove that twenty-four years ago you were given work by him on the understanding that you later paid him a thousand pounds . . .'

'There's really no need to go into details; I can see what I wrote.' He put the paper down on the desk, leaned back in the chair, and studied Thorpe for several seconds. 'Tell me, why are you so intent on seeing the letter published?'

'I've just told you.'

'Don't you appreciate the fact that at the time I had no option but to make the statement to the House that I did?'

'No option?'

'Had I not made it, the Opposition would have had a field day.'

'That's irrelevant.'

'On the contrary, nothing is more relevant. Party politics is the art of keeping the Opposition in opposition.'

'Even at the cost of lying?'

'Who can define a lie when everything is capable of opposite definitions and contradictory interpretations?'

'What you said was a lie, however you define or interpret it.'

'I made a statement, which in essence was correct, since I had no alternative but to make it if I was to retain my credibility and political honour.'

'You can seriously talk about having retained credibility and honour?'

'Once I'd made my statement, in the minds of my listeners I remained the man I had been before. One's credibility and honour lie in the minds of other people.'

'If they'd known the truth, they wouldn't have believed in either.'

'Had known the truth? The truth is that for the past twenty-three years I have behaved honourably by any standards, let alone the standards of success. And for the past twelve years I have represented my constituency to the best of my ability and—not being a hypocrite and therefore being free from false modesty—I know that I have done a great deal for my constituents. And to pursue the matter further, were I forced to resign in circumstances which the ordinary and rather naive voter found discreditable, it is fairly certain that the other side would win the seat.'

'And you really think that that can begin to justify your lie?'

'This is a pragmatic world. The end, therefore, always justify the means.'

'You're totally wrong.'

'I doubt it.'

'For one thing, if your political opponent gained the seat, he might do more for your constituents than you have.'

'His politics are of the far left and so in the name of liberty he would impose tyranny. No tyrant has ever improved the lot of anyone but himself . . . Mr Thorpe, you would call yourself an idealist, but you must recognize that idealism is not only a danger to oneself, it is also dangerous to others. Have you stopped to consider what are the implications of the publication of my letter?'

'Of course.'

'Are you quite sure? Do you know anything about the City?'

'No.'

'The City has a motto—my word is my bond. Naturally, we all pay lip service to such an ideal whatever path we choose to tread in private, because illusions take a stronger hold on men's minds than reality. It therefore follows that we are very quick to condemn anyone seen to fall short of such ideal, irrespective of our own shortcomings. Do you follow me?'

'No.'

'Then I'll try to put things more simply. If my letter is published, my credibility will be severely damaged, both as a politician and a businessman. Character credit is almost as important as financial credit and the one is directly related to the other. So my business will probably be ruined.'

'It deserves to be.'

'Evidently you don't realize that it will not be I who will suffer if my business is ruined, it will be all those who are directly or indirectly relying on my skills and business acumen in order to earn their living.'

'Why won't you suffer?'

Barnham showed surprise, then slight contempt. 'Naturally I've made certain that whatever happens, my own financial future is assured.'

Thorpe remembered his promise to Pamela, made only minutes before, that her life would never be affected by this visit.

'You look as if you're beginning to appreciate that the problem is not as simple as it first appeared to be. Few problems are. Take yourself, for instance. You would call yourself an idealist . . .' Barnham checked his words as he saw Thorpe shake his head and prepare to speak. He frowned and his tone became impatient. 'It is stupid to try to deny it. You believe yourself to be an idealist. But are you really responding only to the highest motives? As you know, I paid a firm to investigate your life. From them, I learned of your friendship with Miss Susan Fifield. You say it's not your intention to use the letter to blackmail me, but to see it's published so that the world learns what happened twenty-four years ago. Then why didn't you go straight to one of the national newspapers and hand them the letter? Why come here and tell me of your intentions first? . . . You know the answer as clearly as I. You've no intention of ever seeing my letter published because despite that blindfold of idealism, you retain sufficient common sense to put your own interests first. You will not, therefore, take any action which must result in the exposure of Paul Fifield and the real reason why you've come here is because you believed that I'd find the means to convince you that publication is not in the interests of anyone, least of all yourself.'

Thorpe stared at him, hating him; and surprised that he could be so acute in most of his perceptions and yet so wrong in one.

'Why be bitter? Because it forces you to acknowledge that your motives are less high-minded than you'd wish? Be grateful, not bitter. There's nothing so potentially destructive as high-mindedness . . . I imagine you have the original of my letter on you?'

Thorpe said nothing.

'Give it to me now and I'll destroy it and bring an end to all your problems.'

After a while, Thorpe brought a second envelope out of his inside coat pocket and put it on the desk. Barnham picked it up and extracted the letter. 'It's strange, isn't it,' he said in a reflective tone, 'how stupid one can be when young and hungry for success.'

'You'd do the same thing again now, if the stakes were high enough.'

Barnham smiled. 'I wasn't thinking about the bribery, but about the fact that I wrote this and gave it to Phillip Barber because he said he wanted an insurance that I would never tell anyone about his corruption. It never occurred to me then that when I became far more successful than he, this weapon of defence could be turned into a weapon of attack.'

Thorpe turned and walked over to the door.

'Thank you for bringing me the letter.'

He went out.

*

He parked in front of Alding House and as he stepped out of the borrowed car, Tilly appeared and began to bark. He called to her and she came up, tail waving energetically.

Susan came round the corner of the house and the late, weak October sunshine, reaching down through a gap in the clouds, lent depth to her face and added highlights to her hair. Her expression became angry. 'I said never to come here again.'

'I had to tell you something.' He walked over, ignoring Tilly who was trying to demand attention.

'Tell me what?' The light wind flicked at two curls which leaned over her forehead and she tried to brush them back with her fingers.

He didn't know how to say it gently, so he said it baldly. 'Your father is alive.'

Her face became white and strained. 'I put flowers by his grave. I arranged to have his flat sold. How can you be such a swine as to come here and say that?'

'He's in a hospital in Carcassonne and although he was made to suffer a lot, they think he'll make a full recovery.'

'He's dead.'

'His death was faked. Then some men found out where he was living and tortured him to tell them where he'd hidden a letter.'

'Letter?'

'The letter which was taken from the vaults before the robbery and murder and which was used for blackmail.'

'Are you trying to say . . . It's a filthy lie.'

'I did not sell the information to the gang who robbed the vaults and the fact that your father is still alive proves that.'

'He's dead.'

He brought a piece of paper out of his coat pocket. 'Here's the telephone number of the hospital.'

She grabbed the paper, scrumpled it up, threw it on to the ground.

'You can't change the facts, doing that,' he said sadly.

'He's dead.'

'Please, telephone and confirm for yourself. I know he badly wants you to go to Carcassonne to see him.'

'He's dead.'

He remembered the times he'd tried to convince himself that it was understandable she should believe him guilty, even though he'd been so hurt that she would not accept his innocence as an article of faith, as he would have done had the roles been reversed. She had to distance herself as far away as possible from trouble because for her the world must always run smoothly. So if now she acknowledged that her father was alive, she must also acknowledge that he was a criminal. Then her world could never be smooth again . . .

'What are you going to do?' she demanded shrilly.

He said sadly: 'Are you frightened that I'll tell the police and then your father will be arrested and charged and you'll be forced to feel the disgrace? . . . Don't worry. The police haven't enough evidence to arrest anyone, not even me, so if nothing's said, nothing will be done. And in my book, your father's suffered enough for what he did, particularly when he had to tell Vera Vinay that her husband had just died, knowing that he was responsible. But I don't suppose you can understand that?'

'I don't understand anything.'

'You don't surprise me.'

'What are you going to do?' she demanded for the second time.

'Get the first flight I can to Mallorca.'

'But you said he was in a hospital in Carcassonne.'

'My date is with someone who's learned to meet life full face on and fight back, not turn tail and run.'

He returned to his car and drove off.

A Question of Principle

CHAPTER 1

The dining-room, which led directly off the kitchen, was small and the low, beamed ceiling and the wide, open fireplace made it seem even smaller still. There really was no room for the Elizabethan court cupboard, but this had come from Anne's home and she kept it because of the memories it held.

The four of them sat around the reproduction refectory table, Anne nearest the kitchen door. Elham brushed his lips with a serviette. 'That was a truly delicious piece of pork,' he said in his deep, fruity voice.

'Yes, wasn't it?' echoed Penelope. She turned to her sister. 'I just don't know how you learned to cook so well.'

'Necessity,' replied Anne, a touch of light irony in her voice.

'But Mother never taught us a thing. I mean, I simply wouldn't know where to begin.' 'Simply' was verbally underlined. She seldom spoke without underlining one word or another.

Rickmore had drunk enough not to guard his tongue as carefully as Anne would have had him do. 'If the need ever arises, no doubt you'll manage very successfully.'

'I don't think she needs to worry,' said Elham pompously.

An oblique reference, wondered Rickmore, amused, to the fact that Terence Elham was a man with credit while Dennis Rickmore was a man of credit—mortgage, overdraft, strained relations with the credit card firm . . .

'Let's clear the table, Dennis,' said Anne, 'and bring the sweet in.'

He looked briefly at her. There was a warning gleam in

her eyes. Don't start sniping at them. She was right, of course, but it was a pity not to pull the legs of two people who were so self-satisfied that they seldom realized their legs were being pulled. He stood, saw that Elham's glass was empty and picked up the bottle of wine. He went round the table to top up Penelope's glass.

She put her hand over the rim. 'Not for me, thanks. I'm on cloud nine already.'

More affectation? She seemed totally unaffected by what she'd drunk. Or were the effects merely well camouflaged? Anne had told him that Penelope was drinking heavily nowadays and always had a couple of vodkas before going out to a party in case the hospitality was poor. She claimed that vodka wasn't really alcoholic, not like gin or whisky. She had the useful ability of being able to believe whatever it suited her to believe.

'Come on back to earth,' said Anne.

He refilled Elham's glass.

'The Spaniards,' said Elham, 'seem to be improving the quality of their wine these days.'

'They are. You ought to try all the different Riojas one can buy now.'

'I most certainly will.'

He most certainly wouldn't, thought Rickmore. He emptied the bottle into his own glass after Anne had shaken her head to show she didn't want any more. It wasn't smart to drink Spanish wine; French, of course, German provided it didn't contain too much anti-freeze, and Californian if one were slightly eccentric. He raised his own glass and drank. Bad manners to drink standing up. It was fun confirming their opinion of him . . . He checked his thoughts, vaguely astonished to discover that they were becoming slightly incoherent. He carried the now empty bottle and the meat dish through to the kitchen.

The kitchen, part of the outshut, was very small and there

was little working surface; what there was, was now crowded with the bowls, dishes and utensils, used in the cooking and preparation of the meal. He stood in the centre, his head only an inch beneath the ceiling. 'Where . . . where shall I put the meat dish?'

Anne, her dark blue eyes expressing amusement, murmured: 'You, sir, are half sloshed!'

'Absolute nonsense.'

'Repeat after me, I've sipped solely a sustaining sufficiency, certainly insufficient to succour a social solecism.'

'Like hell!'

'Probably very wise of you.' She moved a mixing bowl and then took the meat dish from him and put it down.

'You wrong me.' Even when completely sober, he occasionally mispronounced his R's.

'I doubt it.'

'Very well. I will prove I can speak in many tongues. I see . . . I saw sea shells . . .'

'If I were you, love, I'd look some other time, when the sea's not quite so choppy . . . The pud's in the fridge, along with cream. Are you up to whipping that?'

'Any more cheek and I'll show you exactly what I am up to whipping.' He went across to the refrigerator and, very carefully, brought out four individual bowls of chocolate orange mousse, putting each one on top in turn. 'Where's the . . . the cream?'

'In front of your nose.'

He lifted out the carton, shut the refrigerator door—a little more enthusiastically than he'd intended—moved over to the food mixer.

'Dennis, you know that's not working.'

He remembered.

'Use the beater.'

He poured the cream into a plastic bowl and whisked it, bothered for most of the time by the bowl's tendency to crab sideways. When the cream held a point, he tapped the whisk to clear it, then began to walk over to the doorway.

'Are you thinking of serving the cream in that bowl?'

He looked down and was immediately amused by the thought of his sister-in-law's and brother-in-law's expressions at the sight of whipped cream being served in a kitchen bowl . . . He corrected his thoughts. Terence was a man of precision. So it was sister-in-law and sister-in-law's husband . . .

'For heaven's sake, wake up. Here, give it to me.'

He handed her the bowl. 'I'll get the white wine.'

'Don't you think . . .' She stopped. They didn't drink wine very often and it seemed a pity to suggest he left the third bottle unopened merely because he'd obviously had enough. Since the pre-dinner drinks, some of the lines had disappeared from his face and his manner had become light and ironic, reminding her of when they'd first known each other and the world had been all sunshine . . . She sighed as she opened the cupboard to the right of the sink and brought out the small silver dish, another legacy from her parents' home. Normally, other people's prosperity was no cross to bear, but when those other people were close relations who made a point of underlining their prosperity . . . There was laughter from the dining-room. Had Dennis been misguided enough to tell them about the judge who stuttered? If so, Terence's laughter had been very false. For him, the law was not a subject about which one joked . . .

'Not your chocolate orange mousse?' said Penelope, as Anne walked through the doorway, carrying a tray with the four glass bowls and the cream on it. 'Didn't I say before we left home, Terence, that we'd have the most perfect meal?'

'You most certainly did.'

'Much nicer than if we'd gone to the Gordons' . . .' She stopped abruptly.

'What's this?' asked Rickmore. 'It sounds to me, Penny, as if you had a second invitation for tonight.'

'Well, we . . .' She looked at her husband.

'As a matter of fact, we did,' said Elham, now at his most urbane. 'But since we didn't receive it until after yours, and since we'd no doubts about which one we'd rather accept, we naturally refused the Gordons.'

'We're flattered.' Even Rickmore accepted that this was a moment to keep quiet, but the wine was too lively for him to do so. 'And very highly honoured!' Never let it be forgotten that Sir Francis was a high court judge and therefore an invitation from him was to be regarded in the light of a royal command. So could Terence, a man who knew the value of every relationship (but the price of none), have willingly turned down this invitation? Surely not. Penelope must have persuaded him that they could not go back on their prior acceptance. Although every bit as much of a snob as he, she did make a point of honouring family ties . . .

Penelope, aware that there was a danger of something being said that could not easily be laughed off, changed the conversation and talked about a cocktail party to which she and Elham had recently been. Her remarks were amusing and only slightly catty.

Think what you like about her, Rickmore decided, as he poured out the white wine, you had to admit that her social skills were second to none.

The sitting-room was on the far side of the massive central chimney about which the house had been built. Like all the other rooms in the house, it was heavily beamed and the central one was deep so that anyone with any height had to duck to pass under it unscathed. Roughly square, the room had a single small window and was naturally rather dark. A modern fireplace had been built within the very wide inglenook one and although from any æsthetic point of view this should have been ripped out, since it gave out so much more heat than the original would have done, it had been left. As Anne had once said, it was much easier to be an æsthete when one was well off.

Rickmore got up from one of the armchairs, crossed to the fire and threw on a couple of split logs; there was a rush of flame which caused a patch of soot to sparkle briefly as it caught fire. He turned. 'How about the other half?'

'No more for me,' said Penelope. 'One more drop of alcohol and I'll be seeing quadruple.'

'You'll be seeing what?' Elham, who'd begun to slump in the armchair, jerked himself upright. 'What did you say, Penelope?'

'I said I can't possibly drink any more or I'll be seeing quadruple.'

'Nonsense. Do think before you speak.'

'But you're always saying that thinking is dangerous for me.'

'You're talking ridiculously.'

She was hurt by his bad-tempered words.

Rickmore said: 'You'll join me in another brandy, won't you, Terence, even if the girls have chickened out?'

'But we brought it as a present for you,' protested Penelope, 'not for us to drink.'

'A present shared is a pleasure doubled.'

'What a marvellous sentiment. I just can't think how you can be so clever as to think up something like that.'

Anne said drily: 'He adapts the original.'

Rickmore made a face at her. 'Can't you leave any illusions in other people's minds?'

'Don't you mean delusions?'

He laughed, went over to the small mother-of-pearl inlaid table and picked up the bottle of Martell VSOP the Elhams had brought. 'You didn't get the chance to answer me, Terence. Will you have another snifter?'

'Snifter?' replied Elham. 'It's a long time since I've heard that expression.'

'I'm firmly rooted in the past.' He collected Elham's glass, poured into it a very generous measure, returned it. He collected his own glass and helped himself equally liberally. When he sat, he did so much more heavily than he'd intended and a little cognac slopped over the edge of the glass. He licked his hand. 'As my mother always taught me, waste not, want not.'

Elham sententiously thought it was a pity that Rickmore's mother hadn't also taught him that a gentleman did not lick his hand in public.

It was a clear night and the sky was alive with stars; the rising moon was beginning to cast vague shadows. In the distance, a vixen began to cry, in reality calling for a mate, but sounding as if in agonized torment; much nearer, a roosting pigeon was disturbed and the clap of its wings carried far.

Penelope passed through the outside doorway of the porch, then turned. 'It's become very much colder,' she said, from within the comfort of her full-length silver fox coat. 'Don't stand there with the door open, go on back into the warmth.'

'You're right, it is colder,' said Anne, 'so I think I will.'

Penelope stepped forward to embrace her sister and kissed her on both cheeks. 'It's been an absolutely perfect evening. I haven't enjoyed one so much in years and years.'

'Good.' Anne freed herself.

'Good night, Anne,' said Elham. 'The meal was truly delicious.' From their first meeting, he had correctly judged that, in direct contrast to her sister, she eschewed all affectation and he never made the mistake of showing her more than genuine respect. This respect occasionally made him wonder why she'd married Rickmore. With her attractive looks and warm personality, her reasonable and logical approach to everything, and her determination, she surely could have found a husband with a much sounder financial background.

Anne said one last good night and then closed the outside door of the porch; since it was glass, light continued to spill out on to the brick path to help them until they came within range of the outside light on the corner of the house.

Elham's dark green Jaguar was parked outside the garage —a World War Two army hut which was beginning to look as if it dated back to World War One. The Jaguar was an XJ-S, breathed upon and customized by Steerson; the V12 engine had been developed to produce 340 bhp, the suspension had been modified to accept this extra power, and the interior was even more luxurious than was that of the standard model. It was impossible to mistake the fact that this was a rich man's car.

'How's it going?' asked Rickmore.

'As smooth as silk,' replied Elham, with deep satisfaction.

'From what I've read, the engine is built like a Swiss jeweller's watch.'

'I wouldn't know how it's built; only how it goes.' He went to pull out the keys from his pocket and was surprised to discover how clumsy his fingers had suddenly become.

'She does use rather a lot of petrol, though?'

He shrugged his shoulders. He couldn't be expected to concern himself about that; if a man had to worry about the fuel consumption, he had no business buying the car. He finally managed to bring out the keys and went to insert one in the lock of the door; somehow he missed and the point of the key briefly scraped along the paintwork. He swore, conscious he was making a bit of a fool of himself. He tried again and this time the key went home. He turned it and the four doors unlocked. He pulled open the door and

Penelope, after kissing Rickmore on both cheeks, climbed in and sat.

Elham went round to the driver's door. 'Thanks again, Dennis.'

'It's been a pleasure.'

But for whom? he wondered as he settled behind the wheel. He started the engine and then blipped it, unable to resist the satisfaction of showing how much power lay under his command. Then he engaged Drive, released the handbrake, and accelerated.

The drive, perhaps more accurately described as a slightly upmarket yard, ended at wooden gates which were always left open; in the headlights, the broken bottom crosspiece of one of them was obvious. Rundown, like so much about the place, he thought. As they turned left on to the road, there was a muted squeal from the tyres. He was vaguely surprised to discover that they'd been travelling that quickly.

The slightly undulating road ended at a T-junction. He turned right, came to a halt at crossroads fifty yards further on. On their right was a pub. Rickmore had said that occasionally he went in there and had a drink. A typically pointless exercise since only the local yokels would use it—but his brother-in-law had no grasp of priorities.

The road was clear and he accelerated, fiercely enough momentarily to pin them back in their seats.

'Don't drive so fast,' she said petulantly.

'You call that fast?' He laughed. When he'd been young . . . He corrected his thoughts, which had been about to indulge in fantasy. When he'd been young, he hadn't owned a Jaguar and burned up the roads. He hadn't even owned a clapped-out Mini. He could still remember the scorn of a girl he'd met at a bottle party when he'd confessed to being carless. She'd turned down a suggestion of another meeting. That, surely, had been some time during his pupillage, when every penny had had to be made to do the work of four . . .

'For God's sake, Terence, slow down and keep to your side of the road.'

'Stop fussing,' he snapped. It was generally supposed by their friends that she couldn't be as vacuous as she appeared and that therefore it was all a pose. But the pose was that she couldn't. But she was beautiful and when he saw the envy and desire in other men's eyes, he was content, except . . .

'Do look what you're doing.' Her voice was now shrill.

He steered for the nearside as he stamped on the brakes. The car skidded very slightly on the damp road, but then corrected itself without any action on his part; indeed, he didn't even become aware that they had begun to skid until it was all over.

Despite his braking, they still entered the left-hand corner too fast, especially remembering that there was a sharper right-hander a hundred yards further on. He was considering the need to brake again—and to return to the left-hand side of the road—when from a rough copse on their right a man ran out. Elham swung the wheel to the left, but the off-side wing hit the man and sent him flying, a Catherine wheel of arms and legs.

CHAPTER 2

Elham braked as he looked up at the rear-view mirror. The soft moonlight was just strong enough for him to be able to make out the dark bundle in the middle of the road. He tried to assure himself that it was moving.

'What are you doing?' she demanded shrilly. 'You fool, don't stop.'

'But . . .'

She gripped his shoulder and shook it, careless of what effect this had on his driving. 'For God's sake, keep going.'

'He may be hurt,' he mumbled.

'Someone else can cope.'

The car had slowed to little more than a walking pace. He half-turned and looked at her as he desperately tried to force his mind into focus. 'But I daren't just drive on. The law . . .'

Her voice rose still higher. 'Can't you understand? If you report it, they'll breathalyse you.'

He realized that she was right. It wouldn't matter that the accident had not been his fault, that the man had run into the car rather than that the car had hit him. They would insist on checking his blood/alcohol level and they'd find it was over the limit. From that moment on, it would prove impossible to maintain that the collision had been unavoidable because insobriety raised a presumption of guilt which was almost impossible to rebut . . . So if he stopped now, he must inevitably end up by being charged . . .

The Bar was jealous of its reputation and demanded that those who practised at it were beyond criticism. To be found guilty of any criminal offence was likely to lead to disbarment; to be found guilty of a serious one inevitably did. So disaster lay ahead. And this at a time when he had applied for Silk and his future seemed set to attain heights which thirty years ago had appeared unrealistic day-dreams . . .

His mind was trained to cut through confusion and to recognize essentials and now, despite the acohol, despite the shock and panic, he understood that disaster need not lie ahead if only he could conceal his part in the accident. Could he?

Hit-and-run cases presented the police with difficult investigations and their clear-up rate was not high. Usually, they only solved them when someone was able to give an initial indication of the vehicle's identity—only then could they call in experts to make the necessary positive identification. This initial indication normally came from one of three sources—an eyewitness (who might be the victim), the sighting of a vehicle damaged in a manner consistent with the accident, or as a consequence of a report from the garage called upon to repair such damage (ironically, requested in an attempt to conceal it). Here, there had been no eyewitness other than the victim. He had run out from the copse so carelessly that it was impossible to believe he could have taken any notice of the approaching car through the glare of the headlights. After the impact, shock must surely have prevented accurate observation? So if he drove on now, the odds were heavily against the victim being able to give the police any useful evidence. And once back at Popham House, he could check the damage the car had suffered and decide what steps needed to be taken to conceal it . . .

Although this was never a busy road, there was bound to be another vehicle along fairly soon, so the injured man would not be long without help . . .

He accelerated. They rounded the right-hander and drew level with the cricket pitch, fenced off from the sheep which grazed the outfield during the winter. Ahead of them, another vehicle approached, its headlights picking out the pollard willows which lined the stream which separated the road from the field. He realized that if he'd hesitated even a few more seconds, he'd have been unable to escape disaster and he felt sick at the thought.

'I do believe that Terence is getting even more pompous,' Rickmore said, as he used a pair of tongs to lift a partly burned log to one side of the fireplace.

'What lies behind that observation—sour grapes?' asked Anne.

He put the tongs back on the stand, picked up the fire-guard and set it in front of the fireplace. As he stood upright, he said: 'You really think that?'

She regarded him for several seconds, then answered as she ran her fingers through her thick curly black hair which refused to be constrained or styled and had filled her with despair until she had learned to leave it to grow as it demanded. 'Not in the sense that you envy him his pos-sessions. But maybe yes in the sense that you envy him the security that those possessions give him.'

'I suppose I have to admit I'd like to be able to forget the more mundane problems of life, such as how can we afford to live next week.'

'We always manage.'

'But I can't buy you all the new clothes you need . . .'

'If you're thinking of that silver fox, forget it.'

'The what?'

'Wasn't it Penny's new coat which made you say that?'

'I didn't realize it was new—I thought it was the old one.'

She laughed as she came forward and rested her forearms on his shoulders and linked her fingers behind his head. 'If she knew that you never realized she was wearing a brand new silver fox coat, she'd be spitting six-inch nails.'

'I'm just dead unobservant and ignorant.'

'When it comes to fur coats, undoubtedly.' She kissed him. 'That's one of your attractions.'

'Then you're prepared to admit I do have some?'

She kissed him again, then released him and stepped back. 'You know what I think of fishing for compliments?'

'The bait's never right?'

'The fish you catch are rotten . . . Come on, instead of talking nonsense, let's go to bed.'

'Right,' he said with enthusiasm.

'You've had too much to drink to think along those lines; aren't you remembering your Shakespeare?'

'At this time of night? Anyway, didn't he also say that he always hath a way?'

She knew a warm happiness that she was married to a man who could talk stupidities instead of stocks and shares and futures. She yawned. 'I thought that pud I made was quite nice.'

'So now who's fishing?'

'All right, I am. So you can damn well tell me what you thought of my chocolate orange mousse.'

'Lumpy.'

She whirled round, picked up a cushion from the settee, and hurled it at him. He ducked and the cushion swept across the top of a small occasional table, sending objects flying. 'Damn!' she exclaimed.

'No doubt you expect me to apologize for ducking?'

'Of course.' She went over and knelt, to discover exactly what, if any, damage she'd caused. The chased silver snuff-box was undented. 'That's all right, thank goodness . . . I do wonder what's happened to Uncle Paul? It's strange to have a blood relative who took off from home and hasn't been seen or heard from since.'

'One day he'll turn up, looking for his favourite niece because he wants to leave her all those vulgar oil wells he owns back in Texas.'

'When I was young, I used to have that kind of daydream. But when I mentioned it to Mother, she said that Paul would only reappear if he were broke.' She returned the snuffbox to the table. 'He gave me this two days before he disappeared. I often wonder why he did.'

'Perhaps he thought he was about to snuff it.'

'God, your sense of humour doesn't improve! . . . What's this? Blast!'

'Now what's the matter?'

In answer, she held up a blue spectacle case.

'Are they Terence's?'

'Can't be anyone else's, can they? And he's bound to need them tomorrow, so he'll have to come back now and fetch them. Ring him up, will you, while I finish tidying up?'

He went through to the hall—like the kitchen, originally part of the outshut—and across to the corner cupboard by the doorway into the kitchen. He lifted the receiver off the telephone and dialled. The call was unanswered. 'They can't be back yet.'

She stood in the doorway of the sitting-room and looked at her watch. 'It's nearly twenty minutes since they left here. They must be back by now if they went straight there.'

'They're not likely to have done anything else at this time of night—Terence reckons that a late night leads straight along the path of unrighteousness.'

She thought for a moment, her features slightly blurred by the combination of light and shadow which softened them and added a touch of beauty to a face which normally held too much character to be termed beautiful. 'Try again.'

He dialled and there was still no answer.

'D'you think something's happened to them on the way back?'

'Very unlikely. The devil always looks after his own.'

'But they couldn't possibly take more than a quarter of an hour . . . I think I'd better drive over to see if they're all right and to return the glasses.'

'Why can't we just leave it . . .'

'Because we can't.'

'They would, if the roles were reversed.' He sighed. 'I know, they aren't.'

'That's not very fair.'

'Facts often aren't.'

'Now who's being pompous?'

'The final insult! OK, OK, I'll drive his spectacles back so that in the morning he can appear in court with his usual brilliance.'

'Are you sure you're up to driving?'

'I'm as sober as a judge.'

'Then heaven help justice . . . Darling, please go carefully.'

'On tiptoe, fairy-like . . . On second thoughts, not a very safe expression in this gay day and age.'

'Don't worry, you'll never be mistaken for one of them.' She returned to the sitting-room, brought back the spectacle case which she handed to him. 'Don't stay on for a nightcap, or anything.'

'Not a dram shall pass my lips. And as far as the anything is concerned, Penelope has never bewitched me while Circe weaves.'

'Idiot! Sometimes I think you're certifiable.'

'But charming.'

'God, you don't dislike yourself!'

'What cause have I ever had to? . . . I'll be back in a rush.'

'Just go and return at a sober pace.'

'Is our old banger capable of any other?'

He left the hall and went through the small porch to the outside. He was about to shut the porch door, when she called out: 'What about a coat?'

'Don't need one,' he replied, forgetting how cold it had become.

He walked along the brick path, round the corner of the house. He was, he thought as he opened the wooden gate, a very lucky man to be married to Anne. Life would be perfect if only he could earn a bit more money . . . It was funny how life usually made certain there was an if. Take Elham. He had success, money, and a very beautiful wife. Yet it had become clear in only the last few days that his life might hold an if. The previous Tuesday, over a drink in the Reckton squash club, Hugo Beeston had over-casually mentioned seeing Elham in a restaurant just off the Fulham Road, lunching with a sculptor who'd created a hullabaloo with her work. Beeston, a born gossip, had obviously been fishing for information as to whether the relationship was possibly more than a casual one. He'd gone away empty-handed. But could Elham be having an affair with a sculptor who was, apparently, noted for depicting the male member in unusual guises? It was a delightful thought . . .

He reached the garage, opened the right-hand set of doors and clipped them back. He didn't bother to switch on the light, but edged his way between the workbench and the Escort to the driving door. He settled behind the wheel, turned the key, and the engine churned over but did not fire. He tried again, with the same result. He remembered how the Jaguar had fired immediately and how the exhausts had burbled with the tenor of a running brook which might, at whim, be transformed into a raging torrent. When Anne had said that perhaps he envied Elham his sense of security, but not his material possessions, she'd forgotten that cus-tomized XJ-S.

The Escort's engine finally fired; the engine ran lumpily. Only recently, the garage had said that he couldn't expect much from a car which had been right round the clock once and seemed to be heading for its second century. He needed a new car. They hadn't added where he was to find the money to buy this new car.

He backed out, turned, drove on to the road and turned left to go down to the T-junction. Seven minutes later he approached the left-hand corner just before the cricket field to find that traffic cones had been set up on the road, together with a police notice to slow. Round the bend were parked two cars. Clearly, there had been an accident. He slowed down to a crawl, suddenly very conscious of the fact that he had drunk more than enough to be driving.

A policeman in uniform, reflector tabs on his sleeves and a reflective lollipop in his right hand, waved him on, his quick movements suggesting impatience. Probably, Rickmore thought, some of the passers-by had tried to rubberneck. He dropped down to second gear, hugged the left-hand verge, and drove past the policeman. He was aware of a group of people, but could not make out what they were doing. He reached the right-hander and passed a policeman who was ready to slow traffic coming in the opposite direction. By the time he was through the corner, all signs of the accident were gone from the rear-view mirror.

The road, turning this way and that for no obvious reason —the course of the rolling English drunkard?—crossed the tributary of the Wort and then climbed up over the railway line and into the village of Ailsham, a haphazard collection of centuries-old cottages, a few ugly modern council houses, a general store, and a pub. Beyond the village the road forked and he turned left.

Popham House lay a mile outside the village. Originally a typical farmhouse, probably built for a yeoman farmer of some consequence, with high-pitched roof, peg tiles, bricks made from clay dug nearby, and beams cut out from locally felled oaks, it had been enlarged and modernized by previous owners. Since they had had considerable taste and sympathy for period, the result had not been noticeably incongruous or anachronistic. Lacking such constraining influences, the Elhams had, when in turn they'd decided to have the enlarged house enlarged, demanded size and luxury irrespective of any other standards. Popham House was now the home of wealthy people who wanted others to admire and envy.

The large, fussily designed wrought-iron gates were open. So they had returned, thought Rickmore. Then why hadn't they closed them? Was Elham tighter than he'd seemed?

He drove through the gateway and into the macadamed drive. To the left was a three-car garage. The Jaguar was parked outside and Penelope and Elham were standing by it. Elham had a torch in his hand and this was switched on even though the outside lights on the garage were also on. As the Escort came to a stop, Rickmore was momentarily struck by the expression on their faces; it looked like fear, but since this must be an absurd flight of fancy, he dismissed the idea.

He opened the door, climbed out, and approached them. 'We tried to phone, but there wasn't any answer.'

They said nothing, but continued to stare at him. 'Is something wrong?' he asked.

'No,' Elham mumbled.

'You forgot your specs and we reckoned that as you'd need them tomorrow, I'd better run them over.'

'What . . . what's that?'

'Your spectacles—I've brought them.' He held out the case.

Elham took it and then there was a silence, which Rickmore finally broke. 'I'll be getting back home, then.'

Penelope made an effort to behave normally. 'Thank you so very much for bringing them. It's wonderfully kind of you.'

Despite their previous denial, Rickmore thought, they were behaving as if something were very wrong. But obviously they didn't want to discuss what that something was. He began to turn away when a brief fleck of light drew his attention to the offside wing of the Jaguar. He saw that there was a slight dent in it. Then his gaze moved down and, thanks to the angle at which he stood, he could just see that the offside light pod was smashed. Obviously Elham, his judgement affected by drink, had bumped into something as he drove in. No wonder the atmosphere was strained! And ten to one Penelope, whose second name was not discretion, had not had the sense to keep her opinions to herself . . .

Rickmore returned to the Escort and left.

Anne was in bed, the duvet drawn up half over her head as she often liked it—squirrelling warm, she called it. 'Was he grateful?' she asked sleepily.

'I wouldn't know.'

'What d'you mean?'

'When I arrived, both of them were still outside, standing around the Jag and staring down at a dent in one wing and a smashed headlamp.' He chuckled. 'For once, Terence's driving obviously wasn't up to genius standard.'

'Why's that so amusing? You have a mean sense of humour.'

'Like as not,' he replied complacently.

CHAPTER 3

Detective-Sergeant Ridley read through the brief typewritten report. At 11.17 the previous night, a man driving from Reckton to his home in Ackley Cross had come across a body lying in the road just past Ailsham cricket ground. He'd telephoned for help from the nearest house and the ambulance had arrived at 11.39, a couple of minutes after the first patrol car. The victim had suffered a hit-and-run accident. He had been taken to the Latimer General Hospital in Reckton, where his condition had been diagnosed as serious; he had a broken arm and two crushed ribs, but his main injury was a fractured skull and internal cranial bleeding. No prognosis had yet been given. Patrol car Tango Bravo Seven had gone to the hospital and PC Fielding had tried to identify the victim, but without success.

At the conclusion of the report was the usual compressed

description. Name, unknown; sex, male; colour, white; nationality, unknown; occupation, unknown; age, between 20 and 30; height, about 5ft 11ins; weight, about 160 lbs; build, medium; complexion, fair, freckles on cheeks; hair, brown, straight, bottle-brush style; eyes, small iris, light brown; eyebrows, arched, thin; nose, straight, very narrow saddle; face, long, clean-shaven; chin, square, dimpled; lips, thick, upturned corners; mouth, large; ears, large, close to head; forehead, slightly receding; distinguishing marks, tattoo 'BA' on right forearm; clothes (all without makers' tabs), black wool sweater, green shirt, navy blue jeans, vest, pants, socks, woollen gloves, plimsolls; jewellery, gold ring, plain, left middle finger; habits, heavy smoker, no sign of drugs. No papers. Prints taken and sent on.

He dropped the single sheet of paper on to the desk, yawned, ran the fingers of his right hand through his wavy brown hair. He lit a cigarette, looked at his watch. Five minutes to reporting to the DI.

Elham entered the first-class carriage and settled in the only vacant corner seat. ''Morning,' said Templeton, from immediately opposite. He nodded in reply. Templeton resumed reading his newspaper. Their conversation seldom went beyond this briefest of greetings. The train started and quickly gathered speed and soon they were rattling over the complicated system of points by the large marshalling yard which was used by passenger trains. Beyond this, the countryside stretched out, bare and dedraggled from the recent heavy rain.

Normally, Elham opened *The Times* at the law reports, studied these and agreed or disagreed with the decisions reached; then he spent the rest of the hour's journey learning what new mess the politicians had led the country into. Today, however, he left the newspaper unopened and stared out of the window. As the telegraph poles flicked by and the carriage rocked steadily, without any audible rhythmic accompaniment since here the line was continuously welded, he suffered a growing sense of resentment which, for the moment, even subdued his fears. There had been no need for Penelope to become so aggressively—and contemptuously?—commanding. He'd been shocked, of course, but he had not lost his wits. Why had she treated him like a child and spelled everything out? He'd appreciated the situation just as well as she. Given a little more time, he'd have done all that it was necessary to do. He'd always worn the trousers in their household and he'd no intention of handing them over now . . . This morning, when he'd said he was feeling too rotten to go to chambers, she could have shown sympathy instead of sarcastically asking if he really wanted people to wonder why he hadn't gone to work on the morning following the accident . . .

The train flashed through a small station so quickly that it was quite impossible to read the name; he didn't have to read it to know where it was because he'd been born four miles away—in a small, dingy semi-detached, one of a row of ten, inhabited by women who walked around in public in carpet slippers with curlers in their hair and men who sat down to meals in their braces. People born in such streets usually only left them in their coffins. But he'd had the drive and ambition to claw his way up and out into a different world and that was something Penelope shouldn't ever forget . . .

When he'd first met her, she'd had a circle of admirers, how large a circle and how admiring he'd been careful never to determine. But by then he'd discovered self-confidence —some might have described it as arrogance—and he had decided to marry her even though he was considerably older than she and totally lacking in the feckless, to-hell-with-tomorrow attitude towards life that her other male friends had possessed and which, in their stupidity, they'd considered one of the charms of their gilded circle. His self-confidence had been well founded. He'd had something to offer which none of them had: a glittering future . . .

Such reminiscences, with their underlying theme of self-approval, had the effect of lessening his resentment. And as it lessened, so his fears returned. What were the police doing at that moment? Searching the road and the grass verge for anything that would help lead to the identification of the hit-and-run car? The fleck of paint which could be matched with the paint from the suspect car (every car manufacturer cooperated with the police and sent in samples of the paints they used; the exact composition of the layers of anti-rust, undercoat, and topcoat, could identify the model); the sliver of glass from the headlamp which could be matched with the remaining glass; the tyre impression which could sometimes be nearly as damning as a fingerprint; the pellet of mud, knocked off from the underside of the wheel-arch, which possessed peculiar characteristics and so identified an area where the car had been? . . . Certainly the police would have already circularized all garages and repair shops, asking to be informed if any car were brought in with damage that was consistent with its having hit a body . . . He'd explained all this the previous night, after the third whisky, when the horror of what had happened had gripped his lungs until he'd had difficulty in breathing. He'd said that running away hadn't solved anything because there was that dent in the offside wing of the Jaguar, together with the broken glass of the headlamp pod, and they didn't dare leave them as they were for fear of their being seen by a patrolling constable, and they didn't dare try to have them repaired because if they did then a report would be made to the police . . . He could still 'hear' the scorn with which she'd said that he was supposed to be the one with the brains, so hadn't he realized that the safest place in which to hide something was in full view? So all he had to do was drive the Jaguar into the corner of the garage, making certain that he caused enough further damage to erase all previous signs . . . He'd stared at her, slack-jawed, wondering how in the hell she, of all people, could have come up with the solution? And an answer had come to him. She had realized that the whole of her way of life was at stake and so she was fighting to preserve it with all the ferocity and ingenuity of a mother defending her young . . .

It was drizzling when they arrived at Cannon Street. He took a taxi to chambers and when he paid the fare and added to this his precisely calculated tip, the driver showed his contempt for such parsimony.

Haldane Buildings had originally been a large Edwardian block with four floors. During the war it had suffered some bomb damage which had left the top floor untenantable and as soon as possible after the war the block had been demolished and in its place a more elegant building, in Georgian style, had been erected, with much better use being made of the available space so that now there were six floors.

He climbed three flights of stairs, beginning to puff as he started on the third one. At the head was a small landing, on either side of which was a set of chambers. He turned left. The outer door was pinned back, displaying on its upper half a list of members; the names of those who were practising being in bold letters, while those who were merely associated with chambers were in light lettering. His name headed the list; occasionally, he spent a few seconds recalling the times when it had been at the bottom of the list of his first chambers. He opened the inner door and went in.

There was a passageway off which led five rooms, a cloakroom, and the clerks' room. A murmur of conversation came through the doorway of the clerks' room. He walked on, although normally he stopped to say good morning, a routine that started his working day.

He entered his room. Until he'd decided to apply for Silk, he'd always had a pupil who'd shared the room with him; since a Silk was not allowed to have a pupil, he'd not replaced the last one when that self-opinionated young man had reached the end of the year; now he had the room to himself—the only member of chambers to do so.

He hung his umbrella and hat on the mahogany stand, added his overcoat. He crossed to the desk and looked down at the several briefs, then walked past the shelves of books to the single large sash window. He stared out at the small square which consisted of grass and four small flowerbeds surrounded by a gravel path. Had the police found anything of significance? Was there anything they could find . . . ?

His thoughts were interrupted by a quick knock on the door. Arnold, the chief clerk, entered. He closed the door, carefully so that it made no noise, walked with his strange, almost mincing gait up to the desk, coughed once, and said: 'Good morning, sir.' His first greeting was always formal. After that, it would be 'Mr Elham'.

It struck Elham—with complete inconsequentiality— that he'd never before realized quite how ungainly Arnold was; as if head, arms, body, and legs, had not originally been meant for each other.

'Not a very nice morning. And the forecast is that the rain will become quite heavy.'

Elham returned to his desk, pulled out the chair, and slumped down on it. He was conscious that Arnold was looking at him with concern. 'I had a bit of a thick night, Tom.'

'Then there's no need to worry. You're not in court today.'

'I'm not?'

'I did mention it last thing last night. Wicks and Chamfers has been moved to Monday. Of course, that meant I had to do something about Stevens and Stevens, so I rang Mr Baldwin and explained and asked if it would be all right if

Mr Young took the brief. After a bit, he agreed.' Arnold sucked in his thick lower lip, then let it go with a plopping sound; a frequent mannerism of his when he was pleased with himself. 'I did suggest at the time that the brief wasn't really marked high enough.'

For once, Elham was uninterested in the markings on his briefs. Let the police gain even a hint that it might have been the Jaguar . . . But there'd been no eyewitnesses and now the original damage was completely masked . . .

'Are you all right, Mr Elham?'

Arnold, looking like a dehydrated dugong, was peering down at him with an expression of concern. 'Of course I'm all right,' he snapped.

'A very thick night!' Very occasionally, Arnold permitted himself a touch of familiarity; it was as out of character as a Stradivarius playing rock. Penelope often referred to him as Uriah Heep, but this nickname was inappropriate since however unctuous his manner, however ungainly his appearance, his sense of loyalty to Elham was unbounded.

The phone rang and Elham picked up the receiver. The caller said that he was passing on unofficial word that Elham's application to be granted Silk had been accepted. Congratulations and that was going to cost a couple of glasses of champagne at their next meeting.

Elham replaced the receiver and stared at the nearest brief on his desk. It was marked £500, of which Arnold would receive ten per cent. As a fashionable and successful Silk, briefs marked £5000 would be far from unusual. He said: 'I'll be taking Silk.'

'Congratulations, Mr Elham. Indeed, many, many congratulations. Not that I ever had the slightest doubt. It was merely a question of choosing the right time.' He was filled with excited pleasure and pride.

CHAPTER 4

The PC parked by the side of the road, stepped out and slammed the door shut. He looked at the oblong house and correctly judged that it had once been two primitive, semi-detached cottages which had been converted into one reasonably comfortable home. There were still two front doors, but no path across the lawn to either of them. He went along the cinder path to the back door. This was half glass and through it he could see a woman standing by a solid fuel cooker. He knocked and she walked across and opened the door. 'Mrs Daley?'

'That's right.' In contrast to his Kentish acent, she had a much harder, sharper London one.

'I'd be glad of a word with Mr Daley, if he's around.'

'He ain't. He's at work.'

'Where would that be?'

'At Mill Farm.'

'Which is where?'

She told him how to drive there, then her manner became slightly easier. 'I suppose it's on account of last night.'

'It is.'

'It real shook him.'

'It would.'

'Coming round the corner and seeing someone lying in the road . . . How is the poor man?'

'The last heard, he was still not conscious and they don't really know yet how badly injured he is.'

'And it was someone in a car what hit him and didn't stop?'

'That's right.'

'D'you know what I'd do to people like that?'

'No, missus, I don't, but I do know what I would ... Thanks a lot, then, sorry to have disturbed your work.'

'I hopes you find the driver.'

'We will.'

He turned away and walked back to his car, hardly aware of the distant view of farmland and woods. He'd been born in the country, but was happy to live in a town. In winter, the countryside was either knee deep in mud and muck or frozen solid.

Mill Farm—there was no stream and no sign that there had ever been a windmill—was on the right-hand side of the road; a square, red brick house, uncompromisingly functional, lay close to the road and leading past it was a concrete drive which ended at a range of farm buildings which dated from the same time as the house. Three wings jutted out from the long, central building and the dairy was in the near end of the middle one of these. Inside, a man was cleaning down the sides of a large stainless steel bulk milk tank. The emptying valve was open and the waste water was gushing out on to the concrete floor; the PC had to step carefully to avoid getting his shoes soaked. 'Mr Daley?'

Daley nodded. A tall, thin man with a face tanned by sun and wind, he spoke sparingly and moved with the slow, regular action of someone who'd spent all his working life with animals.

'I'd like a word if you've the time?'

He nodded again. He looped the hose over the side of the tank so that the jet continued to play into it, went over to a tap and turned this off. He moved across to a control panel, opened a couple of valves and switched on a pump to circulate cleaning fluid around the milk lines.

'D'you smoke?' asked the PC, producing a pack of cigarettes.

'Not in here I don't.'

The PC grinned. 'Sorry.'

'It's not me, it's the boss . . . D'you feel like a coffee?'

'I wouldn't say no to a cuppa.'

Daley led the way out of the dairy and round to the far wing and a small side room in which were a couple of wooden chairs, a butane gas-ring, and an old, deep stone sink above which was a tap. On the far side of the sink was a stained and battered table on which were a kettle, a jar of instant coffee, a jug of milk, a packet of sugar, a couple of teaspoons, and four earthenware mugs. He filled the kettle, lit the gas-ring, and put the kettle on this.

The PC sat, somewhat gingerly since the chair looked less stout than in fact it was, then said: 'It was you who found the injured man near the cricket field at Ailsham?'

'It were.'

'So maybe you can help us trace out the car which knocked him down?' He again brought out the pack of cigarettes from his pocket and this time Daley accepted one without demur. 'As I understand it, you came round the corner by the cricket field and there was the man in the road?'

'That's how it was.'

'And a bit before you reached the corner, you met a car going in the opposite direction?'

'Yes.' The kettle began to steam and Daley turned off the gas. 'How d'you like it—strong?'

'Not too strong, but then neither too weak. A bit like a Piccadilly whore.'

Daley did not smile. He spooned instant coffee into two of the mugs, lifted up the kettle, and poured in water. 'There's the milk and sugar. Ain't no call to worry how much milk you use.'

'You can always pump yourself up some more?' The PC stood, went over, helped himself to three spoonfuls of sugar and a generous measure of milk. He returned to his chair.

'This other car—d'you think the driver of that had seen the man in the road?'

'Can't think of no way he didn't.'

'How was the car being driven?'

'Fast.'

'What d'you mean by that?'

'What I says.'

The PC smiled. 'Would you like to give an estimate of its speed?'

'No, I wouldn't.'

'Was it going straight or weaving about a bit?'

Daley shrugged his shoulders. 'No saying. Never dipped his bloody lights so all I was worried about was seeing where I was going.'

'How many headlights did it have?'

'One.'

'One?'

'That's what I said, ain't it?'

'Which side was this?'

'Nearside.'

The preliminary findings were that the man had been hit by a car driving in the direction of Ailsham, well over on the wrong side of the road—the offside light would have taken the force of the blow. There had been a doctor who'd travelled with the ambulance and he'd judged that the accident had taken place within a short time—say a quarter of an hour—of his examination, so the accident had occurred very shortly before Daley had reached the scene. While the driver of this other car with only the nearside lights working might have been someone unwilling to become involved, it was, on present evidence, more reasonable to assume he was the hit-and-run driver. 'Can you suggest what kind of car it was?'

Daley spoke scornfully. 'I said, he never dipped. Blinded me, even if they was yellow.'

The PC didn't say that this was fresh evidence. The French always had yellow lights. If this had been a French car, the chances of identifying it became very slim unless the driver was caught at the port of embarkation with a smashed headlight and a dented wing (forensic evidence suggested the car must have suffered obvious, but not heavy, damage). 'You got no impression at all of what sort of car it was?'

Daley showed himself to be a stubborn man. 'Didn't you hear—I was blinded?'

'Sure. But even under those conditions one can still sometimes gain some sort of overall impression of a car. Have a go. Was it big or small?'

Daley drank, drew on his cigarette, then said, with some reluctance: 'Big.'

'What kind of big? Something like a Land-Rover?'

'No. It were one of them smooth jobs.'

It took a little time to determine that in this context smooth meant curved and sporty.

'A bit like a Ferrari, for instance?'

'What's that?'

'You must know what a Ferrari looks like.'

'Well, I bloody don't.'

Such ignorance was, in the eyes of a car enthusiast like the PC, quite heretical. There was something about having much to do with cows which addled a man's brains. He asked a few more questions, but it had become obvious that there was nothing more to be learned.

Rickmore crossed over to the window of his office and stared out. On the far side of the street, two boys were playing marbles under the bare branches of a large horse-chestnut tree. The course of their game eluded him since it bore no resemblance to any of the variations he had known in his youth. He turned, a shade too energetically, and winced.

The aspirins he'd taken after breakfast—a breakfast restricted to coffee—were having little effect and his head still thumped at about 9 on the Richter scale. It was damnably unfair that he should suffer so much since he hadn't been drunk, he'd merely drunk too much. When he'd complained to Anne, she'd shown a callous lack of sympathy. Alcohol always reacted badly on him, so why drink as much as he had?

He returned to his chair and carefully sat. He read what he'd written ten minutes earlier, scrumpled up the sheet of paper and threw it at the wastepaper basket. It dropped outside. It was just one of those mornings. He picked up his ballpoint pen, squared up a fresh sheet of paper, and thought. He thought that his headache was becoming worse and his stomach was revolting. The telephone rang and the assistant sales manager, overseas, asked him if he'd heard from Julot in Paris. He said he hadn't and as he replaced the telephone, he thought that that was hardly surprising. Selling refrigerators to Eskimos was a simple task compared to selling English perfumes to Parisians . . .

An old friend had said not long ago that all right, the job wasn't the best paid in the country, but who was he to complain when his life was spent in the company of glorious, glamorous, half-naked women? Impossible to make Mike understand that as PRO he was seldom, if ever, in the company of the frolicsome ladies who appeared in the firm's advertisements.

How to say something fresh about the firm's products? How to fill up the monthly newsletter with little snippets of information that would attract the attention of the press and so lead to a mention of those products in the newspapers? How to persuade the glossy magazines to add to their list of acknowledgements, perfumes by Teerson Products. Teerson Products sounded more like the manufacturers of pot scourers than seductive perfumes for exotic women. A suggestion he'd made soon after joining the firm had been that they change the name of the brand products to something more suited to the image they wanted to capture. The suggestion had been received with frosty disapproval. Mr Teerson was very, very proud of his name and wanted it heralded far and wide. A chemist by training, he'd discovered a way of making personable perfumes using wholly synthetic and cheap materials; the discovery had made him rich. Rich men paid poor men to glorify them, not to extinguish them under pseudonyms. Realizing that here was a verity which might repeatedly prevent him doing his job as effectively as he'd want to do it, he'd considered resigning and looking for a position where his ability would not be stifled by pride. But the recession had begun to bite hard and jobs had not been as easy to find as before and he simply hadn't been prepared to take the risk of finding himself unemployed for months on end ... And to look on the cheerful side, the job was not demanding—one learned to overcome, or ignore, the frustration—and it did leave him time and energy for his writing ...

He often wished he'd as much confidence in himself as an author as Anne had. Then he wouldn't ask himself if her confidence rested on loyalty rather than critical honesty. The public had received his one published book with a notable lack of acquisitive enthusiasm and his royalty returns had looked rather like a census of Jews living in Mecca —but his editor was always encouraging him and had stated with apparent honest authority that one day his books would become a critical and popular success ... It was a strange fact that the only time Elham had treated him without the slightest condescension had been when he'd offered him one of the six free copies of his book. It did seem that somewhere within Elham's breast there lurked a faint respect for things other than financial success and social standings ... He smiled. Since the book had, indirectly, questioned the integ-

rity of success and the merit of wealth, Elham must have
found the book very distasteful. Or perhaps he'd never
bothered actually to read it. Certainly Penelope wouldn't
have done. She never read anything but her horoscope and
probably that occasionally taxed her intelligence . . .

He checked the time. Ten minutes to coffee. Two hours
and ten minutes to lunch. Five hours and ten minutes to
packing-up. And the end of another day devoted to further-
ing the future of Mr Teerson, private egotist, public phil-
anthropist, and staunch defender of free enterprise's right
to exploit its workers.

CHAPTER 5

Elham put the last of the accompanying documents down
by the side of the twenty pages of instructions. At stake in
this action was the contingent liability arising from alleged
malfeasance under a contract in which the terms were
ambiguous. Both sides had a case and one of the points of
law at issue was highly arcane. Normally, it would have
been just the kind of brief to please him. To begin with it
was highly marked, and beyond that he was a born lawyer,
enjoying the subtleties of shades of meaning and seeing
nothing odd in spending endless time pondering the true
significance of a single sentence. But today this case merely
irritated him to the point where he wondered why the two
parties couldn't summon up sufficient common sense to
resolve their own difficulties. Today his mind repeatedly
returned to that moment when the man had run out into
the road, to be sent flying by the Jaguar . . . If only they'd
left Oak Tree Cottage five minutes earlier or later. If only
he'd driven a little slower or a little quicker . . .

How far had the police now got in their investigations?

Whatever happened, they couldn't possibly trace the car. Could they? There'd been no one else on the road, the victim could have seen nothing . . . Those whose work brought them close to the police knew that, often through no fault of their own, far from the highly successful crime detection force many believed them, they were frequently all at sixes and sevens. When there was no direct evidence of identity, it was probably true to say that they didn't solve four out of five hit-and-run cases. But that still left the one that was solved . . .

Years ago, soon after he'd been called, he'd defended a man from a good background who'd been accused of swindling the firm for whom he'd worked. During the course of one of the interviews, the man had said: 'I've discovered something. The worst thing is the fear, not the fact.' At the time, he'd not fully understood what the man had meant, but now he did.

He looked at the telephone. There must be someone he could speak to to discover what progress the police were making . . . Only a fool drew attention to himself by asking such questions . . . But he'd soon go bloody mad from the stress . . .

The question suddenly formed in his mind: Why didn't he see Lucy? However mentally tired he might be, she fed fresh life into him. Surely, then, she could also banish his fears? Never mind for once that it was the middle of the day. (He'd never been to her place during the day, only at night. Buried within his subconscious was the belief that daylight adultery was sordid.)

He collected his hat and overcoat and put these on, picked up his umbrella. He looked at the briefcase, but left it. He walked down the corridor to the clerks' room. Allwyn, one of the younger members of chambers, was talking to Betty Greer, Arnold's assistant. ''Morning T. E. I hear from the grapevine you're taking Silk. Congratulations.'

He muttered a few appropriate words.

'Don't forget, I never mind being led. Especially astray.'

Elham ignored that weak attempt at humour. He said to Betty: 'Where's Tom?'

Betty, fast approaching middle age, plumpish, level-headed, reliable and efficient, if slow, replied: 'He had to go across to the courts a moment ago; he'll be back soon.'

'When he does, tell him I've gone out and won't be returning until some time in the late afternoon.' He nodded at Allwyn, left. He wondered if Betty and Allwyn were now trying to guess what had caused him to act so out of character? If so, Allwyn would doubtless hint at something salacious, little realizing how right he was . . .

He walked along the road, past Middle Temple Hall, to Fleet Street. He stood on the edge of the pavement and hailed every approaching taxi; the fourth one was free and it stopped. 'Twenty-two, Cuthbertson Road,' he said, as he opened the back door.

'Is that at the back of Harrods, Guv?'

'That's right.' He settled on the back seat. In ten days' time, he thought, it would be a year since he'd first met Lucy at a cocktail party, given by acquaintances rather than friends, to which he'd not wanted to go, but had because Penelope had insisted they did. It was ironic that Penelope's insistence had been fuelled by the possibility that some rather important people would be present—they'd never turned up. There was even more, and harsher, irony in the fact that Penelope was so beautiful and desirable that at that party no man under the age of senility had looked at her without desire, yet she was totally uninterested in sex. At first, after their marriage, he'd put this down to shyness —even in a permissive age, perhaps not every woman permitted. But then, unwillingly, he'd been forced to under-stand that she just was not interested in the physical act of love because she gained no pleasure from it. She'd never actively rejected him. She didn't refuse his demands while inventing headaches, she simply never responded and nothing he had ever said or done had altered that fact. Finally accepting that that was the situation, he'd tried to come to terms with it logically. He gained physical pleasure from her body, so why should it matter to him that she gained none from his? The loss was hers, not his. But while the law might cherish logic, emotions did not. The more she denied him her passion, the more he longed for it, at the cost of his own pleasure . . .

At the cocktail party—composed, as he'd previously guessed, of people right outside his milieu and of little consequence to him—he'd been cornered by a man who had been castigating the latest negotiating platform of the printing unions with boring fluency when Lucy had come up and said that his wife wasn't feeling too well and she wanted to go home. 'Not again, for God's sake!' the man had exclaimed bitterly. After he'd left, Lucy had said: 'I do so hate that kind of comment. It leaves one vainly wondering whether she's tight, pregnant, or just a hypochondriac.'

'Don't you know?' he'd said, surprised that he responded to her uncalled-for comments instead of ignoring them.

'How on earth could I when I've only just met the woman?'

'Then wouldn't it have been better . . .' He stopped, realizing—just in time—that now it was he who was in danger of ignoring a basic rule of social conversation.

She'd grinned, a mischievous, challenging grin. 'Wouldn't it have been better if I'd minded my own business? Of course. But then think how much more boring . . . Are you Lloyd's, lawyer, or layabout in the Foreign Office?'

'Why should I be any of those?'

'The mould's unmistakable.'

'I've no idea what you mean.'

'Then there's no point in my explaining, because you'd never understand.'

That night, as he and Penelope had prepared for bed— separate beds—she'd said: 'Who was that extraordinary women you were talking to for such a long time? The one dressed so outrageously in stretch pants.'

For some reason, which he'd not then attempted to ana- lyse, he'd answered with defensive brevity. 'God only knows! I was stuck with her when she came across with a message for someone I'd been talking to before.'

'Oh!' Penelope had ceased to be interested in the woman whose social tastes were so obviously lacking.

Lucy had haunted his mind. She'd appear without warn- ing when he was shaving, when Penelope asked him what he thought of her new frock, when he started to read the law reports in the train, when Arnold spoke about the latest brief to come in to chambers. Since he tried to hide himself from himself as well as from other people, it had been quite some time before he'd accepted the fact that she was haunting his mind because he was convinced, even on so short an acquaintance, that in her the fires of passion didn't just burn, they raged. Once this acceptance was made, her images became lascivious.

He'd managed to hold the haunting images in check for a time, then they had become too febrile to be contained any longer. One Thursday he'd set out to identify the small, sparkling, outrageous woman whose eyes had suggested, whose mouth had demanded, whose body had promised. He'd telephoned the host of the party, spent several minutes discussing matters of no consequence, then had casually introduced the one that had come to concern him so deeply.

'You mean it was Lucy you were talking to?'

'That's right.'

'I wish I'd known that. I'd have listened in.'

'Why?' he'd asked, with pompous stiffness.

'Because I can't imagine a more disparate duo and it would have been amusing to hear you misunderstanding each other. Did she shatter your remaining faith in femininity?'

'As a matter of fact, I did find her rather forthright.'

'What you mean is, plain bloody rude. Her trouble is, she's fruity.'

For some reason, impossible to recall, he had accepted this as a slang word, not met before, for lesbians. He'd known a sharp, and clearly illogical, sense of loss. 'Is she? I must say, she didn't strike me as one, but you just can't tell these days, can you?'

'She didn't strike you as one what?'

'Lesbian.'

'Lucy? She'd die of laughing if you told her that. What ever gave you such a crazy idea?'

'You said she was fruity.'

Another bellow of laughter. 'I've always said that you lawyers know less about the world you live in than a newborn babe . . . As fruity as a nut cake. Nutty. As mad as they come.'

'She's rather unusual?'

'My God, you've only got to see some of her sculptures to know that. Why d'you think one of the Sunday papers keeps referring to her as an up-and-coming sculptress?' An even louder bellow of laughter, the reason for which Elham only discovered later. 'So why all the interest? Thinking of joining her lists?'

'Good God, no!'

'It makes a lovely thought. From what I hear, in five minutes flat—' a pause, for that to be appreciated—'she'd have a misogynist renouncing his faith.'

For a time, he'd struggled with himself. He was a sober, decent, respectable husband; sober, decent, respectable husbands did not betray their marriages, even in modern times . . . It was, of course, true that Penelope refused him her passion—but many men were refused not only passion but body as well, and yet they continued to honour their marriages . . .

Now that it had been confirmed that by repute she was every bit as passionate as he'd imagined, the mental images became too painful to be borne. He'd telephoned her on the Friday. 'My name is Terence Elham. I don't suppose you'll remember me . . .'

'Then you lack supposition. Ever since that ghastly cocktail party, I've been wondering if you really can be as starchy as you appear.'

He'd taken a taxi to her flat and as he'd climbed out on to the pavement, he'd become aware of the fact that he was clammy from sweat. He'd almost returned into the taxi . . .

She'd been wearing a loose pair of overalls and—it seemed to him—little else, since the day was warm. The gently outlined flesh beneath the overalls, changing shape as she moved, had excited him to the point where his breath became short . . .

She'd led the way through to her studio because, she'd said, she'd a spot of work to finish before she showered and changed and they went out to dinner. She'd suggested they had a drink right away and had asked him to pour her a Campari and whatever he wanted for himself. Several bottles and half a dozen glasses had been on a tray on a table against the far wall. Next to that table had been a second and much larger one and on this had been a few of her sculptures. He'd examined them with an interest which initially turned to puzzlement, then to consternation, when he realized he was looking at the male member, in virile state, cast in the form of Cleopatra's Needle, the Eiffel Tower, the Post Office Tower, Nelson's Column, the Empire State Building, and the Leaning Tower of Pisa.

'Wonderful!'

Slack-jawed, he'd turned and stared at her.

'I bet myself you'd react exactly as you have. I am going to enjoy getting to know you very, very much.'

For dinner, she'd chosen a nearby restaurant, dimly-lit and smoochy, on the grounds that it would be as different as possible from the places to which he normally went. It was. Afterwards they'd walked to her flat arm-in-arm—something he hadn't done in years—and the smile on her face had been tantalizing, promising, and triumphant . . .

The taxi came to a stop. He climbed out and paid, adding an exact tip. He went up the stone stairs to the front doorway, recessed under a portico, and pressed the top button on the answerport. Lucy's voice came through the speaker loud and clear.

'I've got to see you.'

'Terry?' From the first day, she'd used the diminutive because he'd told her that no one else did. 'What the hell's up?'

'I . . . I need you.'

There was a buzz as the door catch was released. He went inside and climbed the stairs to the third floor. She was standing in the doorway and he saw she was wearing the same overalls as she had on his first visit. She stared at him, her expression intense. 'You really do need me?'

'Yes,' he said hoarsely.

She put her arms round him and pressed him to herself. 'Shall I tell you something, my lovely lawyer? Those are the sweetest words you could say to me.'

CHAPTER 6

Ridley left his office and went along the passage to the lift, found it was up at the top floor, and decided to go down the stairs. These brought him to the outside door on the north side of the building. The wind had become stronger and colder and it made him wish he'd had the sense to bring his mackintosh; for a moment he thought about returning to get it, but decided it wasn't worth the bother.

He walked briskly up Bank Street, turned left into High Street and the pedestrian precinct, and continued along this to the laundry. The redhead behind the counter greeted him with a smile. ''Afternoon. Getting chilly, isn't it? Bart says he thinks we're in for snow.'

'Tell him from me that he's a miserable old b.'

'Don't you like snow?'

'Well, do you?'

'If there's enough of it. Then the roads get blocked and I can't come in to work.'

'It's all right for some! If I had a six-foot drift all round my house, the boss would just expect me to grab a shovel and start digging . . . Have you got my jacket?'

'Where's the ticket?'

'Sorry and all that, love, but I forgot to bring it from home.'

'Then you're out of luck.'

'Sports jacket, a kind of a check in green and grey, with black stripes in all directions.'

'Suppose I tell you we've fifty jackets like that?'

'I wouldn't believe you.'

'Men!'

'Where would you be without 'em?'

'Happier.' She sighed. 'All right, I'll see what I can do.'

'That's my girl.'

'Yeah. Just so long as I do what you want.'

'Is that an offer?'

'Didn't you once tell me you was married?'

'She's generous.'

'I'm not.' She left and went through swing doors, careful to move her hips with grace.

He remained by the counter and stared out through the glass door. Still nothing on the hit-and-run victim, despite reference to the local and national missing persons' lists . . . Odd that so far no one had come forward to report a husband, son, or lodger missing. The man had been in good physical shape, so he hadn't been living rough—someone must know he hadn't returned to his home, even if that someone was only an inquisitive neighbour. Another odd thing, there'd been no means of identification on him; most people carried around with them personal papers of one sort or another. And where had he been going at that time of night on foot (there'd been no parked car nearby) . . .

The redhead pushed open one of the swing doors and returned into the shop, in her right hand a flimsy wire hanger on which hung a sports jacket. 'This is the only one like you described.'

'Thought you'd got fifty? That's mine, all right; straight from Savile Row. You're a marvellous girl.'

'I know.' Expertly, she extracted the hanger, folded the coat, and wrapped it in brown paper. 'That's four quid.'

'Christ! Started cleaning 'em in champagne?' He paid her and left.

Lucy gently ran the tips of her fingers down Elham's chest. 'Now tell me what the matter is.'

'Nothing.'

'Don't be silly. When you said you needed me, I thought you were just extra horny. But you needed to screw me because you're in some sort of trouble and it's a way of getting some relief.'

He hated it when she spoke so crudely.

'Come on, tell me what's biting you—apart from me . . . Nothing's ever so bad as it seems when you keep it to yourself.' She leaned over and gently nibbled his right breast.

'Last night . . .' He stopped.

'What about it?'

'We went to dinner with my brother-in-law.'

'I don't suppose that was enough to knock you sideways, so what went wrong there?'

'I was driving back afterwards and . . . and there was an accident.'

'Your wife was hurt?'

'It wasn't like that, it was . . .' He stopped once more, then spoke quickly. 'I was driving very slowly and carefully, I swear I was. But suddenly this man ran out from some trees, straight in front of the car. There wasn't anything I could do. You've got to understand, there wasn't anything at all I could do because there wasn't the time. It all happened too quickly.'

'You hit him?'

'Only a little,' he answered, quite unaware of the absurdity of his words.

'Was he badly hurt?'

'Not really.'

'Surely no one can begin to blame you, if you didn't even have time to brake?'

'I swear I didn't.'

'Love, you mustn't torture yourself like this, if there was nothing you could do.'

'There wasn't.'

'Well, then . . . Sometimes things happen which there's just no way of avoiding. And if this man wasn't seriously hurt, you've no need to go on worrying about him.' She kissed him, full-mouthed, hungrily. 'Are you going to remember that now?'

He wanted to tell her the full story so that she could agree he'd done the only sensible thing and that it would have been absurd for him to risk the destruction of his career, but he couldn't be certain that he'd still hold her sympathy; she had some odd ideas . . .

She nibbled his ear. 'Are you going to remember that now?'

'Yes.'

'Then maybe you'll screw me because you want to, not to help you forget last night?'

Emmery was twenty and ambitious. And he possessed the instinct which told him a story was stronger than the facts so far in evidence suggested which was the hallmark of a good journalist.

He said, over the phone: 'Then you've still no idea who he is?'

'That's right.'

'He doesn't fit anyone on the missing list?'

'No.'

He asked a few more questions, to which he received unsatisfactory answers, rang off. He didn't think the police were deliberately playing it close to their chests—they really had no idea who the injured man was. But who, other than a drop-out, could go missing without someone trying to trace him?

He told the news editor that he'd a lead which looked promising, OK to follow it up? The editor agreed. Emmery left the square, dirt-stained building, crossed to the much-used Nova, climbed in, started the engine, and drove out on to the road.

It was an eighteen-mile drive to Reckton, through gently rolling, well farmed countryside with the North Downs as a backdrop. At the large roundabout immediately outside the town, he took the second exit.

Thirty years before, Reckton had been a market town, unremarkable, but possessing a quiet, rather sleepy charm. Then the railway line to London had been electrified, bringing the town within the commuter belt, and the planners had been let loose, their brief to modernize and enlarge in order to cope with the projected increase in population. With unerring instinct, they'd destroyed all that was worth preserving and preserved all that should have been destroyed. Now, the town was without a soul.

They'd changed the course of the ring road since he'd last used it and he missed the turning he wanted. He found there was no right turn at the next junction so had to take the one after that and, swearing freely, finished up in an area he did not know. Inevitably, the first person he asked for directions was a stranger, but the second was not and she directed him to the hospital.

He spoke to a sister who answered his questions as briefly and generally as possible. The patient was still in a coma, in intensive care. He had suffered chest and arm injuries, but these were relatively minor; far more serious had been the blow to his skull which had fractured it and caused internal bleeding and possibly further injury, the extent of which could not yet be determined. It was impossible to give any sort of prognosis. No one had visited him.

Emmery returned to the Nova. It was odd, he thought, to be lying in hospital, in a coma, unidentified—it made of him a no-man. Which suggested the heading, The Abominable No-man . . .

He drummed on the wheel with his fingers. He'd discovered nothing solid that would build a story. At best, unknown man lying in a coma after hit-and-run accident might make for a small filler in next Tuesday's *Gazette*. But, now that he was here, it seemed a pity to return to Etchinstone without following up his hunch a bit further . . . Surely it was worth questioning the man who'd discovered the victim?

Daley was milking. Five at a time, the Friesians came into alternate sides of the herringbone milking parlour where they were fed automatically while he clamped on the clusters.

'I wonder if you've time for a word?' shouted Emmery, as he stood on the steps leading down to the pit.

Daley looked briefly up at him. 'Does it look like I've nothing to do?' He removed the cluster from the end cow on the right-hand side, glanced along the row of bags (which, from the pit, was almost all he could see of the cows), pulled down on a lever which opened a gate and allowed the cows to make their way out of the standings and the parlour. He closed that gate, opened the far one, pulled on a rope which slid back the door into the collecting yard. Cows came through and he shut the door behind the fifth one, then the gate. He sponged down the bags. A cow urinated and the hot liquid splashed down on the concrete and rebounded. Emmery hurriedly retreated and Daley showed his sarcastic amusement.

'I'm from the *Gazette*,' Emmery said, once satisfied he was safe.

Daley dropped the cloth back into the bucket of disinfectant. It took all sorts to make a world.

'You found the injured man after the accident, didn't you?'

He picked up the first of the clusters from its hook, arranged the cups over his hand in a star pattern with the rubber tubes twisted to block the vacuum, placed the cluster under the first cow's bag, in turn untwisted each cup and slipped it over a teat.

'It was you who found the injured man, wasn't it?'

He nodded.

'It must have been a bit of a shock?'

He moved down to the second cow.

'And you also saw the car that hit him?'

'I saw a car; that's all.'

'But the police think . . .'

'What they think is their business; it ain't mine.'

Emmery smiled; he rather liked awkward characters.

'They say that you said one of the car's headlights wasn't working, so since the man could only just have been knocked over, it like as not was that car. What make was it?'

'How would I know?'

'I thought you told the police?'

'Then you thought wrong.'

'What did you actually tell 'em, then?'

'Same as I'll tell you now, before you clear out of here and leave me to do me work. It was a big, smooth car and it was going fast.'

'You can't make a guess at what kind it was?'

'No. And the police can say it were a Ferrari from now until Christmas and it won't make no bloody difference.'

'Then it probably was a Ferrari?'

'I said I don't know.'

Emmery left, glad to escape the dangers of urinating cows. He walked through the dairy to his car. A Ferrari was a rich man's car . . . Unknown victim seriously injured by wealthy hit-and-run driver . . . That could make a story. And if it was angled adroitly, one or more of the London papers might pick it up, with financial advantage to himself.

They were watching a nature programme on BBC1 when the telephone rang. 'I'll get it,' Rickmore said. Anne loved films about birds, but he'd seen so many recently that they were beginning to bore him. He went out into the hall and crossed to the corner cupboard on which the telephone stood.

Penelope said: 'Dennis, I just had to ring and say how very much we both enjoyed last night. It was such fun to be with just the two of you.'

Was that an oblique way of saying that a dinner-party should always be composed of at least two couples other than the hosts? 'It was fun seeing you,' he replied.

'Anne's a wonderful cook; that mousse was simply the nicest I've ever eaten. You're a very lucky man.'

'And perhaps she's a lucky woman?'

'As I've always said, you're the perfect husband.'

Even Penelope ought to have choked on that piece of hypocrisy, he thought. 'Sounds to me as if we'd start favourites for the Dunmow flitch.'

'I'm sure you would.'

He was convinced she hadn't understood the reference. It occurred to him that she sounded even falser and more brittle than usual. 'How's Terence?'

'He's all right. Why shouldn't he be?'

'No reason, except I thought maybe he's still suffering from the remains of a hangover.'

'Don't be ridiculous. He had nothing of the sort.'

Even if he had been slightly tactless in his words, it seemed odd that she should have responded so sharply. He tried to pour a little verbal oil. 'If he was lucky, I wasn't. I spent most of the morning wondering whether to cut my throat to end the agony.'

'Terence did not have too much to drink last night.'

'Lucky man.'

'He was perfectly sober when we left you.'

'Couldn't have been more so.' He managed to keep the irony from his voice.

There was a brief pause. 'Will you tell Anne how much we enjoyed ourselves?'

'I will.'

'Goodbye.'

He'd never before known her to end a telephone conversation so abruptly. Usually, there were protestations of regret at having to ring off and promises to meet again just as soon as the so-crowded social calendar permitted . . .

He returned to the sitting-room. The nature film was finished and the credits were showing.

'Turn off, sweet,' she said.

'Let's just see what's on next . . .'

'It's that awful series where people get beaten up every five minutes. I can't stand so much violence.'

He switched off the television set.

'Who was that on the phone?'

'Your sister, making her bread-and-butter call.'

'How is she?'

'Same as ever, except not quite.'

'A very intelligent answer!'

He went over and rumpled her hair and she grabbed his hand and dragged it down, then pressed it once in a silent message of love before releasing it. 'What's wrong with Penny?'

'Nothing definite, but her manner was a bit odd.'

'I thought that as far as you're concerned, it always is?'

'Maybe I should have said, odder than usual. When I asked her how his lordship was because he might have had a touch too much vino last night, she took considerable um.'

'For goodness sake, what d'you expect? You really are quite hopeless.'

'If she'd said that about me to you, would you have become really huffy?'

'Of course not, but I'm not Penny.'

'For which the gods be thanked.' He crossed to his chair. 'Come to think of it, they were both a bit odd when I returned his glasses last night.'

'If you want my opinion, in the state you were in everyone and everything was odd. I should never have let you drive. There could so easily have been another terrible accident.'

He stared at the wood fire, flames dancing high. 'Have you heard any more about that?'

'No, but then I've only been to the local shops.'

'Usually, that's the source of all news.'

'Gossip, not news.'

He yawned. 'How about making tracks for bed? . . . Rejoice! Tomorrow's Friday, the last working day of the week.'

'Do you really hate the job all that much?'

'I suppose not. After all, it's no more unnecessary and vapid than most and as far as I know the firm's products haven't ever actually killed anyone.'

'But you wish you were at home, writing?'

'That's the masochistic streak in me.'

'Don't be so stupid, and stop denigrating your own work. One day, you'll be famous.'

'But for what?'

CHAPTER 7

The laboratory assistant stared at the ancient Olympia typewriter with dislike. His training assured him that it was ridiculous to credit a piece of machinery with a diabolical sense of humour, but this machine had one. Why else should it type Y every time he meant to strike T?

He pulled out the form from the roller, scrumpled it up, and threw it into the wastepaper basket. He threaded in a fresh form and started typing once more. Reference number, source of exhibit, remitting police officer, date of receipt, date of examination, name of examiner . . . So far, only one typing error and that easily covered up since an n could be turned into a reasonable h. He resumed typing. Description of exhibit, results of examinations . . . One very small sliver of glass recovered from sweater, sample too small for comparison tests but consistent with glass from a vehicle's headlamp; quantity of dirt, pulverized and forced into jeans, probably by impact, containing traces of brick dust and very fine sawdust—type of wood . . .

He reached the end of the report, gratified by the fact that in all he'd made only three unimportant errors. He signed with a flourish, then noted that the time recorded was 110P hours. He swore, as he changed the P into a 0 with a pen. That bloody typewriter!

The Detective-Inspector was a man who suffered constant frustration because he tried to have almost every case which came in fully investigated, even though he knew that there was neither the manpower nor the time available to do this. The trouble was, MacMahon had joined the CID in an era of much less lawlessness when it had been possible to deal efficiently with all but the very minor crimes and he'd never been able to come to terms with a time when even a burglary might be left to a uniform PC.

He scratched the top of his head, then tried to smooth the remaining hair to hide his baldness. 'How's the Pierce job going?'

Ridley answered: 'John's got that in hand, but so far he's not had any breaks.' Had he ever been asked, he'd have said that the DI was soft to work himself so hard; there were no medals for growing ulcers. Not that Ridley viewed his work with a cynical detachment. But he did divide it into crime against property and against the person; the one was a fact of life, the other an obscenity. No one could work harder than he in a case involving the mugging of an old woman or the raping of a young one, and had he had his way those guilty would have been punished with physical violence so that they could taste the pain, the terror, the humiliation, of what they had inflicted.

'John?' The DI looked up. 'Doesn't the case call for someone a bit sharper?'

'Maybe. But do we pull that someone off something else?'

One of the two telephones rang and the DI picked up the receiver. He listened, muttered a few words, replaced the receiver. 'The victim of the hit-and-run at Ailsham—he's just died without ever regaining consciousness.'

'Poor sod!'

'Not heard from Dabs yet?'

'Not a word. But we'll be near the bottom of their priority list on that job.'

'And there are no other leads as to the man's identity?'

'None.'

'It's strange he's not been reported missing.' MacMahon fiddled with a pencil. 'And nothing leading to the car?'

'You've got my report mentioning the yellow headlights? And the one which arrived from the lab this morning?'

The DI indicated the uneven pile of papers in front of himself. 'None of that takes us very far.'

'Doesn't take us any bloody where.' Ridley's tone was hard. The driver of the car hadn't given a damn about his victim; all he'd been interested in was saving his own skin. The car could well have been large and expensive, in which case the driver was a wealthy man. If there was one type of person Ridley scorned more than a coward, it was a rich coward.

Lucy's father had been a creative potter of a somewhat anarchical turn of mind and before her marriage her mother, daughter of a shopkeeper, had happily worked in a bank. It was, so Lucy claimed, this dichotomy of parental characteristics which left her a walking encyclopædia of contradictions.

She believed she was entitled to say and do whatever she wanted; but there were some things that she would never say and some she would never do. She believed that social conventions were ridiculous and so deliberately flouted them; but there were one or two she always observed and there was no logic in the distinctions. She went out of her way to shock; but would never shock if to do so might cause hurt. She was a pacifist and very CND, but she was extremely patriotic. She despised wealth, but liked the things that money bought. She demanded that each person be independent, yet allowed no exception to the rule that every individual on earth owed a love and a duty to every other.

She started breakfast at half past one, not because it was now everybody else's lunch-time, but because she had enjoyed a couple of joints the previous night and they always made her sleep like the dead. The simile bothered her. What was death? Would she know she was dead? If so, part of her mind must have lived on and therefore she could not be dead; if not, how could death have any meaning to the person it most concerned? . . . Such thoughts troubled her deeply and depressed her and it was then that she created her priapic sculptures. After all, one couldn't get any further away from death than the start of life. And ever since that first *succès de scandale* such sculptures had sold well, which meant she could spend and spend and prove to herself that she was alive . . .

She buttered a piece of toast, cut a large section of Edam and put this on the toast, reached across the debris-laden table for the jar of Hero black cherry jam. She claimed it was her Welsh ancestors who gave her her liking for jam with cheese. As far as she knew, she didn't have any Welsh ancestors.

As she ate, she skimmed through the *Guardian*. As a person of unimpeachable liberal outlook, she would have countenanced no other daily paper. On Sunday, however, she had the *Sunday Telegraph*. On Sundays, she was a re-actionary.

Wars, threats of wars, politicians behaving like children, children behaving like politicians . . . And a brief report on a road accident near the village of Ailsham on Wednesday night in which an as yet unidentified man had been knocked down and seriously injured by a hit-and-run driver. Nothing was spelled out, yet everything was there for those who could read between the lines. The driver was wealthy, the victim was poor. The driver had been drunk, the victim hadn't had a chance. The driver had fled, careless of the fact that medical attention might be essential to save the victim's life . . .

Elham had told her that he'd been in an accident on Wednesday night, near Ailsham. But he'd said he'd been driving very carefully, it had not been his fault, and the man had not been seriously injured; his silence had implied that he'd naturally stopped and done what he could to help. All lies. He'd been drunk, the accident had been wholly his fault, and he'd abandoned the severely injured victim without a second's thought. He'd lied to gain her sympathy and she'd given it, whereas had she known the truth . . . A woman of sharp, occasionally overpowering emotions, she knew the anger and contempt which swept away all rational thought. Without giving herself time to consider her actions, she went across to the desk, picked up the telephone receiver, dialled 999, and when the operator asked her which emergency service she wanted, replied 'Police' in a tone which turned the word into one of moral violence.

CHAPTER 8

MacMahon drove into the courtyard at the back of the concrete and glass divisional HQ and parked in a free space. Before climbing out of the car, he raised the collar of his overcoat to try to ward off the north wind which had started blowing. He saw Ridley approach, obviously wanting to speak to him, and he gloomily decided that this meant more trouble.

'I'm glad I've caught you, sir.'

MacMahon was intrigued by that 'sir'. Most of the young-sters eschewed such a form of respect these days; instead, being television fans, they called him 'guv'nor'. But at their first meeting of the day, Ridley usually called him 'sir'. He would have liked to know why. He doubted it was a sign of respect. 'Don't tell me what the trouble is, let me guess. The mayor's been shot, the chairman of the county council has been found chasing little girls, and the police committee has named me fascist pig.'

Ridley didn't smile. 'We've had a call from London to tell us that a woman, who refused to identify herself, has been in touch to say that if the police want to know who was driving the hit-and-run car at Ailsham, they need to talk to Terence Elham.'

MacMahon walked towards the building, hurrying be-cause the wind was giving his balding head a bad time. 'Elham . . . The name rings a bell, but for the moment, I'm damned if I can remember why.'

'I've asked around. He's a fairly prominent barrister.'

'Hell!' said MacMahon, just before he opened the door to go inside. The building was well heated and as they came to a stop by the lift, he lowered the collar of his coat. 'My old sergeant used to say that if you had the chance to choose between the Devil and a lawyer, settle for the Devil every time . . . What more d'you know?' He pressed the call button.

'Apart from the fact that he lives in Ailsham, nothing.'

The lift arrived and they took it to the fifth floor, walked along the corridor to the DI's room. MacMahon hung up his overcoat, then went round the desk and sat. 'Tim might be able to fill the picture in a bit.' He looked up a number, dialled it, spoke briefly. He thanked the other, replaced the receiver. 'Elham's a prominent junior barrister who's expected to take Silk very soon. A good all-rounder, hot on contract, well known at the criminal bar. He's rated as tough and clever and never hesitates to knock the police when he's defending.'

'One of them! Then it'll be a positive pleasure to land him.'

MacMahon leaned back in his chair. 'Maybe. But just remember that when you're dealing with a man with his background, if you've got any sense you'll go carefully.'

Typical! thought Ridley, with sudden anger. Just because the man didn't come from the slums, he had to be treated with kid gloves. Hadn't the DI realized the world had moved on? If it was Elham who'd knocked the man down and had then run, he deserved . . .

'His kind defend themselves with very heavy guns,' said MacMahon quietly. 'I'm trying to protect you, not him.' He saw that he was not believed. He sighed. Some people never learned, except the hard way. He hated violence and the waves of suffering it generated, just as much as Ridley, but he had learned long ago that meeting it with any kind of further violence was seldom satisfactory. He looked at his watch. 'The odds are, Elham's up in London. Tomorrow's Saturday, so he'll be at home all day.'

'I'll drive there . . .'

'We'll drive there,' MacMahon corrected.

Saturday was overcast. The clouds were dirt-coloured and they threatened rain or sleet; the increasing north wind suggested that sleet was the more likely.

In the room he used as a study—it had originally been the housekeeper's bedroom—Elham looked through the window and saw Juana, shopping basket in her left hand, come through the gateway into the drive and walk towards the back door, passing out of sight as she drew abreast of the small greenhouse. They'd been fortunate to find the Carvajals, he thought, with the complacency of someone who believed he was entitled to good fortune. Juana was an excellent cook and Miguel a reasonable gardener and neither believed in wasting time. Originally, he remembered, he'd been slightly reluctant to employ them because they might have left Chile for political reasons and he'd had no desire to support a couple of reds, but at no time since then had either of them ever shown the slightest sign of political awareness. And perhaps, his thoughts continued, considering how difficult it had become to find any servants, let alone good ones, a few left-wing sympathies—as opposed to activity—were not all that important.

He looked away from the window and down at the nearest brief on his desk. It was from Marsden & Slingfolds. Craig, the senior partner, had asked Arnold whether Mr Elham was thinking of taking Silk. Arnold's reply had been evasive and thus, in effect, an answer. Craig had then said good, there'd be quite a bit of work for Mr Elham, QC . . . To take or not to take Silk was a question which usually caused much heartburning. That one was a busy junior was no guarantee that one would become a busy Silk, since the junior was the all-rounder, the Silk the specialist. Further, Silks, to all intents and purposes, never appeared in court on their own, but always had juniors. This meant two sets of fees, with the Silk's noticeably higher than the junior's. So Silks were only briefed in major cases or where the client was wealthy, and therefore the amount of work potentially available was far less than when they'd been juniors; successful Silks made far more money than successful juniors, unsuccessful ones, far less. Many had discovered the bitter truth of this, but always too late. That ambition dug its own pit became very clear when one saw an underemployed Silk earning far less than he had, yet prevented from reverting to being a junior . . .

His thoughts changed course. It wasn't too fanciful to compare himself now with a man who'd awoken from a terrifying nightmare thankfully to find himself surrounded by the familiar, safe world. There'd been a short article in one of the papers about the hit-and-run case and this had named the car as a Ferrari. If that was what the authorities believed, then he could stop worrying . . .

He heard the front doorbell chime. Stephanie? Penelope said she might be calling. If so, he'd stay right where he was. Stephanie was loud-voiced; she was horsey and, like so many horsey people, had the manners of a groom; she was often downright rude to him. If she had not been so closely connected with one of the county families, Penelope and he would have had nothing to do with her.

He heard footsteps approach just before Penelope came into the room. 'Terence, two detectives have called and want to have a word with you.'

The icy waves of shock swept over him.

She closed the door and came up to the desk. 'For heaven's sake, pull yourself together.'

'But . . . but . . .'

'They'll be questioning everyone. But if they see you as you're looking right now, they won't need to question anyone else.'

'Why have they come here?'

'Why not? It's the biggest house in the village. They're bound to start with us.'

Were they?

'Just answer their questions. Don't volunteer anything.'

With a sense of bitter irony, he identified that as the advice he had given to many of his clients.

'And act as if you've absolutely nothing to worry about.'

He was again surprised to discover how sharp and cool she was, qualities with which, before the accident, he would never have credited her. In the face of such determination,

he forced himself to subdue and overcome his fears . . .
They could ask all the questions they liked, but he'd taken
steps to make certain that no one could ever prove the
truth . . .

Both men came to their feet as he entered the sitting-room.
MacMahon was dressed in an old, badly cut, heavily creased
suit; he had a round face, pleasantly featured, which looked
drawn, as if from long-term fatigue. A typically hardwork-
ing, but not over-intelligent middle-aged detective-
inspector. The detective-sergeant was much younger and
clearly far less tolerant and far more self-opinionated. Elham
spoke carefully, not hurrying his words; he was satisfied that
he sounded confident. 'I understand from my wife that you'd
like a word with me? Do sit down. And may we offer you
something to drink? Or, if it's too early, some coffee?'

'That's very kind of you,' replied MacMahon, as he sat,
'but we had a cup before we left.'

Elham walked over to the fireplace, turned to face the
room, and joined his hands together behind his back. By
taking that pose, he was reminding them that he was the
master of the house, successful, and wealthy. 'I'm a busy
man, so perhaps you'd tell me quickly how I can help?'

'That's easily answered, Mr Elham. We're looking for
someone who can tell us something about that hit-and-run
on Wednesday night . . . I don't know whether you've
heard, but the victim has unfortunately died.'

'Has he?' He was very conscious of the fact that his tone
had changed.

'So we are dealing with a very serious case. Is there any
way you can help us in identifying the driver of the car
concerned?'

Penelope was looking at him with an expression he had
no difficulty in reading. The death of the man altered
nothing; keep calm. 'No, I'm afraid I can't. If I had been
able to, I'd have been in touch with you before now.'

'Yes, of course.' MacMahon spoke so easily as to sound almost deferential. 'And you haven't heard any rumours?'

'I do not listen to rumours.'

'You don't? I suppose that's fair enough. Although just once in a while we find that a rumour does have some truth in it.'

'Really?'

MacMahon smiled. 'You remain unconvinced.'

'I do. And I am quite unable to suggest who might have been driving the Ferrari.'

'Ferrari?'

'That is the make of car the paper mentioned.'

'Oh, that! A typical load of cod's. Right now, we've no idea what make it was, except that it was a sporty model.'

'What does that mean?'

'Some kind of sports saloon; or maybe even an exotic.'

'Then it might have been a Ferrari?'

'Indeed. But, as I said, we've nothing as yet to suggest a make . . . That seems to be that, then.'

Ridley, sounding annoyed, said: 'What about—'

MacMahon interrupted. 'But I suppose we'd better just ask you the same question we're asking everyone else. Where were you on Wednesday night?'

'Has that any relevancy?'

'Only to this extent, that if you were out and returned here roughly about the time of the accident, you might have seen something that could help us. Were you out that night?'

'Yes.'

'Do you mind saying where?'

'We dined with my sister-in-law and her husband.'

'Where do they live?'

'Yew Cross.'

'So they're almost in the next village . . . It's like my brother-in-law. And, frankly, I never know whether that's a good thing or a bad one.' He smiled briefly. 'Have you any idea what the time was when you got back here?'

'No, not really.'

'We left there just after ten-thirty,' said Penelope firmly.

'Which road would you have returned on?'

'The usual one.'

'I'm sorry, Mrs Elham, but I'm afraid I don't know which is your usual road,' MacMahon said good-humouredly.

'Three Oaks crossroads and then direct to here.'

'Would that take you past the cricket field?'

'Yes.'

'About what time d'you think you'd have passed there?'

She shrugged her shoulders. 'Sometime between twenty and a quarter to.'

'In other words, a little before the accident. Did you by any chance see anyone walking along the road near the cricket ground?'

Elham answered. 'There were no pedestrians.'

'Did you observe any car which, in the broadest sense, could be termed sporty?'

'We met only one car that I can remember, at the cross-roads, it was an ordinary saloon.'

'Then now that finally is everything and we don't have to bother you any longer.' MacMahon stood. 'Thanks very much for your help.'

'I've hardly been able to help,' said Elham, a shade more forcefully than he'd intended.

'Maybe not directly, but indirectly, yes. We now know for certain that just before a quarter to eleven there was no sign of the victim walking along the road, or of a sporty car . . . Which does jog my memory. Just for the records, what kind of car do you run?'

'A Jaguar and my wife has a Volvo.'

MacMahon came forward and held out his hand. 'Good-bye.'

Elham led the way out of the sitting-room and across the

hall to the front door, which he opened. MacMahon smiled as he stepped past, Ridley merely nodded, his expression surly.

Elham closed the door and turned, to see Penelope standing in the doorway of the sitting-room. He went to speak, but checked the words because he couldn't be certain where Juana was. He hurried towards his wife. He needed to know whether he'd sounded convincing.

As he drew out on to the road, MacMahon turned right instead of left, which he would have done to return to Reckton. 'Well?'

Ridley did not try to hide his resentment. 'You went soft on him.'

'Did I?'

'You didn't follow up the fact that he was on the road just before the accident, you didn't ask him about the dinner-party and how much he'd drunk, you didn't—'

'Steve, are you too young to have heard the expression, "Softlee, softlee, catchee monkee"?'

'I've heard it, yes, but what's that to do with some poor sod getting knocked down by a car that didn't stop?'

'He's our man, isn't he?'

'That stuck out a bloody mile. Which is why I can't understand why you didn't squeeze him.'

'And immediately cause him to shut up tight, since with his experience in court he knows that the police's best friend is the accused's tongue. As of now, we've nothing that can be called proof—you know that as well as I do—so we need to keep him talking. And by letting him think he was clever and we were dumb and awed, we had him talking without ever realizing he was. How many cars were there in the garage?'

'Two.'

'A Volvo and a Metro, which probably belongs to staff.

Since both he and his wife are at home, where's the Jaguar? At a garage, being repaired?'

'We've asked to be notified about any repairs consistent with the accident and no reports have come through.'

'Quite. But take this scenario. He turns up at his usual garage and spins them a yarn of how his car got crunched. They know him as a pillar of the establishment. They'll believe him and it won't cross their minds that it could be his car we're interested in.'

'All that because he's Mister Bloody Elham?'

'Because it's an automatic reaction with ninety-nine people out of a hundred to believe that those who've really made it in life are like Cæsar's wife.'

'Who was probably a right old bag.'

Ridley, MacMahon thought, had this fatal blind spot which was fuelled by jealousy. Sooner or later, it could get him into trouble; probably, it would deny him the promotion that he deserved. 'When we get back, check the local garages for his Jag. In the meantime, we'll pay a call on the brother-in-law. I'm banking on the fact that Elham was too satisfied he pulled the wool right over our eyes to think of warning him to keep a tight mouth.'

Yew Cross consisted of several old cottages, three modern bungalows, and a pub; they were grouped around cross-roads. MacMahon braked to a halt in front of the entrance to the saloon bar of the Black Swan. 'Nip in and find out the brother-in-law's name and where he lives.'

Ridley's sense of humour took its first airing of the day. 'That requires a pint of best bitter.'

'Half a pint and you're paying.'

Ridley went inside, returned in just under five minutes. He settled in the front passenger seat. 'The woman behind the bar's not a bad bit of crackling; not bad at all. Wearing one of those dresses that make you want to drop a quid on the floor and watch her pick it up.'

'In between assessing her cleavage, did you find time to ask questions?'

'His name's Rickmore, he lives in the first house on the right down that lane, there, and he's an author.'

'We shouldn't treat him as untrustworthy just because of that.'

CHAPTER 9

Rickmore stared through one of the hall windows and convinced himself that the garden was far too sodden for him to be able to dig it, despite the fact that the day was dry. He heard a car door slam, thought it was Anne returning from the shopping, then heard a second door slam and knew it almost certainly wasn't her. He went through to the porch and after a moment two men, neither of whom he'd seen before, came round the corner of the house.

He opened the porch door as they came to a stop. 'Mr Rickmore? My name's Detective-Inspector MacMahon and this is Detective-Sergeant Ridley. Could we have a word with you?'

'Of course. Come on in.'

They entered and he pulled open the panelled door into the sitting-room, but MacMahon did not immediately move forward. 'A lovely old house, Mr Rickmore.' He stared up at the sloping ceiling which made the hall triangular in shape.

'I like it, when I can remember the ceilings are so low . . . And talking about that, keep your heads down as you go through and do mind the central beam; that's the most deadly of all.'

They settled in the sitting-room.

'I don't know whether you've yet heard,' said MacMahon

in his slow, friendly voice, 'but the man who was injured in the hit-and-run at Ailsham on Wednesday evening has died?'

'No, I hadn't. The poor devil.'

'His death obviously makes the case even more serious than it was. In fact, to put it bluntly, we'd really like to get our hands on the driver who just cleared off.'

'Yes, of course.' Rickmore's voice made it clear that he hoped they succeeded.

'So now we're trying to draw up a list of those who were on the road just before and just after the accident; that way, we may find someone who saw a car which could be the one we're looking for, while equally we'll be able to eliminate others. We've just had a word with Mr Elham and he told us he was here on Wednesday night.'

'That's right; he and his wife.'

'And he was in his Jaguar, which is . . . What model did he say it was, Steve?' MacMahon turned to Ridley, who looked uncertain.

'An XJ-S,' said Rickmore.

'Of course! A beautiful job. One needs to be a first-class driver to get the best out of that sort of machinery. Presumably, your brother-in-law's a very good driver?'

'He'll certainly agree with the assessment.'

'But you'd rather not add yours. What do they say? You can question my daughter's parentage, but not my driving skill . . . And Mr Elham also told us that when they left here, he was driving?'

'Yes, he was.'

'Neither Mr Elham nor his wife could be quite certain what the time was when they left. We need as accurate a time as possible when it comes to plotting out the cars we've had reported, so is there any chance that you can give us a sharper time than they could?'

'I don't think I can . . . Although, hang on, I've just

remembered. I went out and saw them off, then returned into the house and my wife remarked that it was just after eleven.'

'How long d'you reckon the drive back would take?'

'Quarter of an hour, give or take.'

'So he'd have arrived at his place at a quarter past eleven?'

'That's about it . . . You're trying to identify all the cars that were on the road near the time of the accident?'

'That's right.'

'Then you need to include mine. I drove over to Popham House.'

'Do you mean, after Mr and Mrs Elham had left here?'

'We found he'd left his glasses behind. We knew he'd need them the next day so tried to ring to tell him, but there wasn't any answer so I drove over.'

'What sort of time are we talking about now?'

'It must have been well after half eleven when I left here.'

'What was happening at the scene of the accident?'

'The ambulance was just pulling away.'

'That'll enable us to fix the time exactly . . . Presumably, you found Mr Elham when you reached Popham House?'

'Yes. They were outside the garage.'

'Having just arrived back?'

'I don't really know.'

'Was the Jaguar inside the garage?'

'No, it was still outside.'

'Then you can confirm that as far as you could see, it was quite undamaged?'

Rickmore hesitated. 'No, I can't.'

'Why not?'

'They'd recently bumped into something.'

'You mean, the car was damaged?'

'Slightly, yes. There was a bit of a dent in the offside wing and the light was smashed.'

'I imagine you asked what had happened?'

'I reckoned that that wouldn't have been at all popular. I don't want to make too much of this, but Terence is always very proud of his possessions and if anything of his gets damaged or refuses to work, he feels as if . . . Well, this probably sounds ridiculous, but I'm sure he feels as if he's being deliberately mocked. Can you understand what I'm trying to get at?'

'Indeed. Lots of people are like that. Steve, here, positively believes a car hates him when it won't start!'

Ridley's expression was sour.

MacMahon stood. 'Many thanks, Mr Rickmore. 'You've been a great help.'

Rickmore saw them out of the house, then shut the outside porch door and returned inside. He thought about what had been said and the impression grew that right at the end, when he'd been expressing his thanks, MacMahon had been trying to hide some emotion; a sense of triumph? But why, when he'd learned nothing pertinent to his investigations? Unless, that was . . .

'Softlee, softlee, caughtee monkee,' said MacMahon with satisfaction, as he drove on to the road and turned left.

'What a slice of luck!' said Ridley.

'Luck?'

'Sorry, masterly interrogation . . . With Elham's brother-in-law testifying against him, even the stupidest jury will have to convict.'

MacMahon changed into top. 'He obviously couldn't see the significance of the questions . . . Like I said earlier, with people in Elham's position there's an automatic and instinctive assumption which it takes a hell of a lot to destroy. But if Rickmore's as intelligent as I judge him to be, by now he'll have had to realize where our questions were leading. So will he stick with what he's told us, or will he change his tune because Elham's his brother-in-law? The answer to that will, to a large extent, depend on how they get on with each other. After meeting the two of 'em, I'd say they've very little in common.'

'They can't be too different or they wouldn't have been having dinner together.'

'Doesn't follow. Like as not, it'll have been the sisters who arranged things. The brothers-in-law just did as they were told.'

'You're being pretty cynical. For once,' Ridley added.

'My wife has a sister. Doesn't yours?'

'She's an only.'

'That you should be so lucky!'

They reached the T-junction, turned right, and came to the crossroads, where they stopped. There was no traffic coming in the opposite direction and MacMahon drove on. He enjoyed a certain sense of complacent satisfaction. Thanks to an anonymous telephone call and then to a brother-in-law too innocent and too conditioned to realize what was really happening until it was too late, Elham was now fingered for the hit-and-run. Provided nothing blew up in their faces, they ought not to have much trouble in finding the evidence to prove his guilt.

Anne, a shopping basket in her right hand, entered the house. Rickmore took the basket from her. 'Thanks, that's heavy,' she said. 'Tinned peaches were on offer and I bought three because you like them so. Incidentally, I met old Mrs Peacock in Sainsbury's and she asked how your writing was going. She seems to think you're a cross between Dickens and Zola.'

'Then obviously she hasn't read my book.'

'You'll be buried in Poets' Corner yet.'

'A consolation too delayed to be enjoyed.'

'You sound as if the world's all grey.' She walked into the kitchen. 'Have a drink and cheer up. You and Terence didn't drink us dry, did you?'

'Not quite.'

'Love, is something wrong? When I left, you were all chirpy, now you're acting like a man who's just discovered a large bill.'

He put the shopping basket down on the nearest working surface. 'While you've been out, a couple of detectives called. They're questioning people in order to try to draw up a list of who was on the road on Wednesday night at around the time of that fatal accident so that they can eliminate cars which couldn't have had anything to do with it. At least, that's what they claimed.'

'Why d'you say that?'

'I'm certain now that the real reason was solely to question me about Terence.'

'If so, why get uptight about it? He must have gone past the accident spot not long before it happened. You'll have been able to corroborate his times.'

'It was more than that.'

'More?'

'They wanted to know if I'd say anything to confirm their suspicions.'

'Suspicions about what?'

'That it was Terence who was involved.'

'My God! That's a horrible thing to say. All right, you don't like him, but really . . .'

'Whether I like or dislike him has nothing to do with it,' he said harshly.

'Yes, it has. If you didn't dislike him, you couldn't begin to think so nastily.'

'He'd had too much to drink . . .'

'And so had you, but you drove there and back and didn't knock anyone down. Thousands of men are so bloody stupid that they drink too much and then drive, but they don't knock people down.'

He said quietly: 'Do you remember what I told you when I got back? That Terence must have hit something because one wing was dented and the light was bust?'

'Well?'

'I went outside with them when they left here; the car was undamaged.'

'Oh my God! But . . . but if he'd run into someone, he'd have stopped and called for help.'

'Realizing that if he did so he'd inevitably be breathalyzed. That he'd be found to be over the limit and so he'd be accused of drunken driving, or worse; worse, as it's turned out.'

'You've got to be wrong.'

'I hope so,' he answered, without conviction.

'What do we do?'

'First tell Terence what's happened. I'll phone him now.' He left the kitchen, stood by the corner cupboard, lifted the receiver, dialled the number. There was no answer. 'They're out.'

'It's Saturday, isn't it? I've just remembered, Penny told me they were going to friends for lunch. At least, I think she did.' She was speaking disjointedly, her mind not on what she was saying.

'Then I'll try again later on.'

'Dennis, it's impossible. Terence and Penny couldn't just drive on after something like that, knowing what that could mean to the injured man . . . Oh, God, I really need that drink,' she said, in little more than a whisper.

CHAPTER 10

Titchbourne's Garage lay on the boundary of the smaller of Reckton's railway station's car parks. Originally a small, family-run business, it had been taken over twelve years previously and a four-storey administration and spares building had been erected to the right of the repair sheds. The garage held Rover, Jaguar, and Vauxhall agencies. In the forecourt, to the right of the pumps, were a number of secondhand cars for sale and amongst these there was sometimes a replica D-Type Jaguar, built by a small local specialist.

Ridley, glad to get out of the wind which had started blowing a couple of hours before and which felt as if it was coming straight in from the Arctic, went into the main shed and asked for the foreman. He was directed over to a Rover Vitesse whose bonnet was raised and into whose engine compartment two men in overalls were peering. 'If you can't get it to work, send it over to Stradley's,' he said, naming one of the three rival garages in town.

The foreman straightened up. 'What's it this time? On the bum for a rotor arm for that wreck of yours?'

'Are you offering me one?'

'Do I look that stupid?'

'No comment. How about having a chat in your office?'

'Come on, then. And maybe we can find a cup of coffee.'

They threaded their way past numerous cars being serviced and repaired, and reached a small office, built out from the wall of the shed. An electric fire was on and the interior was warm and muggy. The foreman went over to the desk and searched through a number of forms, found the one he wanted and put it by the telephone. 'I've got to ring up the owner of that Vitesse to say she can't have it back today. She'll scream. Bloody old bitch.' Two steps took him across from the desk to a small gas-ring set up on bricks, on which stood a kettle. He checked there was enough water in the kettle, lit the gas. 'So what brings you snooping about the place?' He went round the desk and gratefully slumped down on the chair behind it.

Ridley picked up a couple of loose-leaf service manuals from a second chair, put these on the floor and sat. 'Is Terence Elham one of your customers?'

'Yeah.'

'Have you got his car in for repair now?'

'Can't say off-hand.'

'Will you check?'

'When the coffee's inside me.'

The kettle boiled. The foreman reluctantly stood, went over and made two mugs of instant coffee; from the bottom drawer of the desk he brought out a half-pint bottle of milk, a jar of sugar, and a teaspoon which looked as if from time to time it was used to repair cars. 'Help yourself to what you want.'

Five minutes later he wiped his mouth with the back of his hand, belched, returned the milk and sugar to the bottom drawer, wiped the spoon on the leg of his overalls and dropped it in the drawer which he pushed shut with his foot. He reached across his desk for a thick loose-leaf file. After checking through several pages, he said: 'Elham's Jag is in for repairs.'

'What's the trouble?'

'A smashed-up offside front; wing, bonnet, wheel, radiator, suspension . . .'

'Any idea how it happened?'

'According to his wife, when they got back at night and he was driving into the garage, they ran onto some black ice. Went straight into the wall.'

'Did you collect the car?'

'With that sort of damage, d'you think it drove itself in?'

'So was it still where it had crashed when it was collected?'

'That's right; hard up against the garage wall.'

'Shit!'

'Watch the language. I've got cultured ears.'

'Have you done the repairs?'

'Can't say off-hand, but I doubt they'll have got much further than stripping down. There's a lot of work there.'

'What will have happened to the damaged bits?'

'They'll have been thrown out at the back, ready for the scrap merchant; he's maybe already collected 'em.'

'Can we find out if he has?'

The foreman closed the file with a snap. 'So what's all this in aid of?'

'Routine inquiries.'

'And my second name's Getty ... There was a nasty hit-and-run at Ailsham recently, wasn't there?'

'It's dangerous to draw conclusions.'

'So it could have been him!' He whistled. 'A bloke in his position, eh?' He stood. 'Isn't he something to do with the law?'

'A barrister.'

'Doesn't say much for being a barrister.'

'From where I stand, there never has been.'

They left the office and went through the first shed to a yard which was littered with empty oil drums, cardboard cartons, parts of cars, and a wreck which looked as if the light van had fallen over a hundred-foot cliff. The foreman checked briefly, then said, as he kicked a badly crumpled green panel: 'All the bits and pieces are still here. You were born lucky.'

'And handsome to boot. Put 'em on one side, will you? I'll see they're collected p.d.q. . . . Can we go and have a look at the car?'

The front end of the Jaguar was on stands and two mechanics were fitting a new shock absorber. Ridley walked round to look at the nearside light pod. 'Yellow bulbs!'

'He swears blind they give a much better light. I told him they didn't and it was just a gimmick of the Frogs, but he wouldn't listen. Knows it all, that one does.'

'He doesn't know the half of it yet.'

Back at divisional HQ, MacMahon, grey-faced, obviously tired, was in his office. Ridley told him what he'd discovered.

'So he was smart enough to realize that the only way of concealing the first and incriminating damage was to overlay it with further and far more extensive damage.' MacMahon plucked at a couple of hairs on the side of his chin which his electric razor constantly missed. 'What's happening about the damaged bits?'

'I've already sent a couple of lads along to pick 'em up. I've alerted the lab and they've promised to take their fingers out. If there are any incriminating traces, they'll find 'em.'

'It'll all depend on how good a job he made of the second crash . . . Let's be pessimistic. The lab boys can't come up with anything definite enough for the court. Then Rickmore's evidence is going to be crucial.' He let go of his hairs. 'What's he going to do now he knows it's his brother-in-law's skin at risk?'

Rickmore braked to a halt in front of the garage at Popham House and the headlights of the Escort picked out the damaged brickwork. 'I wonder when that happened?' Anne said.

He ignored the question. 'D'you think we're doing the right thing, coming here now?'

'Yes, I do.'

He sighed. 'I hope you're right . . . I'm not looking forward to it.'

'You don't imagine I'm jumping with joy, do you.'

He switched off the lights and then the engine. They left the car and walked across, past the small greenhouse, to the back door. She rang the bell three times, opened the door; Elham disliked their entering by the back, but she refused to go all the way round to the front just to satisfy his social pretensions.

They passed through the deep-freeze and laundry room and entered the kitchen, which was empty but in which all the lights were on. 'Is anyone at home?' she called out. The door from the kitchen into the hall was open and they could just hear the louder notes of a Duke Ellington record. She called again and this time was answered.

They went into the blue room. The smaller of the two sitting-rooms, it possessed charm—which the larger one did not—despite the over-use of the colour which was Penelope's favourite.

Penelope was welcoming. 'What fun having you both drop in like this! I was getting so bored with my own company. Dennis, turn the record down, will you, and then you must pour us some drinks.'

She'd managed to sound as if she really were glad to see them, he thought, as he went over to the stacked disc-player and slid the volume control to its minimum setting.

'There are all the usual drinks in the cupboard, or bubbly in the fridge. Let's have that?'

He said: 'Penny, we've come to have a word with Terence. I think we ought to do that before we drink.'

'But he's upstairs, working; he never does anything else these days . . . I tell you what. We'll open one bottle and finish that before you call him down. Then he'll have to open a second one.'

'It is very important.'

'Oh, very well. I'll go and tell him to come down and be sociable. I said only the other day that when he's a Silk, I'm not having him spend all his time at home working . . .

Oh!' She touched her cheek in a quick gesture of dismay. 'I wasn't supposed to breathe a word of that to anyone. For goodness sake, do remember to forget it . . . That's rather a mix-up, isn't it?'

'Yes,' he answered.

'Penny, for God's sake, get Terence,' said Anne.

She showed both astonishment and fear and they realized that she had been trying to delay what she knew, or guessed, was going to be a painful meeting. 'All right,' she said stiffly. She stood, left.

He looked round the room. It spoke of success. The French print curtains, the Shiraz and Daghestan carpets, the authenticated Raffaelli and Dawson, the unauthenticated Modigliani, the eighteenth-century display cabinet with its lovely collection of early Staffordshire pottery, the silver, some of which was reputed to have come from the Tsar's Winter Palace . . .

Elham, followed by Penelope, entered. He said, ''Evening,' then crossed to stand in front of the fire, in the pose which came so easily to him. 'Penelope seems to think there's some sort of trouble you want to talk about?' He spoke pugnaciously, as if ready to contradict everything that was said.

'I had a couple of detectives along this morning asking questions about Wednesday evening.' Rickmore could not have missed the effect his words had had. The last, slender hope that his suspicions might, after all, be wrong, was gone.

'What questions?'

'What the time was when you left us Wednesday evening?'

'What did you answer?'

'I said that it was around eleven.'

'That's ridiculous,' snapped Penelope. 'It was only just gone ten-thirty.'

He shook his head.

'I know it was ten-thirty.'

He looked at Elham and saw that Elham's pugnacity had been replaced by fear. 'They explained why they were interested—they were trying to identify all the cars on the road before and after the accident so that they could clear all those which definitely didn't have anything to do with it. To help them, I told them I'd driven over here later on.'

'What did they say to that?' asked Elham.

'They wanted me to confirm that your Jaguar was undamaged.'

'Which you did?'

'I could hardly do that, could I? The offside wing was dented and the light pod was smashed.'

'You told them that?'

'Yes.'

'How could you?' shouted Penelope.

Rickmore didn't answer.

'Did they ask you what you meant by "dented"?' asked Elham.

'No.'

'Then you didn't explain that the whole wing was wrecked and the wheel was buckled?'

Rickmore said tightly: 'The wing was only dented and the wheel was undamaged.'

'We'd skidded on black ice and went into the corner of the garage. Both the wing and the wheel were completely wrecked.'

'The corner of the garage was undamaged.'

'Go and look at it now and see for yourself.'

'I know that when I came here Wednesday night, the corner of the garage was untouched.'

'And I'm telling you, it wasn't.'

There was a silence, which became more painful for each of them the longer it lasted. Rickmore finally broke it. 'Terence, was it the Jaguar which hit that man?'

'No,' replied Elham violently.

'Then why does it matter quite so much to you exactly when the garage was damaged?'

'Because if the police believe you're telling the facts, they may start beginning to suspect me of having been the driver.'

'If you're innocent, you'll soon clear yourself.'

'For God's sake, how can you be so stupid? Don't you know that acquittal and innocence are two different things.'

'That's one hell of a thing for someone like you to say.'

'D'you think innocence has a shining ring of truth about it that can't be missed? D'you believe that old saw; Witnesses may lie, but circumstances cannot? Are you so naive that you accept that the police are more interested in a man's innocence than their own clear-up rate?'

'But you're saying . . .'

'I'm saying that if you persist in telling the police what you've just said here, they're going to suspect me; and once that happens, every piece of evidence that is turned up will be carefully angled towards confirming my guilt.'

'You do realize something, don't you? The man who was knocked down has died. Doesn't that mean something to you?'

'I had nothing to do with his death.'

'When you left our place, you weren't in a fit state to drive.'

'No? I'd had no more to drink than you, yet you drove over here. Were you in a fit state to drive?'

'I . . . If I'd knocked someone down, I'd have stopped to do what I could for the poor devil.'

'Are you so certain?'

'What d'you mean?'

'Would you be seized by quite so much righteousness if it weren't someone else who was involved, it was you?'

'The principle's the same.'

'Principles are never the same for oneself.'

'That's an extraordinary thing for you to say.'

'It's an extraordinary fact that you liberals can never . . .' He stopped. He ran the back of his hand across his forehead. 'This is quite ridiculous. We're arguing and becoming quite heated, yet there's nothing to argue about . . . I am not trying to say the police would ever deliberately set out to inculpate a man they know to be innocent. What I am pointing out is that they're human, grossly overworked, and unfortunately judged by results. So if the evidence in a case appears to point to one conclusion, they're sometimes over-ready to accept that conclusion and do not exert themselves to find out if it might, after all, be incorrect.

'You can see what that means here. They're searching for a car that was near the cricket ground at the relevant time and which bears signs of damage compatible with an impact with the victim. The moment they find such a car, they'll tend to concentrate on that one to the exclusion of all others . . . Because of what you've already told them, they're bound to think it could be my car they're looking for. So they'll have checked with all the garages and will have found that the Jaguar is being repaired in Titchbourne's. They'll have examined the damage and inevitably have come to the conclusion that it is far greater than would have been sustained in the accident. But because, by now, they'll have come to the conclusion it could have been my car, they're going to claim I deliberately crashed my car into the garage after the accident in order to hide the signs of damage resulting from it. So if you insist, wrongly, in maintaining that when you were here the Jaguar was only lightly damaged and the garage wall was untouched, their false accusations are going to appear to be corroborated.'

Rickmore said very slowly: 'The wing was only dented, the wheel was not buckled, the garage was untouched.'

'You filthy swine!' Penelope shouted.

'I . . . I have to tell the truth.'

'Hypocrite.'

He flushed. 'I do happen to believe that justice means justice for everyone . . .'

'Justice? You don't give a damn for justice.'

'Penny . . .' began Elham.

'If you won't tell him, I will.' She faced Rickmore, her expression ugly with hatred. 'All you're interested in is in getting your own back on Terence.'

'Doing what, for God's sake?'

'Getting your own back because he's a success and you're a failure. The police didn't come to you, you deliberately went to them and tried to implicate Terence with your filthy lies.'

Anne stood. 'I think we'd better leave.'

'Then go.'

Elham gestured with his hands, looked at Rickmore, then at his wife. He turned away, shoulders slumped.

Anne and Rickmore left the sitting-room and went through the hall, the kitchen, and deep-freeze room to the yard. They climbed into the Escort and, for once, the engine started at the first turn of the key.

He drove slowly, his thoughts jumbled and painful. All his thinking life, he'd accepted that for a country to have freedom, it must have justice. Justice depended on just laws and people who observed their duty to obey them. Each time such a duty was dishonoured, justice suffered and therefore freedom was imperilled . . . But could Elham be right? Was there for every individual a line which drew the boundary between duty and self-preservation? Could he, hand on heart, honestly affirm that in Elham's position he would have done his duty at no matter what cost to himself?

Anne said: 'It was Terence who hit the man, wasn't it?'

'Yes.'

'Oh God!' She put her forearm on the back of his seat so

that she could touch his neck, needing the comfort of physical contact. 'What's going to happen?'

He shook his head. He knew only one thing. He would do his duty, which was to tell the truth, no matter what this cost in emotional terms.

CHAPTER 11

Monday was dry and fine, with only good weather clouds; but for the temperature, it might have been the beginning of spring.

Rickmore stared at the cuttings from the French agent which had arrived from Paris by the morning's post. Each cutting contained a reference to Teerson's Products and was presumed to have appeared in response to the newsletters which Rickmore sent out; as such, the cuttings were held to provide an indication of how effective his newsletters were and it was his job to translate the relevant passages into English so that they could be read by the directors. Had he, as he'd claimed when he'd applied for the position of PRO, been fluent in French it would not have been a difficult task; as it was, it was one that invariably taxed his ingenuity and patience. But he'd learned to work on the principle that if the references were never less than complimentary, no one would ever bother to check the translations.

The intercom buzzed and he pressed down the appropriate switch. 'Yes, Daphne?' He shared his secretary with Advertising. She was dumpy, yet dressed as if she had the figure of a model. Parkes had once asured him that she was a girl with potential. Since then, he'd always considered Parkes rather odd, even for someone in Advertising.

'There are two gentlemen who'd like to see you, Mr Rickmore. They're detectives.'

'OK, send them in.' That would start the rumour mills turning, he thought.

MacMahon and Ridley were shown into the room by Daphne, who was wearing a pleated skirt in a bright tartan which added inches to her already generous waist. She tried to stay to learn at least a little of what was going on, but he thanked her in a way that left her no option but to go.

MacMahon, he thought, wasn't looking fit, Ridley appeared aggressive. They shook hands with careful formality, then he set two chairs in front of the desk.

'I'm sorry to bother you during working hours,' said MacMahon.

'As far as I'm concerned, don't apologize.'

MacMahon smiled. 'Even so, we won't keep you for long . . . When we had a word with you before, you mentioned that on Wednesday night Mr Elham and his wife had dinner with you and that he left his spectacles at your place. You tried to ring him to say so, but couldn't get through, so you drove them over. Have I got that right?'

'Yes, you have.'

'Will you tell us again, as exactly as you can, what happened when you arrived?'

He described the events, his voice hard because there was no way now of avoiding the knowledge of what might be the consequences of his words.

'I'd like to get a mental picture of this dent in the wing. How deep would you say it was?'

'I don't think I can make a reliable estimate.'

'Why not?'

'One needs some sort of yardstick and I didn't have one.'

'Fair enough. Then how would you describe it in general terms?'

'Not very large and not very deep.'

'You place it on the turn of the wing, some way back from the lights. And the bonnet was untouched?'

'That's right.'

'This was night-time, but the outside lights of the garage were switched on. Do they give a reasonable light?'

'A good one.'

'Then if the wing had been buckled and torn, instead of being merely dented, and the bonnet had been crumpled, you'd have noticed the fact.'

'Yes.'

'Did you look at the offside wheel?'

'Not specifically, no.'

'You can't say if it was badly buckled?'

'Not directly. But if it had been, I'd have thought I'd have noticed it.'

'Was the corner of the garage in any way damaged?'

'No.'

'You are quite certain about that?'

'Positive.'

'Then that, I think, is all we need to know for the moment.' MacMahon stood. 'I'd like to thank you for being so frank. It can't have been very easy for you.'

'It hasn't been.'

'I hope it'll help if I tell you that you've done the right thing.'

After they'd left, Rickmore resumed his seat. MacMahon said he'd done the right thing. But had he? Could consequences be ignored? Yes, he decided; they could and must be when justice demanded that.

An hour and a half later, Ridley walked into MacMahon's office. 'You're looking rotten,' he said, as he came to a stop in front of the desk.

'Just tired.'

'Are you quite sure? Wouldn't it be an idea if . . .'

'I am quite sure.' MacMahon pulled himself upright.

'If you say so . . . I've had a bloke from the lab on the

phone. Damage to the various bits is consistent with running fairly hard into a brick wall. They've recovered traces of brick dust and want to know if we'd like 'em to run comparison tests with samples taken from the wall?'

'Not much point to that. It's Elham who claims to have rammed the wall.'

'That's what I reckoned . . . One interesting bit of news. At one point of the offside wing, the force of the impact split and folded the metal back on itself, forming a pocket that was never in direct contact with the wall. The lab's managed to raise an impression on the paintwork inside this and they say that in their opinion the impression was formed by an article of clothing of woollen texture.'

'The sweater the victim was wearing?' said MacMahon, his voice suddenly sharp.

'They're testing. But the chap I spoke to warned me that the impression was blurred and, because of the deformation of the metal, distorted. He said the odds were against their being able to make a unique comparison.'

MacMahon began to tap on the desk. 'Then at best it'll be no more than corroborative evidence and a good defence lawyer could probably turn it inside out.'

'If it's on its own, maybe. But if it's in there with other evidence, the jury will get the right idea.'

'Provided there's some central, unshakable fact on which to hang all this.'

'Rickmore's evidence, surely?'

MacMahon stopped tapping. 'What about the sliver of glass—did the lab mention that?'

'Similar to the control glass, but the crime sample was too small for any definite comparison.'

'I suppose if we'd given them half the headlamp glass, they'd have shouted for the other half before they'd commit themselves . . . Every time defence counsel makes an expert witness look like a wally, the lab boys expend a bit more energy on defending their backs and a bit less on doing their job . . . We've not yet checked out the dirt forced into the victim's clothes, have we?'

'There's not been time.'

'There never is. Find out if there've been any repairs carried out recently on the house or garage; if there have been, get samples of the brick and wood. And find out if the Elhams employ full-time staff. If they do . . .'

'They will. Too bloody lazy to do the work themselves.'

MacMahon leaned back in his chair. 'I've said it before and I'm about to say it again. If you go on carrying around that chip on your shoulder, sooner or later you'll end up in right royal trouble.'

'What chip?'

'Your resentment of anybody who has more than you.'

Ridley's expression became sullen.

'No one ever will invent a society where there aren't have-nots as well as haves.'

'So the haves aren't complaining.'

MacMahon sighed. Ridley would never understand. 'If any staff were around on Wednesday night, find out what they heard or saw. And try to discover if we're ever going to be told whether the dead man's dabs are on file. It's four days now since we requested a search.'

'I got on to 'em earlier and was given a lecture. The present computer is so slow that it can take up to ten days to go through its database of three hundred and fifty thousand prints. But some genius is working on a new computer that'll cut the time down to one day.'

'Always jam tomorrow,' said McMahon.

Juana opened the door and Ridley introduced himself. He then explained what he wanted, speaking very simply because he'd never overcome the teachings of his mother that all foreigners were stupid. Juana was worried, since neither the señor nor the señora was in the house to guide her as to what to do, but Ridley could be charming when bothered to take the trouble and soon she had forgotten her worries and she asked him into the kitchen for a cup of tea.

While he was eating a second wholemeal biscuit, a man came into the kitchen and was introduced by Juana as her husband, who worked in the garden. That, thought Ridley, was fairly obvious; Cavajals had brought part of it in with him.

'Have you had any repairs done recently?' he asked.

Cavajals looked at his wife, who spoke more English than he did. 'You wish to know the garage?' she asked.

He shook his head. 'No, not just for the moment. Have any repairs been done, to a window or a door maybe? Has anything been made or altered?'

'There is the . . .' She came to a stop.

'The what?'

'I do not know how is called.'

'Is it part of the house?'

She shook her head. 'It is . . .' She stopped again. Then she said, very impatient at being unable to express herself clearly: 'Please to come with me.'

He followed her out to the yard and the garden immediately beyond this and she showed him a cold-frame, newly put together by her husband—if he understood her correctly —from a kit supplied by a local firm. Her husband had had to alter one corner. Her husband was a very clever man with a hammer, saw, or screwdriver . . . Yes, he had had to do a bit of sawing. And because it had been cold and the Jaguar had been out, he had done it inside the garage . . .

The floor of the garage was concreted and in one place it had cracked; in this crack—which, she said, was about where her husband had worked—was a sprinkling of saw-dust. He used an old and battered tablespoon, found on a workbench, to lift out the sawdust and drop it into a plastic bag she brought him.

They returned to the kitchen. Cavajals had left and the coffee in their mugs was cold. Ridley said he didn't mind cold coffee, but she emptied both their mugs and switched on the electric kettle.

He asked her about Wednesday night once she'd made fresh coffee and was seated at the kitchen table. She explained that they'd been in their house which was beyond and behind the garage.

'What was the time when you went to bed?'

As usual, they'd gone to bed early. Because he didn't understand the television, her husband only watched sport and if she tried to watch anything else he became annoyed, so they seldom stayed up at night.

'Did you hear the Elhams return?'

'They come back, yes.'

'Have you any idea what that time was?'

She shrugged her shoulders.

'Was it soon after you'd gone to bed?'

'Not soon. Miguel is asleep. I could not be sleepy and I read.'

'Have a guess what the time was.'

She was silent for so long that he thought she wasn't going to answer, then she said: 'I think it was a good time after eleven.'

'Did another car arrive after them?'

'I stop the reading and turn the light off. Then it come.'

'Was it here for long?'

'Not long. And after it go, there is a crash. I think something bad is happened. But there is no more noise.'

'Can you describe what kind of a noise it was?'

'I think was the señor to hit the garage.'

'And this was definitely after the other car had left?'

'Please?'

He repeated the question and she confirmed that the crash had been after and not before.

They were, Ridley thought with deep satisfaction, gradually tightening the noose around Elham's cowardly neck; soon, they'd pull it tight.

CHAPTER 12

Rickmore left the garage and walked towards the garden gate. Even on a winter's day, Oak Tree Cottage was attractive. Not because the proportions were good—they weren't; the cottage was unreservedly boxy—but because three centuries had made it as much part of the countryside as the large and majestic oak whose upper branches could be seen to the right and beyond. He sometimes wondered who'd been the original occupants and what kind of a life they'd led. A thought which other authors had exploited . . .

As he opened the gate, he noted that one of the upright slats was still loose and needed nailing back; he assured himself that he'd do that at the first opportunity, knowing that he'd put it off for as long as he possibly could. For him, nails bent and hammers missed. Anne had described his carpentry as Mack Sennett comedy.

Anne entered the hall from the sitting-room and he kissed her.

'Well! It's some time now since you've been romantic on your return from work. Have you had a rise?' She studied his face and her tone changed. 'No, it's not like that at all, is it?'

He hung his lined mackintosh on one of the hooks on the wall to the right of the porch door. 'The two detectives called at the office. I confirmed all I'd told them before, so now I'm left wondering if I'm a rotten bastard.'

'Do you think you are?'

'More to the point, do you?'

Her gaze never left him, her high-boned face expressing conviction, but also sadness. 'Not if you truly believe you had to do what you've done.'

'He is your brother-in-law.'

'Does that alter the principle?'

'Of course not. But it must affect the light in which other people will see my actions.'

'You're worried by what people will think?'

'I don't give a damn about them if I know I've done the right thing.'

'Have you?'

He managed a wry smile. 'Hasn't that brought us round in a circle?'

'What is it, Dennis? D'you want me to agree that you had to do it?'

He was worried by her tone, but tried not to show that. 'I suppose I would like confirmation that my motives for telling the truth are as pure and high-minded as I've been assuring myself.'

'And not as mean and contemptible as Penny suggested?'

'Ouch!'

She stepped forward and kissed him again. 'Listen, my love. If the whole world said that your motives were utterly sordid and despicable, and you assured me they weren't, I'd know the whole world was wrong. You're an idealist and if that sometimes means you're difficult to live with, I don't care. I wouldn't change you for anyone.'

He hugged her. 'I'm a very lucky man.'

'Quite right.'

'No false modesty?'

'None whatsoever.' After a moment, she disengaged herself. 'I'll make some coffee.'

He followed her to the doorway of the kitchen, leaned

against the side. He watched her fill the coffee machine with water and not for the first time wondered how two sisters could be so different in character.

Ridley was late and he hurried up to his room, which was smaller than MacMahon's but which he did have to himself —something that rarely happened in the older stations. He checked the desk top, but there was no ironic message asking him if he'd be good enough to go to the DI's room if and when he had a moment to spare. So MacMahon wouldn't know he'd been late . . . The telephone rang and the caller was Mrs MacMahon. Her husband had been unwell during the night, the doctor had seen him and had called for an ambulance, and he was now in hospital; the hospital doctors seemed to think he might have suffered a slight heart attack. So he would not be in to work for a while. She didn't say so, but she was obviously worried sick that perhaps he never would be back.

Ridley used the internal telephone to tell the divisional superintendent that the DI was ill, then the outside one to give the same message to the detective chief superintendent at county HQ. He was informed that a relief DI would be sent down as soon as possible, but because the Force was so short staffed at the moment, this might take time; until then, he was acting DI.

He went through to the DI's room, ostensibly to find out if any of the morning's mail needed urgent attention, in reality to see how the room fitted him. It fitted him like a glove.

The laboratory assistant telephoned at four fifty-six on Wednesday. By then, Ridley, while no less confident of his own abilities, was prepared to admit that the job of detective-inspector was a more difficult one than he'd supposed. Especially when the detective-constables couldn't—or wouldn't—carry out their orders exactly as he wanted them carried out.

The assistant said: 'Both the control and crime samples of sawdust were softwood, treated against rotting with some fungicide. As you'll know with sawdust, there's seldom much hope of a positive identification and the best we can do here is to say that the samples are similar. There's no chance of specifically identifying the fungicide used.'

'Is that all?'

'What more do you want?'

He wanted a positive identification, but obviously was not going to get one. He thanked the woman and rang off. Every time, it was the same. The two samples were similar, but not uniquely so. They'd still not one single piece of unshakable evidence to complement Rickmore's testimony . . . That left only one way of going about things. Pressure Elham until he admitted his guilt. MacMahon had steadfastly denied that this was the way, but he'd joined the Force in the days when a policeman metaphorically doffed his helmet to the gentry. All that gibberish about softlee, softlee, catchee monkee. A smokescreen, to try to obscure the fact that he could not shake himself free of his instinctive deference . . .

Ridley looked at his wristwatch. When would the old bastard get back from London? Certainly by eight. So hit him then, at the end of his working day, when he'd be too tired to be fully alert mentally. Force him to admit that it had been his car which had slammed into the as-yet unidentified man . . .

Elham had hired a Granada, since the Jaguar would not be ready until the following day. He turned into his drive and saw, with sharp annoyance, that a dirt-stained car was blocking his way into the garage.

Penelope met him in the hall. 'The police are here,' she

said in a low voice. He experienced immediate tension and fear. 'Pull yourself together,' she said fiercely.

He briefly wondered how he could have been married to her for years, yet never have realized that when necessary she could be as hard as nails.

'If you don't tell them anything, they can't prove anything.'

Had she no idea how the police worked; how they uncovered one small piece of evidence here, one small piece there, then stitched them all together to prove the accused's guilt?

'They tried to question me. I told them their suspicions were disgusting and libellous.'

Slanderous, he automatically thought. Into his mind there came the image of the man suddenly appearing in the car's headlights ... A few seconds only, but which now threatened the whole of his future life ...

'Show some backbone.'

He'd said the same thing, more elegantly phrased, to men he'd defended and whose servile attitudes had virtually been admissions of guilt. He was learning it was not so easy when one was the accused ...

She dug her fingers into his arm, so tightly that even through the thick, good quality cloth and the sleeve of his shirt, the grip was almost painful. 'Make them believe you.'

He went into the blue sitting-room. Ridley briefly introduced Detective-Constable Cricks. Elham wondered where MacMahon was and wished he'd come instead of Cricks; MacMahon had been pleasant and understanding.

'I want to go over a few points again,' said Ridley, his manner openly antagonistic. 'On Wednesday evening, you left your brother-in-law's house at around eleven o'clock ...'

'At around ten-thirty,' he corrected.

'Mr Rickmore says that it quite definitely was eleven.'

'He is mistaken.'

'Your maid agrees that you returned some time after eleven.'

'Juana? I fear she's not a good time-keeper, as we soon discovered after she started working for us.' He was surprised how easily confident he managed to sound; just the right amount of casual indifference as to how his answers were received; a man of consequence, naturally willing to assist the police, but certainly not to be browbeaten . . .

Penelope confirmed what her husband had said, in a way that sharply exacerbated Ridley's resentment, since she sounded condescending. Because of this, he made the mistake of claiming too much. He said that the forensic laboratory had definitely concluded that the imprinted pattern on the damaged wing from the Jaguar had been made by the dead man's sweater . . .

Elham, knowing that the detective-sergeant could not be telling the truth—had he been, he'd have come to arrest, not question—understood that the other had thought to panic him into an admission. The knowledge gave him confidence. He asked what proof there was that the impression had not been implanted at some time after the car had been taken to the garage—could the police prove constant reference? What gave the so-called impression its unique quality . . .'

Angrily, Ridley introduced the sliver of glass. This had been identified as coming from the headlamp of the Jaguar. This time, Elham asked only one question. Was the laboratory prepared to say that it had come from the headlamp of the Jaguar and could not possibly have come from any other car? When Ridley did not answer, he ostentatiously shrugged his shoulders as he would have done if addressing a jury.

Ridley spoke with even greater antagonism. What about the sawdust found in the victim's clothing? Had it been proved beyond question, Elham asked quietly, that the sawdust was similar in every respect, uniquely similar in every respect, to the sawdust found in the garage? Ridley said that the car Daley had seen had had yellow lights. So, remarked Elham, did every French car on the roads. But perhaps there had been something about those yellow lights which positively identified them as British, not French?

When Ridley left, his expression was bitter.

As they heard the car leave, Penelope said: 'You were really marvellous!' Her surprise was less flattering than her words.

He went out to the drinks cupboard and poured himself a whisky and her a Campari. He noticed that his hands were shaking. He was like an actor who'd suffered stage fright right up to the moment of appearance, yet had acted superbly as the adrenalin flowed, then suffered badly from reaction the moment the curtain dropped.

He returned to the sitting-room and handed her a glass.

'You completely silenced the insolent man!'

As he stared at her, he noticed several small and wholly immaterial things, as often happened in a moment of mental stress. She was using a different shade of lipstick and was wearing the ear-rings he'd given her the previous Christmas; there were lines about her mouth that hadn't been there before; her dress was tight and her breasts were well outlined, breasts which should have summoned passion . . .

'Terence, have you been struck dumb?'

'No.'

'Then why don't you say something? Why are you still looking so miserable?'

'You obviously don't understand.'

'I understand you sent that man packing, with his tail between his legs.'

He sat down on the nearest chair, drank. 'I'm worried because they've found out so much.'

'They've discovered nothing of importance. Every time he tried to claim they had, you showed he was lying.'

'It's true I could knock each piece of evidence independently. But when they're all put together, they're good enough to strengthen the central evidence. And when that's strengthened, it in turn strengthens them.' He finished the whisky, stood, saw she had not yet touched her drink, left the room and refilled his glass. When he returned, he stood in front of the fire instead of sitting. 'Take the imprint they've found on the wing. Obviously, it's not good enough to prove that a specific sweater must have made it. But it fits in with the central evidence which says that it was my car which hit the man; one moves on from there to the fact that if it was my car, it's probably the dead man's sweater which made it. And if there's other evidence which fits in in the same way, then before long all these pieces of evidence cease to be separate but become part of the pattern. In other words, they corroborate the central evidence—Dennis's.'

'He can't do it to you,' she said fiercely.

'Perhaps, after what you said to him the other night, it's become more of a pleasure than a duty.'

'I was terribly upset.'

'But will he allow for that.'

'My God, he is my brother-in-law, isn't he?'

'And also a man of principles.'

'What's that to do with it? He can't do it to us. You've got to talk to him and make him understand.'

'Since when has any liberal ever understood the nature of the world he lives in?'

CHAPTER 13

Seated in his office, Rickmore knew a painful embarrassment. Elham seemed to have lost all sense of self-respect.

'Can't you realize what it would mean to Penelope and me?'

'Yes, of course, but . . .'

'If you tell the court exactly the same as you've told the police, I'm bound to be found guilty. At worst, I'll be jailed, at best I'll receive a suspended sentence; either way, I'll be disbarred.'

'We've been through all this before . . .'

'I'll be out of work and unqualified to do anything else. For God's sake, think what it would mean to Penelope, even if you've never bothered to consider what it would mean to me.'

'Not considered it? I've not thought about much else . . . All I'm doing is telling the truth.'

'And you think it's right to do that no matter what happens to the family?'

'But the truth . . .'

'Do you hate me that much?'

'For God's sake, I don't hate you at all.'

Elham leaned forward until he was sitting on the edge of the chair. 'Suppose I admitted it was the Jaguar, but I swore by everything I hold sacred that I had absolutely no chance of avoiding him; that even if I hadn't had a single drink all night, it wouldn't have made the slightest difference? What then?'

'How could that alter the need to tell the truth?'

'You'd still think it right to see me ruined over something over which I'd no control?'

'You should have stopped the car after it happened.'

'There was an oncoming car and that reached the man within seconds.'

'You didn't know at the time whether seconds might have made the difference between life and death.'

Elham said, not realizing that he had virtually abandoned the fiction that his last few questions had been hypothetical: 'What gives you the right to set yourself up as the judge?'

'I'm not.'

'Do you imagine that there's another man in the whole country who'd betray his own family like this?'

Rickmore said desperately: 'I don't know; I just don't bloody know what any other man would do in this God-awful situation. I only know what I've got to do.'

'Got to?'

'Yes.'

Elham stood. He stared down at Rickmore, his expresion strained. 'If . . . if I offered you ten thousand pounds?'

Rickmore tried to keep his contemptuous anger under control. 'If the offer was made to get me to change my evidence, I'd tell you just what to do with it.'

Elham's shoulders slumped. He turned, went over to the door, then suddenly swung round. His voice was shrill. 'Every man has his price. I just wonder what yours is?'

Because of the time of day, the train arrived at Charing Cross and not Cannon Street. Elham left the first-class carriage and walked along the platform to the ticket barrier. He showed his season ticket and went through. He felt as if part of him was standing aside and observing, with clinical detachment, his ever-quickening advance towards disaster.

He looked up at the large overhead clock. Half past eleven. He should have been in court, but earlier he'd telephoned Arnold and told him to see if Trent could take the watching brief. He suddenly knew an overwhelming pity for himself. Why? Why had it happened to him?

Lucy, he suddenly thought. She couldn't offer him escape, but she could give him temporary forgetfulness. He turned and went through one of the exits to the pavement and the taxi-rank.

The taxi went through Admiralty Arch and down The Mall. His thoughts raced ahead. Because of all that had happened, it was days since he'd phoned her, let alone seen her. She must have become worried. So she'd be even more passionate than usual and in the white heat of that passion, he'd be able to forget . . . Defining what he'd forget made him remember it. He stared through the glass partition, silently urging the driver to greater speed.

The taxi arrived at Cuthbertson Road and drew up outside No. 22. He paid, crossed to the steps, climbed these, pressed the bell for the top flat. The speaker crackled into life and a man said: 'Who is it?'

Stupidly, he checked that he had pressed the button for the top floor.

'Who is it, then?'

He knew that she employed male models (better never to wonder, remembering those sculptures, what pose she required) and decided the speaker must be one. 'Is Lucy there?'

'Yeah. So now who are you?'

'Terence.'

As he waited, he wondered how old the model was.

'She says she's busy.'

'But I must see her.'

There was a long silence. He pressed the bell again. This time, Lucy answered him. 'Terry, go away. I can't see you.'

'I'm in trouble; terrible trouble. I need you desperately.'

The man spoke again. 'Look, Terry-boy, the lady doesn't want to know you any more. Got it?'

He stood there for over a minute, absurdly waiting for
her to tell him that it had all been a silly mistake and to
come straight up . . . Finally, he turned and went down the
steps, feeling sick and old. It did not occur to him that it
had been shame which had made her refuse to meet him.

Betty returned to the clerks' room and sat behind her desk,
but did not immediately resume work on the Statement of
Claim. 'It was Mr Elham who came in just now. He looks
really terrible.'

Arnold stared at her over the tops of the half-moon glasses
he wore when his eyes were tired. 'What exactly do you
mean?'

'I think he must be ill. Either that or something terrible
has happened.'

He wondered if she was being stupid.

'You know, if you come to think about it, he's not been
his usual self for days.'

There was some truth in that.

'D'you think he's worried about taking Silk?'

'Of course not,' he replied sharply.

'Then maybe it's something which has happened at home.
I mean, with a wife like his, anything . . .'

'Shall we leave his private life private? Suppose you get
on with the work.'

'All right, all right.' She liked him, but that didn't stop
her finding him, at times, a pompous old fool. She wound
a sheet of paper into the typewriter and typed in the name
of counsel, the case, and the name of instructing solicitors.
She looked across at Arnold and saw that his high, greasy
forehead was creased, as it always was when he was worried.
He could huff and puff as much as he liked, but Mr Elham's
wife was a bitch . . .

Arnold tried to concentrate on the fees' book he was
bringing up to date, but his mind kept returning to what

she'd just said. Was Mr Elham either ill or desperately worried over something?

After a while, he left and went along to Elham's room and with even greater disquiet saw that Elham was not working but was slumped back in his chair, staring into space, his expression that of a man under intolerable pressure. 'Mr Trent appeared for your clients; everything went smoothly.' Elham turned and looked directly at him and he was shocked by the expression now in the other's eyes. He blurted out: 'Is something wrong?' Then he added: 'Is there anything I can do?'

Arnold, at the age of four days, was named Thomas Arnold as he had been found on St Thomas's day in Arnold Street. Since the small wooden box had been left at one of the rear entrances of the Clarence Hertchwitz Memorial Hospital, he should, perhaps, have considered himself lucky.

The orphanage in which he'd spent his early life had been well run, but his years there had been filled with dull despair. His nature was of the kind that needed a deep, lasting, and particular relationship if it were to be fulfilled and this he failed to find; the staff were too busy, and trained to be too egalitarian, to give more to him than to the others in their care, and because he was shy and solitary he failed to strike up any deep friendships with his peers.

He'd almost married when he was twenty-two. But a fortnight before the wedding, the woman, seven years older in time, seventy years older in experience, had met a merchant seaman from Glasgow who'd offered her Nirvana and, despite all her experience, she'd gone off with him. The humiliation of this had hurt deeply, although he eventually realized that in fact she would have made him very unhappy. He never contemplated marriage again and very seldom went out with women, even though he was not a homosexual; he usually felt uncomfortable in their presence.

His first job, gained through the influence of one of the governors of the orphanage, had been as an old-fashioned office boy in chambers which had been headed by a QC who'd been as successful as he was objectionable. The QC had died suddenly, the head clerk had retired, and he'd been promoted to assistant clerk. Several years later the building had been redeveloped and the chambers had split up; he'd found work in another set, almost at the same time as Elham joined them as a pupil.

As he was given more responsibility, so he discovered that not only did he enjoy the work, he was very good at it. Solicitors liked him, probably because he treated them with considerable respect and their egos were always finely tuned when dealing with the senior branch of the law; barristers liked him because they found they could trust his judgement; his judgement was good because he had a natural flair for bargaining which seldom let him down and he could tell how high he could demand a brief be marked before instructing solicitors rebelled. At the same time, he also developed an instinct which suggested how successful any barrister was likely to be.

He'd soon judged that the highest posts in the judiciary were not beyond Elham's reach. So he'd carefully hitched himself to Elham's star. And strangely, although this had been a material decision—as Elham's status grew, so would his—he'd found that relationship for which he'd been searching all his life. He didn't know what Elham felt about that, but he didn't care. It was sufficient for him that he could be a part of his life and climb the ladder in his shadow.

So he'd been shocked and frightened when Elham told him all that had happened; so shocked and frightened that for the rest of the day he'd been unable to do any work and Betty had fussed, believing him to be sickening for the 'flu.

He left chambers sharp on five—a unique event—and caught the tube to Clapham. A ten-minute walk brought him to the house in which he'd lodged for the past seven years. He let himself in, called a greeting to the landlady in the kitchen, and went up the stairs to his two rooms. He settled in the armchair in the sitting-room and stared at the blank screen of the large television set he'd bought himself the previous year . . . Desperately, he tried to think clearly. Because he was totally unconcerned with the morality of Elham's actions, the question was not whether he should try to help, but how. How, in God's name, to save Elham from being ruined by his brother-in-law? Because he'd never met Rickmore, he had to imagine him in a villainous guise in order to hate him the more. If only he could be knocked down and killed in another road accident before he gave his evidence in court! Would it be any good travelling down to Reckton and seeing Rickmore and pleading with him not to testify? But Elham had said that Rickmore was motivated by a sense of duty and therefore it was impossible to talk sense with him. Then how to silence the prosecution's main witness? Or reduce the value of his testimony to the point where it was no longer strong enough to support the circumstantial evidence . . .

Frustration squeezed his mind. He longed to sacrifice himself, yet could not discover how. He stood and crossed the room to the small cupboard beyond the television set and brought out a bottle of whisky and a glass. It was his invariable custom to have one whisky before his supper. Tonight, he had three. And because he was unaccustomed to so much alcohol, his mind began to wander, to twist and turn . . . And suddenly he realized that there was one way in which the value of Rickmore's evidence could be fatally weakened . . .

He paced the floor, the alcohol no longer confusing his thoughts but seemingly sharpening and polishing them. Two years back, a brief had come into chambers from solicitors working for a trust which helped people in need.

The scent of charity had kept the markings low and so the brief had gone to Vernay. The trial had not been a long one and Vernay had been extraordinarily lucky with one of the main prosecution witnesses, but the accused, Dean, had believed he owed his freedom to brilliance rather than luck (a common mistake with those who, to their complete astonishment, were acquitted). Dean had come up to them outside the courtroom (Elham had not been in court that day, so Arnold had been free to accompany Vernay to see how he was shaping) and had said: 'If ever I can do either of you gents a good turn, just ask. That's all, just ask and I'll come running.' Later, Vernay had said that they must remember the offer in case either of them wanted to go in for burglary. At the time, Arnold had disapproved of such levity. Now he remembered the words in a very different light . . .

CHAPTER 14

The phone rang and Ridley picked up the receiver. 'DI,' he said, no longer aware that he had promoted himself.

'It's Dabs here. We've an identification for you, reference seventeen six stroke nine.'

That was the hit-and-run victim. So MacMahon had been right when he'd surmised that the victim had been engaged in some criminal activity. Ridley picked up a ballpoint pen. 'Shoot.'

'Richard Tamworth. One conviction, for indecent assault.'

'A sex merchant!'

'His last known address is twenty-six, Updyke Road, Evenham. But that's pretty old, so it may not be worth much.'

'You'll send us a copy of his file?'

'Of course.'

'By the way, he's died.'

'Then I'll transfer him to the gone and unlamented section.'

After replacing the receiver, Ridley stared down at the sheet of paper on which he'd written the name and address. It was now possible to postulate two facts. That Tamworth's disappearance hadn't been reported because whoever knew he'd disappeared also knew the possible reason for his disappearance and was too ashamed, or scared, to draw attention to it. That the reason for his sudden and fatal appearance on a section of road where there were no homes nearby had been that he'd committed an offence of a sexual nature and had been fleeing pursuit . . . Yet against this last was the fact that there'd been no report of any such incident on the Wednesday night . . .

Behind the desk was a large-scale map of the county, with the divisional boundaries marked in red. He found Ailsham cricket ground and the double bend in the road just south of it. Where could Tamworth have come from? Somewhere where there were potential victims. The countryside was populated, but except in the villages the houses were fairly well apart. That could appeal to a sex criminal, since he was less likely to be disturbed and caught; on the other hand, it meant far fewer potential victims from which to choose and a much greater risk of being noted. Ridley visually examined the surrounding countryside, searching for somewhere that would have attracted a sex criminal . . . Hacksley House. Once a rich man's mansion, now a geriatric hospital. Nurses worked in hospitals and nurses' hostels were frequently targets. A long shot, but not impossibly so . . .

He drove the four miles to Hacksley House and parked against the raised flowerbed in the centre of the turning circle immediately in front of the portico. He climbed out of the car and looked up at the large Queen Anne mansion. Once, just one man had owned all that, together with the park which stretched right round it; dozens of servants had catered to his every whim. Ridley knew a brief satisfaction at the thought that the man and his descendants had been dispossessed.

The matron had an office on the ground floor, to the rear of the house. She was a tall, firmly proportioned woman, quiet in manner, with a face which expressed both strength and compassion. She showed no surprise when he explained what he was looking for and he was pretty certain that after a working lifetime in nursing there was little that could surprise her.

Her voice was well pitched and brisk. 'There were no official reports of any incident on that Wednesday night.'

'There weren't.' He was disappointed, but not surprised.

'However, there was something . . . At what time was the road accident?'

'Soon after eleven; say just short of a quarter past.'

'And how long would you imagine it would take a man to get from here to the point at which the accident took place?'

'In the dark . . . Having to find gates . . . Twenty minutes, or maybe a bit more. But that's pure guesswork.'

'If we accept that figure, we're back to roughly five to eleven. And if my memory's correct, that's about the time when Nurse Trott, who was off duty and in her bedroom, caused a commotion by screaming.'

'Because she'd been attacked? But you said there was no incident that night?'

'She screamed because she had a nightmare which frightened her very badly.'

'Then I'm sorry, but I just don't see the relevance of this.'

'Mr Ridley, that is the explanation which Nurse Trott

gave. It was not given directly to me, which from her point of view is perhaps as well. It is my experience that while young children may wake up screaming because of nightmares, adults do not.'

'Then you think . . . ?'

'The circumstances were such that I was not called upon to decide what really happened.' She saw that he was about to speak. 'Nor do I wish to give my opinion now. There are rules which govern not only the working lives of our nurses, but also their off-duty lives. While I demand adherence to the former, I am, I hope, sufficiently realistic to realize that the latter are mostly out-of-date.' She smiled briefly. 'The world is a very different place from when they were drawn up. Yet as matron, it is my duty to see that while they exist, any official breach of them is dealt with.'

'You're saying . . .' He stopped, uncertain how to put the question tactfully.

'I'm saying that a blind eye is an advantage to people other than admirals.'

'Then it would be best if I had a word with Nurse Trott on my own?'

'Probably essential.' Again that quick smile.

'Can you tell me what kind of a person she is?'

'Intelligent, quick-witted, attractive, and something of an iconoclast, which at her age is right and proper.'

'Would you also say she's . . . well, sexy?'

'I feel you are better qualified to answer that than I.' She reached across to the intercom, but did not immediately press down on the switch on which her forefinger rested. 'I think I'll ask her to see you in the almoner's waiting-room. That can fairly be called neutral territory.'

The waiting-room was a lot more cheerful than he had expected. The walls were painted in two shades of green, there were four comfortable chairs and a settee, on the low, glass-topped table were a number of up-to-date magazines of general interest, and the four framed prints on the walls were of attractive, colourful country scenes.

Nurse Trott was an extremely attractive blonde with an artless manner which at one and the same time made a man both protective and hopeful. She was also very wary. She expressed surprise and excitement at meeting a real detective and even more surprise when it turned out that the detective was interested in the night she had screamed. She began to explain just how frightening that nightmare had been . . .

'You're sure it wasn't something else which made you scream?'

'Of course not.' She was very wide-eyed.

'The matron was saying that young kids wake up screaming from nightmares, but she'd never known an adult to do so.'

'She said that?'

'Yes.'

'Oh! . . . Well, she's wrong. I did.'

'You remember I'm investigating the hit-and-run case and one of my jobs is to trace out what the dead man was doing before the accident?'

'Of course I remember you telling me that. Which is why I don't see how I can possibly help.'

'By telling me if you screamed because you were threatened or attacked by a man?'

'If anything like that had happened, I'd have reported it.'

'Unless the circumstances were such that you didn't dare report them.'

'I don't know what you mean.'

'Miss Trott, the matron is quite a woman.'

'She can be an old battle-axe.'

'She probably has to be, with you lot to keep an eye on.' She giggled.

'She's convinced you were breaking the rules that night.'

'Of course I wasn't.'

'But she hasn't been called upon officially to decide whether you were so she's prepared to play at being Nelson.'

'To play at what?'

'To put the telescope to the blind eye.'

She nibbled at her lower lip.

'I'll lay it straight down the line. All I'm interested in is what really happened; how it affects anyone here doesn't concern me. And matron's not asking me to pass on to her what you say to me. But if you don't tell me what I've got to know, I'll have to start asking around and then things can't remain all nice and private and pretty soon matron's going to have to take official note of what's going on. And that means, no more blind eye.'

She looked at him for a while, then made up her mind. She spoke with great earnestness, conveying the fact that she was sharing her deepest secrets with him because she recognized a soul-mate. Everyone was agreed that the rules governing the conduct of nurses who lived in were positively Victorian—just imagine, no visitors allowed except in public rooms and all visitors to be off the premises by seven at night. It positively cramped a girl's style. Especially if the boyfriend hadn't anywhere to take her when they wanted to be alone. So it was accepted practice to smuggle a friend into the nurses' wing; dinner was the best time for getting him in because authority was busy eating, between two and five in the morning the safest time for him to leave. It was, of course, almost impossible to keep a visit secret from one's friends and neighbours, but it was absolutely essential to keep it from the sister in charge of the nurses' wing and the cleaning women. A week ago on Wednesday, she'd smuggled Bill in. Bill was . . . someone special. And this was the last quarter of the twentieth century and only the dodos believed that there was still one law for the man and another for the

woman. And what harm did it do if it was a deep relationship, based on love . . .

'You were in bed together?'

She found that rather too direct and blushed.

The lucky bastard, he thought. 'So what happened to
make you scream?'

She became even more embarrassed, rather upsetting the
image of a daughter of liberation. It seemed that their love
had blossomed, almost to the point of fruition, when she'd
looked by chance at the window and had seen a truly horrific
face staring at her . . . She'd screamed from shock—and,
perhaps, also from a sense of outraged modesty. Whereupon,
she'd found herself faced with the necessity of explaining what had frightened her, without disclosing Bill's
presence . . .

'Where did he disappear to?' Ridley asked, more from
curiosity than because it was of any importance.

'The cupboard. It's rather small and he was terribly
uncomfortable.'

And, perhaps only temporarily, frustrated. 'You didn't
tell anyone you'd seen this face?'

'I couldn't, could I?'

He wondered if she'd ever stopped to realize what the
tragic consequences could have been of remaining silent.
'From what you've said, the curtains weren't drawn. Yet
you and Bill . . .' Tactfully, he did not finish.

'I don't like being closed in and my bedroom's on the first
floor so I never draw them. I didn't think anyone could ever
look in.'

Nobody had told her about ladders. 'How would you
describe this face?'

Her description was poor which, considering the circumstances, was not really to be wondered at, but it did convince
him that the man's face had been concealed by some kind
of a mask.

There was little more she could add and he thanked her for her help and promised her, on his honour as a gentleman, that he'd tell no one else at the hospital what she'd just told him.

He left the building and stood on the lawn outside the nurses' wing and worked out in which direction Ailsham cricket ground lay. Then he returned to the car, opened the boot, and changed into a pair of wellingtons. He walked across the park and went through a gateway, across a lane, and over a metal five-bar gate into a fifteen-acre field that was down to permanent pasture, but too sodden even to carry sheep. The man's route lay almost directly to the opposite corner. He searched the thorn hedge on either side for a distance of fifty feet, then crossed the field and searched there. There was a break in the hedge which had been stopped with a hurdle that now lay on its side. He went through, into another and larger field, down to winter wheat. He thought he could make out footprints which crossed the field. He went round the edge to a thin belt of trees beyond and near a clump of brambles he found a woollen ski mask. The pattern picked out eyes, nose, and mouth, in different colours from the background. He imagined what it must have been like to be making love and to look up suddenly to see that at the window and he wondered if the experience had left Nurse Trott with a neurosis.

On his return to the station, Ridley collected the OC file and carried this through to the DI's room. He read through the summary of cases from all over the country, stretching back over the past year, which had been reported and investigated without success, but not closed, for whatever reason. At the end of forty minutes, he had picked out three rapes, one attempted rape, and one sexual assault, each of which had been carried out by a man who had been described as having a face from a horror film.

CHAPTER 15

On Monday evening, a blustery, rain-threatening evening, Arnold was too preoccupied with his problems to realize what a strange figure he cut in the district. There was no mistaking his clerkiness, just as there was no mistaking the fact that in this part of Lewisham at times the writ of the law might not run very far. Several times in his walk from the bus stop he was eyed speculatively, but his very indifference to what lay about him provided a protection. He reached his destination and spoke to a slatternly woman who said that bloody Fred was down in the bloody pub where he was every bloody evening, spending the money she bloody needed.

The pub, on a corner site, was wedge-shaped. Dean was in the larger of the bars, drinking heavily. He was a small, foxy man who might have looked less untrustworthy if he had cut off his Zapata moustache. It really was astonishing that, two years before, the jury had found him not guilty.

'I can't say I do remember you,' said Dean uneasily.

'We met in court.'

'Never been in no court.'

'When Mr Vernay got you off that charge of housebreaking in Reading.'

'Yeah? . . . Well, maybe now I do remember a bit.'

'I'd like a little chat, if you've time?' He looked at the bar. 'What will you have?'

'If you're asking, it's a large brandy and ginger.'

Arnold bought the drinks and Dean suggested they went over to an empty table close to the outside door. They sat and Dean drank quickly, reckoning that if he had to cut and run for it, he might as well leave an empty glass behind.

'D'you remember what you said to Mr Vernay and me after the trial was over?'

'Can't say as I do.'

'That if ever you could do either of us a favour, we only needed to ask.'

'I said that?' Dean was astonished and disbelieving.

'I've come to ask you to do me a favour now.'

Dean's manner became very much more confident. 'There's favours and favours.' He fiddled with his glass to remind the other that it needed refilling.

Arnold, who hadn't yet touched his whisky, took the glass over to the bar. As the barmaid refilled it, he noticed how grubby her frock was. It completed the picture of slatternly failure and small-time villainy in which he found himself; he would have entered hell and supped with the Devil to help Elham.

He returned to the table. Dean drank, then said: 'So what's it all about?'

'I want you to do a job.'

'Jesus!' Dean was shocked by such stupidity. He looked round, but the table nearest to them was unoccupied and the couple at the one beyond were in a clinch and even the Last Trump might not have disturbed them. 'Are you round the twist, talking like that?' he demanded in a fierce whisper. 'And I don't have nothing to do with that sort of thing.' Then he realized that Arnold would have seen his list of previous convictions and he amended his denial. 'Leastwise, not since I got off when I hadn't done the job.'

'But you'd had plenty of experience before then?'

'That ain't nothing to do with you. I've done me bird. Look, mister, I'm finishing this drink and then I'm clearing off. And don't never come near me again.'

Arnold had not supposed that Dean would help him merely from a sense of gratitude. 'I'm willing to pay.'

'For what?'

'Carrying out a burglary.'

Dean was scared. Scared that this was all a trick, lining him up for the Norwich job which had gone badly wrong and left him only one small step ahead of the law. He hastily stood, picked up his glass and emptied it. 'You try and follow me and I'll do you rotten.' It was a ridiculous threat; he did not have the bearing of a man who would ever use physical violence.

Arnold produced an envelope. Certain it was hidden from everyone but Dean, he opened it and riffled through the corners of the twenty-pound notes. A man of simple tastes, he had for years saved a large proportion of his income and he had several thousand pounds in a building society account. He was prepared to spend everything.

Dean stared at the money and he started to think. The coppers wouldn't ever use someone in Arnold's position. And Arnold was dead serious. Only a right fool turned his back on easy money . . .

The Jaguar turned into the drive of Oak Tree Cottage and came to a smooth halt. Elham climbed out, switched on the torch, and went round the bonnet to open the front passenger door, but Penelope had forestalled him and was already standing on the drive.

'Don't forget,' she said.

'I won't.'

'Don't let him be all nauseatingly hypocritical.'

He wondered whether she still underestimated the strength of Rickmore's convictions or whether her words were merely a sign of how desperately nervous she was.

They walked towards the gate into the garden, buffeted by the gusty wind. The beam of the torch picked out a puddle. 'Mind that, dear.'

'Why can't he get the drive properly surfaced. It's like a slum.'

Had she ever allowed herself to understand what a slum was really like? Almost certainly not. She lived in a world where money put an impenetrable barrier between herself and slums. But if they failed tonight, that barrier would come crashing down . . . How to find the words that would convince Rickmore . . .

He opened the gate and they passed through. She complained about the unevenness of the brick path and said that if she didn't break an ankle, she'd be lucky. He liked this path, which wasn't really uneven, because it was so in character with the house. He'd always gone along with her desire for the new and the smart, but he knew a respect for the past which she lacked.

When they reached the small porch, he shone the torch on the bellpush, pressed it. They could look through the nearest hall window and they saw Rickmore step out of the sitting-room. He was wearing a polo-neck sweater and a pair of creased grey flannels. Elham imagined his wife's thoughts. Dressed like a tramp, as usual. He wondered, surprising himself by doing so, whether she'd ever dressed for comfort rather than effect? But perhaps she couldn't face the world without protection.

The porch light was switched on. When he identified them, Rickmore could not conceal his astonishment. He greeted them and now amazement had been replaced by reserve. Guessing the object of the visit, thought Elham, but not the content. They went inside.

'We hadn't seen you for such ages,' said Penelope in her most social voice, 'so I said we simply must pop in and find out how you both were. Aren't you going to kiss me hullo?' The ugliness of their last meeting might never have been.

Rickmore kissed her on the right cheek.

'Both, continental style.'

He kissed her on the left cheek.

'How's the new book coming along?'

'I'm afraid I've been neglecting it recently.'

She failed, or appeared to fail, to see any connection between recent times and the hit-and-run case. 'We went to a cocktail party the other evening and when I mentioned to our host that you were my brother-in-law, he was very much more impressed than when I told him Terence was taking Silk. So you see, you're famous.

'And so a fool?'

'What do you mean?'

'"As yet a child, nor yet a fool to fame . . ."'

She was confused, yet determined not to appear to be. 'Sometimes, Dennis, you really do say the most amusing things.'

Anne came out of the sitting-room. 'I thought I recognized the voices.'

'It's such ages since we last saw you both.' Penelope came forward and embraced her sister, careless that there was no response; some of the jewels on her fingers sparkled as she moved under the overhead light.

'Come on in here where it's a sight warmer than in the hall,' said Anne, as soon as she had disengaged herself.

In the sitting-room, Penelope, who frequently complained of feeling cold, sat in the armchair nearer the fire. Elham hesitated, then said: 'D'you mind if I stand for a bit? Been sitting all day.' He took up his accustomed position with his back to the fire.

'What will you drink?' Rickmore asked. 'There's sherry, red Vermouth, or Scotch.'

Penelope chose Vermouth, Elham Scotch.

Conversation, while Rickmore moved around with glasses, was brittle; they were four people who were trying to ignore what had been said the last time they met, because that was the civilized way to behave, yet were unable actually to forget.

Elham drank quickly, put his glass down on an occasional

table. He coughed. 'We've just learned something very important.' He paused, but when there was no comment, he added: 'The police have identified the dead man.'

'Who was he?' asked Rickmore.

'His name was Tamworth. He had one conviction for indecent assault. Beyond that, the police are satisfied that he has been responsible for three rapes, one attempted rape, and one sexual assault, although he was not charged with any of these because of lack of evidence.'

There was a silence, broken only by a hiss as part of a log suddenly began to flame.

Elham leaned forward with his shoulders slightly hunched, an attitude he often adopted in court. 'You do realize what that means, don't you?'

'I don't know, not yet. It takes a bit of thinking about.'

'It's obvious,' said Penelope.

'Is it?'

She ignored the worried look her husband gave her. 'He was a filthy pervert. God knows how many women he molested.'

'Almost certainly many more than reported having been raped or assaulted,' said Elham.

'He deserved to die,' said Penelope viciously.

Rickmore said slowly: 'Deserved?'

'That's right.'

'I can't accept that.'

'Why? Because you're a typical man? You think there's no such thing as rape, it's always initially encouraged by the woman who then panics and tries to stop? But it's often not like that and it wasn't this time.' She turned. 'Just tell him, Terence.'

'I know the details of two of the cases,' said Elham. 'In each, the woman was grabbed as she was walking along a street at night, threatened with a knife to her throat, made to walk to somewhere dark where she was forced to strip and then subjected to the most obscene assaults.'

'How ghastly,' murmured Anne.

There was another silence. Penelope broke it. 'He deserved to die,' she said, even more pugnaciously than before.

Rickmore said: 'He obviously was a vile menace. But when you say "deserved to die", where's your authority?' As always, when he became excited or earnest, his slight speech impediment became more noticeable.

Anne, worried by the impression her husband was now giving, said: 'Dennis, all Penny is saying is that that kind of a man is so great a menace that he's better dead than alive. Surely not even you can argue against that?'

'I can start by asking, better from whose point of view?'

'For goodness sake!' snapped Penelope. 'From the point of view of all the women he'd have raped if he'd gone on living. Or are you now so liberal that you think they don't matter at all?'

'It's not a case of being liberal, or anything like that, it's not setting myself up as God. I don't know what motivated him. Suppose he was subjected to overwhelming desires, so overwhelming that he was totally unable to resist them; that morality and self-will simply had no meaning for him?'

'You've not begun to understand. He's better dead because now he can't rape any more women.'

Rickmore spoke quietly to Elham. 'You did say he had one conviction, but in all the other cases there was not enough evidence to charge him?'

'That's right.'

'Then he may well have had nothing to do with them?'

'The police are satisfied he did.'

'Maybe. But thankfully we live in a country where police certainty isn't enough to convict. I repeat, he may not have comitted any of those other offences. In which case, all he'd ever been guilty of was one indecent assault. A man can commit one such act, be caught, and be so shocked by his conviction that he never does such a thing again. Then surely no one can say he deserves to die?'

'Dennis,' said Anne angrily, 'you're being very stupid.'

'Because I refuse to give way to emotion?'

'Because you're arguing just for the sake of arguing.'

'That's unfair and untrue.'

'Dennis,' said Elham, 'the police aren't as blindly biased as you obviously think. They've traced out Tamworth's movements on the night he died. He went to Hacksley House, the geriatric hospital, and used a ladder to get up to one of the nurses' rooms. She saw a hideous face at the window and screamed, which alarmed Tamworth, who fled. In a copse half way between the hospital and the cricket ground, they found a ski-mask, which the nurse identified as having been worn by the man at the window; it also fits the description given by two of the women previously assaulted. His build matches the description of one woman's assailant and she stated that the fingers of the man were noticeably short and stubby and the nails looked disgusting because they were constantly being bitten and so had re-treated part of the way down the fingers—Tamworth's fingers were very short and stubby and his nails had re-treated from constant biting . . . There can be no reasonable doubt that he was guilty of several sexual assaults.'

'Then I'll accept that he was.'

'You're satisfied?' demanded Penelope.

'Satisfied that he was probably a rapist, yes; I've just said so.'

'And if he hadn't died, he'd have continued to commit rape and sexual assaults?' asked Elham.

'I suppose that has to follow.'

'Then he was better off dead,' snapped Penelope.

Rickmore's expression hardened, but he said nothing.

Elham picked up his glass and drained it, replaced the

glass on the table. 'You'll have realized why I've told you this?'

'I imagine so.'

'Without renewing the argument about whether he deserved to die, it's clear that by his death an unknown number of women are saved the most revolting of experiences. Those women would certainly regard his death as an act of providence.'

'That's taking things too far . . .'

'It is not,' cut in Anne fiercely.

Rickmore looked at her. He had lost all her understanding and sympathy.

'I wasn't negligent in hitting him,' said Elham. 'He ran straight out into the path of the car because he was panicking, fearing pursuers were immediately behind him. I had absolutely no chance of avoiding him. It is true that I did not stop. If I had, I'd have been breathalysed and probably would have been found to be over the limit. In those circumstances, it's inevitable that it would have been held that the accident was to a large extent due to my intoxication and there would have been nothing I could have said that would have refuted that presumption. Yet it would have been totally wrong. I could not have missed hitting him if I had not had a drop of liquor for the previous week.

'You said I should have stopped; that it could have been a situation where his life depended on how soon aid could be summoned. But the alarm was given by the other driver very soon after I could have given it, so very little time was lost. In fact, time was not of the essence. Nothing would have changed for Tamworth if I had stopped.

'You have told the police certain facts which identify me as the driver. If you confirm that evidence, I'll be charged, probably with causing death by reckless driving, and will be found guilty. I will be imprisoned or given a suspended sentence. My career will be finished and my life ruined. Can

you now, in the light of what I've told you, bear that
responsibility?'

'You're claiming . . .'

'I am claiming nothing. I am asking you to understand
that the law does not always serve justice; to recognize that
in some cases the law can be as merciless as the criminal.'

'And you're also putting forward the proposition that a
crime can be excused if the victim deserved to be the victim.
That can't possibly be right. Crime is crime and the nature
of the victim is irrelevant.'

'Are you still going to tell the police?' demanded Penelope
shrilly.

'I . . . I don't know.'

'You swine!'

'Penny . . .' began Elham.

'Haven't you the courage to say it to his face? Well, I
have. All he wants to do is to see you in prison and me
reduced to rags. He's always been so jealous of us that he
couldn't even be polite.'

'I am not, and never have been, jealous of either of you,'
Rickmore said angrily. 'And if you won't believe me, ask
Anne.'

Anne looked away, unable to confirm his words.

They were in their bedroom, but had not yet begun to
undress. 'Why won't you understand?' demanded Rickmore.

'Because I can't begin to see how you can believe it's
more important to honour the law than to help Penny and
Terence.'

'You've got to forget what kind of a man Tamworth was.'

'Forget? How can I forget? For God's sake, climb down
from that ivory perch. Penny was absolutely right. He
deserved to die. And if I'd been driving, I'd feel I'd served
justice, not betrayed it. And don't start talking about prin-

ciples. Just tell me why it's so important to ruin your own relations.'

'You really do think it's jealousy?'

'I . . . I just don't know what to think. I can't understand how you can go on and on and on as you are.'

'Because the law is our only defence against anarchy and if we betray it . . .'

'For Christ's sake, stop pontificating; just think on this. If that man hadn't been killed, I could have been his next victim. So what would you have felt about your wonderful justice if you'd come home to find me raped?'

He knew what he would have felt.

CHAPTER 16

Because it was impossible to live for long at a high level of emotional conflict, it was implicitly agreed that the subject should be dropped until Rickmore wanted to return to it. And because he'd been forced to accept that there was no way of escaping both Scylla and Charybdis—he would either have to betray his principles or destroy Elham's happiness and career in circumstances which appeared to make a mockery of his principles—throughout Tuesday he was careful never to broach the subject, even obliquely. But from time to time he'd seen Anne look at him with quick puzzlement and he'd known that she was trying to understand how he could find the decision so difficult a one to make.

On Wednesday morning, he went downstairs to the kitchen where she was cooking breakfast and he made an attempt to break the feeling of restraint between them. 'Eggs and bacon? What about our cholesterol levels?'

She responded to his lighter mood. 'Worry about yours,

not mine. I'm sticking to one piece of toast and an apple. But I decided you were beginning to look pinched around the face and it was time to fill you up a bit. And since we normally have so little fried food, I can't believe this one indulgence will clog your arteries.'

'You know the trouble with one indulgence? It breeds a second.'

'Try using some will-power.'

'In the olfactory face of eggs and bacon?'

'Instead of talking nonsense, see if the coffee's made. It should be, but I haven't heard the machine belch yet.'

He lifted the aluminium lid and coffee, which had been surging up the central spout, splattered him. 'There's a law which states that one always checks at the most dangerous moment.'

'Did it reach your coat?'

'No, only the back of my hand.'

'That's all right, then.'

'Even if I'm severely burned?'

'If you'd been even lightly burned, you'd now be shouting for an ambulance.' She turned away from the stove and kissed him lightly. Then she turned back and used the bottom of the slice to surge hot fat over the yolks of the two eggs. 'I've buttered a piece of toast and it's on the plate—push it over, will you?'

He passed it to her and she began to dish. 'You've got a clean handkerchief to go to work with, haven't you?'

'No.'

She placed the two rashers of bacon to the side of the toast, lifted up the eggs and placed them on the toast. She handed him the plate. 'Go and eat. You're a bit behind time.'

'Not to worry, my hours are flexible.'

'Do Teerson Products know that?'

He carried the plate through to the dining-room and sat

at the table. She appeared in the doorway. 'Did you say a moment ago you did have a clean handkerchief?'

'I said I didn't.'

'That's odd.'

'Why?' But she'd returned into the kitchen and didn't answer him. He cut the yolks of the eggs and let them run over the toast, then started eating.

She came into the dining-room, a mug of coffee in each hand. She passed him one, put one in front of her place setting, then returned to the kitchen for a tray on which were toast, butter, an apple, and a jar of marmalade. She began to quarter and peel the apple.

'You didn't say what was odd about the clean handkerchief I haven't got?' he said.

She ate a piece of apple. 'You know yesterday you needed one for work and there weren't any respectable ones in your cupboard? I knew there was one of the new ones in the load of laundry I'd put on the ironing-board.' She ate another piece of apple. 'But when I went into the spare room this morning, I couldn't find it, so I naturally thought you must have taken it . . . Are you sure you didn't?'

'Quite sure.'

'Then where on earth's it got to?'

'Search me. And I hasten to add that that won't solve the puzzle.'

'Then where is it?'

'A good question.'

'But no answer?'

'Not this early in the morning . . . By the way, the bacon's rather salty.'

'Is it? I'm sorry. I bought it in one of the supermarkets in Reckton and their bacon's never as good as the stuff the local shop sells, but it's a lot cheaper.'

'Champagne tastes, beer income, that's me.'

'Who's any different? . . . And come to that, now I think

about it, the pile of washing was different.'

'Being of a fairly logical mind, I fail to follow you. Or to put it another way, I don't know what the hell you're talking about.'

'I've a funny habit which probably means I'm suffering from some deep and quite unmentionable repression that whenever I move a pile of freshly laundered clothes, I always make certain I put it down exactly square to whatever I put it on. Yesterday I unwrapped the parcel—we had to have the washing done at the laundry because our machine was on the blink—and I put the pile down on the ironing-board, meaning to take it upstairs later, but I forgot. This morning, it was slightly caterwise to the board. Did you move it?'

'Why should I?'

'Looking for a clean handkerchief.'

'Remember something? I haven't got one.'

'Yes, I know . . .'

He ate the last piece of egg and toast, put the plate on one side. 'Shove the toast over, will you?' Then he noticed her expression. 'Is something wrong?'

'I . . . I'm not certain. I suppose really I'm being very silly'

'That sounds unlikely.'

'The thing is, I'm wondering if something funny has been going on.'

'In what way?'

'The handkerchief missing, the pile of washing that's been moved, and . . . Dennis, I woke up in the middle of the night and there just didn't seem to be any reason why. And then I thought I heard a noise in the kitchen.'

'What kind of a noise?'

'I don't know, really. A kind of clink, as if something had touched something else.'

'A mouse charging around in clogs?'

'When I didn't hear anything more, I decided it must

have been a mouse—without the clogs. But now . . . You don't think we had someone in the house last night, do you?'

He was startled by the suggestion. 'Presumably the front door was locked when you came down this morning?'‘

'Yes. And when I opened up, everything was as it should be.'

'Then it had to be a mouse you heard, or the house turning over in its sleep; and for once you did not line up the washing with geometric certainty on the ironing-board, and my one new clean handkerchief has been lost at the laundry and I'll have to go on using an old one with holes in it. People will say my wife neglects me.'

'And you'll agree?'

'Enthusiastically.'

Looking now at Reginald Gilles—pronounced Gil-lays—it was difficult to imagine his winning the 220 yards and quarter-mile for his college because the years had crinkled his flesh and his wife's death had seared his mind. But that did not mean that he was ready to accept the loss of many of his sporting trophies with equanimity.

'The damned scoundrel's taken all the best ones,' he said furiously.

The detective-constable decided he looked exactly like an old bantam cock.

'They're irreplaceable.'

The DC stared at the glass-fronted showcase.

'You've got to get them back for me.'

'We'll do our best.' By now, they had probably been hammered flat and melted down.

'How could anyone stoop to taking something so obviously personal?'

Poor old bastard, thought the DC; never come to terms with the modern world. Perhaps he thought that villains still had scruples.

'And what's more, the damned man helped himself to a drink!'

The DC had to work hard not to smile at that. But he'd been told to treat the old boy with respect. He'd been chairman of the magistrates for a number of years and could almost certainly still raise a stink if he felt the police were treating him with indifference or condescension. 'As far as you know, sir, is anything more missing?'

'I haven't checked. When I came in here and saw me trophies had gone . . .' He stopped abruptly. It was difficult to explain, but a little more of his life had just been taken from him.

'Do you have a safe?'

'Yes, but there's not much in it. Gave all my wife's jewellery to my daughter-in-law. But I don't think she really likes any of it. Bit old-fashioned, I suppose, but it's been in the family for quite a time. As I said to my son, if Erica doesn't want to wear it, keep it and pass it on to your daughter. It's comforting to see something go down the generations.'

It was comforting to have some jewellery for oneself, never mind the next generation; they could look after themselves. The old boy must have been well-heeled. Probably still was, only one wouldn't think so, looking at the way he dressed and the state of repair and decoration of the house. 'Would you check now and see if the safe was forced? And then make certain nothing else is missing?'

'The cups and medals are insured, of course, but it's the sentimental value that matters.'

You keep the sentiment, I'll take the insurance payout, the DC thought as Gilles walked out of the room, his leg movements laboured from arthritis. The DC went over to the nearest of the three windows. One pane had been smashed and then the intruder had reached in and unlatched the window. A crude method of entry into a house in which only one man, hard of hearing, lived. A draught of cold, damp air came through the broken window as he looked out. Stretching away from the outside wall was a flowerbed in need of weeding, and he saw a clear footprint in the soft earth. Chummy was not only crude, but careless. He moved out of the draught and visually examined the room. Furniture had a look of class about it, but the upholstery was faded and in places tattered; the huge carpet must have cost a bomb when it was new, but that was a long time ago; pictures, with display lights, for which he wouldn't have bid a quid, but which might well be worth a lot more than he'd ever see; a carved wooden overmantel which incorporated a mirror that reflected the central chandelier—shades of high life; a mobile cocktail cabinet with a split top that opened out to form two shelves at the same time as a shelf of bottles and glasses rose up to that level . . . He went over and examined it. On the right-hand leaf was a bottle of Haig and a glass. Gilles had said that he hadn't used that glass, so Chummy had. There might just be prints on it; there were still one or two villains who were so thick they didn't know about fingerprints. And if Gilles had to be bullshitted into believing his peasant-sized robbery was receiving the full attention of the police, taking the glass for testing would be a good move . . .

He returned to the show cabinet. The ornamental key had been in the lock, so there'd been no problem about opening the door. Because of the key's design, there'd not be any decipherable prints on it . . .

Gilles returned. 'Found the safe, but he didn't open it.'

'Would you show me where it is, sir?'

They went along one corridor, wood-panelled and dark, turned into another that was even darker, and then almost immediately entered a small room furnished with only a table, a chair, and two paintings. One of the paintings was on hinges and it had been swung back to reveal a safe.

The safe's make was Mackay and the DC knew that the firm had ceased production fifty years or more before; even then, they'd been known more for their fire-resistant qualities than their security. A clever twirler would have cracked it in one minute flat. That it hadn't been forced confirmed that the intruder was useless. Some young punk on hard drugs who needed to buy his next fix and didn't care what risks he took. 'I'll have that checked for dabs, sir, so maybe you'll leave opening it until I say?'

'Of course.'

'Have you any valuables anywhere else in the house that need checking?'

'I don't think so. My wife and I gave my son a great many things when he married. It seemed to us that that was the sensible thing to do, because when one gets old . . .'

The DC blocked. He didn't want to know about old age.

They returned to the drawing-room and the DC had one last look round, and this was when he found the candy-striped handkerchief on the floor behind the sofa. He picked it up. 'Is this yours, sir?'

'No. I never use anything but white.'

The handkerchief had been recently laundered and there was a mark on one corner. It began to look as if Chummy was not only crude and careless, but stupid as well.

CHAPTER 17

Macey, specialists in dry-cleaning delicate fabrics as well as general cleaners, was owned and run by a husband and wife. The wife, a small bustling woman, seldom quite still, said to the CID aide: 'Let's see the handkerchief and I'll tell you.'

He produced a plastic bag, extracted a candy-striped handkerchief, and handed it over.

She examined it very briefly. 'Yes, that's our mark.'

'Can you say who it belongs to?'

'Certainly, once I've checked the records.'

She turned round and opened the middle drawer of a metal filing cabinet, flicked through the cards inside, then came to a stop. 'The name's Mrs Rickmore.'

'How d'you spell that?'

She told him.

'Are there any initials?'

'D.P.'

'What about an address?'

'I haven't one. We don't deliver any more, so there's no call for them.'

He read through what he'd written a second time. He'd been working with CID for only two weeks and was still obsessively conscientious.

Ridley, sitting behind the desk in the DI's room, said: 'Did you say Rickmore?'

'That's right, skipper,' said the CID aide.

That was quite a coincidence. 'D'you get any initials or an address?'

'Initials are D.P. The laundry didn't have an address.'

'I just wonder . . . Right, that's it for the moment. You can get back on to the Swift job.'

The aide left. Ridley searched in the desk for a local telephone directory, found it, and checked the initials of the Rickmore who lived in Oak Tree Cottage, Yew Cross. D.P. So how in the hell had Rickmore's handkerchief appeared in a house that had been burgled?

Lineport, twelve miles from Reckton, had had a flourishing fishing trade until, starting some thirty years previously, spiralling costs had rendered the small inshore boats un-economic. There had never been any quays or docks; the fishing-boats had been winched up the gently sloping pebble beach, their keels protected by a wide metal band known as the Lineport guard. Now, the winch had rusted into immobility and few people remembered what the Lineport guard was.

The town had narrow, twisting streets and a population older than the national average; doctors were reluctant to practise there because so much of the work was geriatric. Sensibly, successive councils had tried to retain the atmosphere and there had been very little development. The largest of the four antique shops was in a Georgian house which had once been owned by a wealthy man who'd seduced his maid and then murdered her when it appeared she was pregnant. He had been tried, found guilty, and hanged. The antique shop specialized in silver, but it also sold miniature scaffolds that were made from the wood of the original scaffold and these had always proved to be very popular. Luckily, despite the large numbers which had been sold over the years, there still seemed to be no lack of the original wood from which to make them.

On Saturday, a man entered and offered to sell a large and handsome silver-gilt cup. The owner of the shop examined this and then asked what had happened to the plinth? The question disturbed the man, who muttered something to the effect that he didn't know whether he did want to sell the cup after all. He returned it to the holdall and hurried out.

The owner called his wife down into the shop and asked her to look after things while he went along to the police. He walked the short distance to the station and spoke to the detective-sergeant.

'Hullo, Mr Chapman, not seen you for quite a time. How are things—going all right? . . . Let's sit down over there and then you can say what's up.' The DS led the way over to a table and chairs. They sat.

Chapman was a precise man, inclined to speak pedantically. 'A little earlier, immediately before I came here, in fact, a man came into my emporium and asked if I was interested in buying a silver-gilt cup. It would be very difficult to explain precisely why, but from the beginning I was rather suspicious of his *bona fides*.'

'You've got a nose for these things, haven't you?'

'It's certainly big enough!' Chapman might be pedantic, but he had a sense of humour. 'The cup had been set on a plinth, but he did not produce this. When I asked him where it was, he became nervous, said he was not certain after all if he did wish to sell the cup, took it back, and left.'

'Went out in a hurry?'

'That is how I would describe his mode of departure.'

'What kind of a bloke was he?'

'He had a moustache, which I must say struck me as looking false, but I'm wondering now whether that impression was perhaps due to my original suspicions. Otherwise he was ordinary, neither short nor tall, with the kind of face which is sometimes said, I believe, to melt into a crowd. Much of his face was obscured by a cap with a large peak.'

'Anything else at all about him that struck you?'

'Yes, there was. He had a very slight speech defect. Once or twice he had trouble in pronouncing his R's.'

'How about this cup he tried to sell you—can you describe it?'

'It was about eight inches tall, six in diameter, and shaped in the style which is known in the trade—erroneously, in my view—as Portland. It was silver-gilt, hallmarked in London in nineteen twenty-one. It bore an inscription, "Two hundred and twenty yards".'

The DS looked down at his notes. 'Your description's got

me wondering . . . Hang on, I shan't be long.' He left and was gone for a little over two minutes. When he returned, he had a sheet of paper in his hand. 'There was a robbery last Wednesday and a load of sporting trophies was pinched. The owner's given a list and this is it—as a matter of fact, you'd have had a copy before the day's out. What d'you think?' He passed the paper across.

Chapman read carefully and slowly, then looked up. 'It is very probable that the item listed as number six is the cup I was shown.'

'I thought it might be. And since there was a whole load of tiny shields listing winners' names, including Mr Gilles's three times, on the plinth, it would explain why you weren't offered that as well . . . I think we'll need a stronger description of this man.'

'I'm afraid I'm not very good at that sort of thing.'

'You're not doing yourself justice. Look how much you've given me already!' The DS was very good at persuading witnesses to tell far more than they'd realized they'd known.

Ridley put the receiver down. He leaned back in the chair and, with unfocused gaze, stared at the window. There was little doubt that the cup which had been offered for sale to Chapman in Lineport was one of those which had been stolen from Gilles. (All doubt would soon be resolved; Gilles had a photograph of himself receiving that cup and this photograph was going to be shown to Chapman.) At Gilles's house, a handkerchief belonging to D. P. Rickmore had been found. The aide who'd taken the handkerchief to be identified had forgotten to ask the cleaners whether they had more than one D. P. Rickmore on their books, but it was a small omission, soon put right—and what were the odds against? Chapman's description of the man who'd come into the antique shop had not been good generally;

specifically, however, it had been promising. The man spoke with a very slight speech impediment.

Ridley picked up a pencil and fiddled with it. The investigating DC had pointed out that the burglary had been carried out by someone with little skill or experience. To offer that silver cup for sale only a dozen miles from where it had been stolen suggested either stupidity or no knowledge whatsoever of how the police worked. Rickmore spoke with a slight speech defect . . . But it strained credulity to imagine that he would suddenly take up burglary unless so desperately strapped financially that he was faced by disaster. Although he obviously wasn't wealthy, equally, he showed no signs of poverty . . . There was something here which Ridley couldn't grasp, perhaps because the conclusion to which the facts pointed was contrary to common sense. For the first time since he'd moved into the DI's room, he felt unequal to the job and wished there were someone he could go to for advice and instruction. He swore. It was not a feeling he liked.

Rickmore finished washing down the Escort and squeezed out the leather. Considering the mileage the car had done, it was a reasonable runner, but only an optimist could think it had many more miles left to go. Was he the only PRO in the country who did not have a company car? What was it like to be so well off that one could walk into a showroom and order the car of one's choice? What was life like when money—or rather, the lack of it—ceased to be central to everything one did or considered doing? Which brought him back to Elham.

He picked up the bucket, carried it across to the spile fence, and threw the dirty water into the small orchard which lay between the road and the garden. He left the bucket and leather to dry in the near corner of the garage.

He walked round the house and entered the porch where

he changed out of wellingtons into shoes. Anne was in the kitchen, cooking. 'Are you doing anything?' she asked.

'I have been and I'm about to.'

'Good. Will you chop an onion up for me? They make me cry so.'

'Why not use those goggles you were given?'

'They steam up.'

'Be difficult!'

'You know they hardly ever affect you.'

'If I have tears, prepare to shed them now.' He picked an onion out of the vegetable rack, carried it across to a working surface, reached across for the board she'd been using, and brought down a steel knife from the magnetized strip. 'I've been thinking.' He sliced off the two ends, began to peel away the skin. 'About Terence.'

'Oh!' She looked at him, then quickly away. It was the first time the subject had been broached since the night Elham had told them that the dead man had been identified.

'I can't do it.'

'What can't you do?' she asked tightly.

'Be directly responsible for ruining him, the circumstances being what they are.'

'Thank God for that.'

He finished peeling the onion, cut it longitudinally several times. 'I couldn't face the knowledge that I'd wrecked his whole life. I'm right in principle—but I've learned something you knew from the beginning. Principles can be right, but the observing of them wrong.' He cut the onion at right angles to the previous cuts.

'When are you going to tell him?'

'I'll phone . . .'

'No. It's something you've got to do face to face.'

'I was afraid you'd say that.'

'Will it help if I come and hold your hand?'

'Squeeze it hard.'

'To try to stop you thinking?'

'You know me too well for my own comfort.'

She carried the casserole dish with the mince in it over to where he stood and used a wooden spoon to sweep the diced onion on to the mince. Then she kissed him. 'And love what I know.'

The suggestion didn't come from either of them, and it was without a word being spoken that Anne and Rickmore left the parked car and walked round to the front door of Popham House, instead of the back.

Penelope opened the door and her astonishment was complete. She stared at them, the surprise slowly giving way to tension.

'May we come in?' asked Anne.

She moved to one side and they entered.

'Is Terence in?'

She nodded.

Rickmore said: 'I want to tell him something.'

They went through to the blue sitting-room. Elham had identified their voices and he now stood, not in front of the fire, but by the armchair in which he invariably sat. On the table by his side was a cut-glass tumbler half filled with whisky and soda.

'Dennis wants to talk to you,' said Penelope unnecessarily.

'Well?' Elham tried to give the impression of defiance; an impression denied by his expression.

Rickmore said: 'I'm going to tell the police that after all I can't be certain about the state of the car or the garage.'

Elham reached for the glass and picked it up with a hand that shook. Penelope began to cry silently, tears welling out of her eyes and coursing down her cheeks.

CHAPTER 18

Ridley braked the CID Metro to a halt, switched off the engine, and climbed out. The wind had freshened and he zipped up the front of his parka before crossing the pavement and opening the front gate of No. 64.

The front garden, even at this time of the year, was tidy. MacMahon, he recalled, was a keen gardener who spent much of his spare time cutting this, planting that, digging here, weeding there. Since he lived in a police house and when he retired would have to leave it, Ridley considered all that work a stupid waste of time and effort. But then, it was totally short-sighted to live in a police house and these days a policeman with any sense invested in a place of his own. But in every respect, MacMahon was of the old school.

Ridley rang the front-door bell and Mrs MacMahon opened the door. She was a large, rather coarsely featured woman who had never been physically very attractive, even when young, but who was possessed of an unmistakably warm nature. 'Hullo, Steve.'

''Morning, Mrs MacMahon. Sorry to bother you like this on a Sunday, but I was wondering if it would be all right to have a bit of a chat with the boss?'

'According to the doctor you shouldn't, that's for sure, not if it's business. But I reckon it'll do more good than harm. A bear with a sore head would be better company than he's been since he got back from hospital. Never could stand being idle.'

'How is he?'

'He seems a lot better, but it's going to be a bit more time before we're certain. Seems they still can't tell whether he did have a slight heart attack and they've got to make more tests. Beats me—I thought you'd either had had one or you hadn't . . . But come on in, instead of standing out there in the cold.'

He stepped into the hall.

'He's in the front room. Tell him I'm making you some coffee and warming a cup of milk for him—and whatever he says, he's not getting coffee.'

He went into the sitting-room. MacMahon was on the settee, his legs up. 'Saw it was you through the window. How are things?'

'Not too bad. But more to the point, how are you?'

'Bloody fed up and bored. There's nothing wrong with me and the doctors are a bunch of old women . . . I expect Elsie's already told you that I'm impossible to live with?'

Ridley grinned.

'Sit down; there's no extra charge for a chair.'

He sat on a large, well-upholstered armchair which showed signs of wear. The MacMahons preferred comfort to style. 'The missus said to tell you that she's making me coffee and warming you up a cup of milk.'

MacMahon swore, but without much conviction.

Ridley said, with uncharacteristic diffidence: 'I've come looking for a bit of advice.'

'Let's hear the problem.'

'Old Gilles's place was done on Wednesday night.'

'Reginald Gilles, the man who used to do a lot of running and was chairman of the local bench for God knows how many years?'

'That's the bloke.'

MacMahon chuckled. 'I'll bet he had something to say about things.'

'He did! . . . It was only a small job and really only warranted someone from the uniform branch, but seeing it was him, I sent Alan.'

'Good thinking.'

'Alan says Chummy was a real beginner—stepped on to a flowerbed and left a good print, smashed a window to get in, nicked a load of silver cups that can't be worth all that much, but left a safe with quite a bit of cash in it. The safe was a Mackay and I reckon I could do it with a screwdriver. He helped himself to a drink and dropped a handkerchief with a laundry mark on it.

'Come yesterday, he—or a mate—was in one of the antique shops in Lineport trying to sell a large silver-gilt cup, missing its plinth, and with "Two hundred and twenty yards" engraved on it. Chapman, the owner, was suspicious and the man cleared off. The cup did come from Gilles's place.'

'Was Chapman able to give a reasonable description?'

'Not really. Could have been anyone, wearing a false moustache and a cap. But he did pick out one useful fact. The bloke had a slight speech defect and occasionally couldn't pronounce his R's properly.'

MacMahon saw that Ridley was looking at him intently, as if expecting some reaction. 'That's not much use on its own, is it?' he asked, worried that perhaps his brain wasn't working as quickly and clearly as it should.

'Suppose I add that we've identified the laundry mark and it's D. P. Rickmore's?'

'God's teeth!' exclaimed MacMahon, who sometimes used such ancient expletives when his surprise was too great for mere four-letter words.

'It all fits,' said Ridley exasperatedly, 'but who the bloody hell's ever going to believe that a bloke like Rickmore has suddenly taken up breaking and entering?'

'He could need money desperately?'

'Could he? He's not rolling in it, sure, but who is, except for a few lucky bastards? We both saw his place. He's not getting ready to queue at the soup kitchen.'

'No, he isn't.'

'Then who's going to believe it was him?'

'That depends on how strong the evidence becomes. If you know Chummy had a drink, presumably a glass was left around?'

'Glass and bottle. I've sent 'em both off for dabs.'

'What about comparison dabs from Rickmore?'

'One of the things I want to know is, do you think I should go for them yet?'

MacMahon thought for a moment. 'Probably not; at least, not openly. This has to be treated very, very carefully. After all, we wouldn't want . . .' He came to a sudden stop.

'What?'

There was no answer.

Ridley waited. MacMahon had the habit of disappearing into a brown study, which could be infuriating; but he'd come here to learn if any such brown study could bear fruit.

The door opened and Mrs MacMahon, carrying a tray, entered. Ridley stood and took the tray from her. 'Thanks, Steve. Just wait a moment while I clear a table.' She briefly studied her husband, worried that it might after all have been a mistake to allow Ridley to discuss work with him, but judged from his expression that it had not. She removed some newspapers from a small table. 'Put the tray down here and help yourself. There's milk and sugar and some biscuits.'

'Can I do your cup?'

'Will you? A little milk, but no sugar, thanks.'

'And what about me?' demanded MacMahon.

'No sugar and a whole cupful of milk,' she answered.

'That muck's only fit for calves and babies.'

She laughed and said that she'd rather look after a crèche full of babies than him.

Some fifteen minutes later she collected up the dirty cups, saucers and plates, put them on the tray, and left.

'What wouldn't I give for a double Scotch,' said Mac-Mahon longingly.

'Have you been knocked off that as well?' asked Ridley.

'Been knocked off everything that makes life worth living . . . Look, Steve, let's discuss motive. There's always a motive, except when you're dealing with freaks like psychopaths. Was the motive here financial?'

'What else?'

'You don't think it might have been to create a lever?'

'I don't get it,' said Ridley bluntly.

'Remember the circumstances. Elham, too much alcohol aboard to risk a breath test, runs away after the accident. Unexpectedly, Rickmore turns up at Popham House, sees the damage to the Jaguar and notices that the garage isn't damaged.

'We interview Rickmore and he gives evidence which provides a peg on which all the circumstantial evidence can be hung and which will nail Elham. Elham's a very smart lawyer who can appreciate the value in court of evidence better than we can. He sees clearly that if Rickmore can't be persuaded to change his evidence, he—that is, Elham—is for the chopper. So Rickmore's value as a witness for the prosecution has to be undermined to the point where no jury will believe him. What quicker way of doing that than making him appear to be a criminal?'

'Elham wouldn't do anything like that.'

'Why not? Because of his position? But it's precisely because of his position that he would. Think of all he stands to lose if he's found guilty of a serious crime.'

'But . . .'

'You're the one who's always sneering at the rich; are you sure you aren't now investing him with a sense of justice, honour, and fair-mindedness just because he *is* rich? He was willing to knock a man down and not stop, wasn't he?'

'That's different.'

'Is it?'

To his angry embarrassment, Ridley realized that Mac-Mahon was right—he had been instinctively supposing Elham incapable of deliberately entrapping another person in order to save himself.

'If you're thinking it could be different because they're related by marriage, just ask yourself, when did that ever stop two people disliking each other? Rickmore's never held back on the evidence. On the contrary, he volunteered the news of his drive over to Popham House without any prompting from us and we'd not have learned about it but for him. He's obviously no fool, so we must assume he realized the significance of what he was saying. He's not starving, but financially he's not in the same league as Elham. It can get on a man's wick to have a brother-in-law who goes out of his way to show how much better off he is. He may well have shown his jealousy, which will have exacerbated the ill-feeling between them. And can you imagine Elham's thoughts when he learned that it was Rickmore who'd fingered him? My guess is, he'd laugh all the way to the nearest bottle of champagne if Rickmore's nailed for something he didn't do.'

'I still can't see Elham setting it up. He hasn't enough balls.'

'Suppose you stood to lose everything you have and are faced with a future of poverty instead of luxury . . . Wouldn't your balls grow?'

'Maybe.'

'And remember one thing more. We first homed in on Elham through a tip-off. Who was the anonymous caller?'

'All we know is, a woman.'

'Prompted by Rickmore? Do you imagine that Elham hasn't worked that out?'

'You've got one hell of a mind! You've turned them into a couple of right royal bastards.'

'If I've learned one thing in the Force, it's that everyone can be a right royal bastard, given tight enough circumstances.'

'They're going to find that . . .'

'Steve, I said at the beginning that this was a case to be taken carefully. I'm telling you now, it's a powder keg. Whatever you do, remember Agag.'

'Where's he come into it?'

MacMahon smiled briefly.

'Are you going to ring now?' asked Anne.

Rickmore looked across at her. 'I wasn't, no.'

'You can't put it off for ever.'

'Not when you're around.' He stood, put a log on the fire.

'Get it over and done with. And remember, it's the right thing to do.'

'Is it?'

'You're not thinking of going back on what you said?'

'No. I'm just trying to convince myself that there really are times when circumstances change wrong into right.'

'Yes, there are.'

'Ever the pragmatist?'

'It makes life more liveable.'

He crossed the carpet and kissed her.

'You're lucky you married me, Dennis Rickmore.'

'You're always claiming that. Don't you think it would be more becoming to leave me to say it?'

'Haven't you realized yet that in the wrong hands you'd have developed into an impossible prig?'

'Thanks very much.'

'But as it is . . .'

'Finish and put me out of my agony.'

'You're one of the nicest men in the world.'

'I can resist everything except praise.' He kissed her a second time.

'Then what about temptation?'

'Let's find out.'

She smiled. 'Go and make the phone call and stop trying to lead me astray.'

He went into the hall and across to the telephone. This was his Rubicon; the moment when he betrayed his principles. Quickly, as if delay might make him renege, he checked the number and then dialled it, asked to speak to Detective-Inspector MacMahon.

'I'm afraid he's away ill.'

'I'm sorry to hear that,' he said automatically. 'Is Detective-Sergeant Ridley around?'

'I'll put you through to CID.'

'Duty DC speaking. Can I help you?'

'Will you give a message to Mr Ridley, please? My name's Rickmore. Will you say that I'm afraid I've realized I've made a mistake and my evidence regarding the damage to the Jaguar and the garage is wrong.'

The DC repeated the message.

Rickmore returned to the sitting-room.

'That was very brief,' Anne said.

'MacMahon's away so I left the message for the detective-sergeant.'

'Thankfully? . . . Look, my love, stop questioning and criticizing yourself. You've done the right thing, the only thing.'

He wished he could be half as certain as she was.

CHAPTER 19

Ridley read the message and swore. Rickmore was going back on his evidence. And without that, the case was a non-starter. The lever had worked. Elham was proving once again that money and power were what really mattered in life; if you possessed them, you could kick the rest of the world in the goolies; if you possessed them, you could distort and cheat justice . . .

But, he thought, maybe this time it would turn out to be not quite so straightforward as the bastard imagined. He'd gone to considerable trouble to set up that lever to force Rickmore to recant or, if he wouldn't, to destroy his value as a witness. Might he not have gone a little too far? Clever men were sometimes too clever for their own health . . . By God, he'd get Elham yet! Or if he couldn't, he'd make Rickmore curse the day he'd recanted.

It was the first time that Rickmore had entered the divisional HQ, situated at the back of the parish church and in such hideous architectural conflict with it. He was conscious that he was breathing quickly and sweating. Like visiting the dentist, he thought.

There was a counter at one end of the front room and this was manned by a sergeant and a PC. He spoke to the PC.

'Detective-Sergeant Ridley? I'll tell him you're here, Mr Rickmore. If you'll just sit over there until I can find him.'

At the opposite end to the counter were padded wall seats, a few rather spartan chairs, and two tables on which were several magazines, some with direct connection with the police force, and several pamphlets aimed at helping and advising the general public.

He was reading—and hardly taking in—a pamphlet detailing some of the measures a householder could take to protect his home when he heard someone approaching and he looked up to see Ridley.

''Morning, Mr Rickmore. Nice of you to come along.'

He had expected resentment, but Ridley had sounded pleasant.

'I've found an interview room that's free, so let's go along there.'

They left and went down a corridor to the second of three rooms off to the right. It was small, with a single window high up which was barred; the only furniture was a table and six chairs.

'Not the Ritz,' said Ridley, 'but it's quiet . . . Now, about this message—I thought it would be best if you came along and explained things personally.' He produced a pack of cigarettes. 'D'you use these?'

'No, thanks.'

'I wish I could say the same.' He tapped out a cigarette, but before he had time to light it there was a knock on the door and a PC looked in. 'D'you want a cuppa, skipper?'

Ridley turned to Rickmore: 'Which do you drink, tea or coffee?'

'I prefer coffee.'

He said to the PC. 'Two coffees. And get 'em from the canteen, not that flaming machine that can't tell the difference.'

The PC withdrew and shut the door.

Ridley had brought a folder with him and he now opened this and read the top sheet of paper. 'Your message said that you'd made a mistake over your evidence concerning the damage to the Jaguar and the garage. Would you like to be specific?'

Elham had advised him very carefully what to say. He was not to admit to making too direct a mistake; rather, he was to blame the surrounding circumstances. That way, his change of testimony would be very difficult to challenge in court, should he still be called for the prosecution and named a hostile witness. He took a deep breath. 'This last Saturday night my wife and I had dinner at Popham House. We arrived after dark and parked directly in front of the garage because I knew my brother-in-law wouldn't be going out.'

'Just one moment. As I remember it, that's a fairly large garage, so opposite which part of it were you?'

'Well over to the right. We left the car and were moving towards the house when my wife suddenly remembered that we'd forgotten to pick up a magazine we'd brought over for my sister-in-law, so I started back and then happened to glance at the front end of my car and I was convinced there was a dent in the bonnet which hadn't been there before. Yet when I checked, there wasn't anything and I realized it had been a trick of light.'

'When you say light, does that mean that the outside lights of the garage were switched on?'

'Two were, but a third one wasn't working. It was obviously the mixture of shadow and light which had given the impression of a dent.'

'But I seem to remember you saying originally that all three outside lights were working on the night the accident took place?'

'I'm certain I didn't say one way or the other. In fact, one wasn't, just as it wasn't on Saturday. Terence says it's got one of those irritating faults where sometimes it works and sometimes it doesn't. And every time he decides to call in an electrician, it starts behaving itself again.'

The PC returned, carrying a tray on which were two mugs, a teaspoon, and a bowl of sugar. He put the tray in front of Ridley, then left. Ridley pushed the tray to the middle of the table. 'Help yourself.' After Rickmore had taken one mug, Ridley spooned sugar into the second one and then drank. 'Today, it doesn't taste of either tea or coffee.'

Rickmore smiled.

'At least it's hot . . . Getting back to the accident. Originally, you said the offside light was smashed.'

'I said it wasn't working.'

'Both Mr MacMahon and I heard you say that it was smashed.'

'Whatever you heard, that's not what I was trying to say. After all, I didn't go round the bonnet, so there's no way I could have known how it was.'

'Then how did you know the light wasn't working?'

'The headlights were switched on; the offside one wouldn't come on.'

'Why were they switched on if the car was parked?'

'Terence was trying to see if he could get the offside one to work. Personally, I think that that was being rather unrealistically optimistic. He's about as good an electrician as I am mechanic.'

'Do you know if the light failed on the journey back?'

'It went just before they reached our place before dinner.'

'But you told us that when the car left your house, it was unmarked and undamaged.'

'It was. A malfunctioning light isn't damage; that connotes some structural fault.'

'Somewhat pedantic, surely?' said Ridley, not as lightly as he'd intended.

'I'm sorry. Anne says I'm becoming more and more pedantic; one of the penalties of growing older.'

'Or of trying to explain away the difference between what you are saying now and what you said originally?'

'That's nonsense. I haven't changed a thing.'

'Tell me, don't you think it strange how many lights failed that night?'

'Sod's Law. Things never go wrong singly. That's why, if I break something I hurry to break two matches as well.'

Ridley shut the folder. 'Do you realize the full import of what you've just told me?'

'In what way?'

'Your evidence was central to proving your brother-in-law

was driving the car which hit and killed Tamworth. Now, you're denying all you said before.'

'I'm denying nothing that doesn't need to be denied because of the facts.'

'Facts?'

'Yes.'

'Not very pedantic when it comes to the truth?'

Rickmore didn't bother to answer.

'How much did Mr Elham drink at your house that Wednesday night?'

'As far as I can remember, the same as I did. Which was one drink before the meal and a couple of glasses of wine with it.'

'That seems considerably less than your previous estimate.'

'I talked it over with my wife and she has a much better memory than I.'

'So if I asked her, she'd say the same?'

'Yes.'

'As, no doubt, would Mr Elham?'

'I can't answer for him.'

'I expect you can,' said Ridley, no longer bothering to sound pleasant.

Rickmore waited, then said: 'Is there anything more I can tell you?'

'A hell of a lot. But I'm certain you won't.'

'Then I think I ought to get back to work.' Rickmore stood.

'It's a funny thing,' said Ridley, 'how your type always thinks that you've a divine right to escape consequences . . . It must come as a hell of a shock when you discover you haven't.'

As Rickmore went down the passage and into the front room, he wondered uneasily why at the very end there had been an abrupt change of tone in the detective-sergeant's voice—almost as if he'd remembered he'd reason to gloat. He left the building to find that the clouds had lifted and there was some weak sunshine.

Back in the interview room, Ridley used his handkerchief to pick up the mug from which Rickmore had drunk and pack it in a cardboard box, carefully wedging it in place with pieces of foam. He carried the box up to the DI's office. A couple of minutes later, the PC who'd brought the coffee into the interview room, entered. 'Got him as he was leaving, skipper.'

'Let's see it.' The PC handed him a Polaroid snap. Rickmore was three-parts full face on to the camera. It was a good, clear snap.

Unusually, but as previously arranged, Rickmore returned home for lunch. When Anne met him in the hall, she studied his face. 'How did it go?'

'Not nearly as bad as I'd feared.'

'Thank goodness for that . . . Tell me exactly what happened.'

'Over a drink. It may not be the weekend, but I need a strong one.'

'Then have two. The meal's Cumberland hotpot, so it won't spoil.'

He poured out a gin and tonic and a sherry and they settled in the sitting-room. 'Ridley didn't start shouting, or anything like that. In fact, right until the end he seemed to be taking it all in his stride. Then he did show his teeth; said that my sort thought we'd a divine right to escape consequences.'

'If only he'd known a bit more.'

'"Whose conscience with injustice is corrupted."'

She shrugged her shoulders impatiently. 'Did he believe you?'

'Not for one second. Terence said he wouldn't. But apparently they're so used to witnesses going back on their evidence that they learn to treat it as one of the hazards of the profession. My job wasn't to convince him, it was to convince him that I'd be able to convince a jury I was telling the truth.'

'And you think you did that?'

'I'm pretty sure I did.'

'Thank God!'

'I'll drink to that.'

Because Lineport was in a different division, Ridley had first to telephone the local DI and ask permission to carry out the inquiries; on arrival, he had to report to the DI.

'The Guv'nor's been called out,' said the detective-sergeant, 'but he said it's OK to carry on. I've detailed a bloke to go with you.'

'There's no need for anyone.'

He laughed.

The PC who accompanied Ridley was young and quiet and Ridley gained the impression that perhaps he wasn't very smart. That suited him. 'All I'm aiming to do is see whether Chapman can identify from a photo the man who tried to sell him the cup,' he said as they walked briskly up the side road that led into the High Street.

The PC nodded.

'D'you know Chapman?'

'Can't say I do, skipper.'

'So you wouldn't know how quick on the ball he is?'

'No, I wouldn't.'

'Well, we'll sure as hell soon find out, as the young lady said when her boyfriend discovered the rubber was torn.'

The PC hardly smiled.

They entered the antique shop and Ridley introduced himself to Chapman and explained the reason for this visit.

'You want me to recognize him from a photo? I'm afraid

that's going to be difficult. You see, because of that cap he was wearing . . . I believe it has a name, but I don't know what it is.'

'Baseball cap?'

'Perhaps,' he answered doubtfully. 'Certainly, it didn't look very English . . . Anyway, the brim which was very large was pulled right down and the man's moustache was rather large, so much of his face was obscured.'

'But you were able to see his eyes, nose, ears, and chin?'

'I still don't think I'll be able to identify him from a photograph.'

'Have a look at this, will you?' Ridley handed him the Polaroid photograph of Rickmore.

Chapman studied the photograph briefly, then said: 'Just a minute.' He went through to the room behind the counter, returned with a pair of gold-rimmed glasses. He examined the photograph again. 'I can't see any real resemblance.'

'Then I'll just touch things up a bit. Let's have the photo a moment.' Ridley used a pencil to sketch in a baseball cap and a thick moustache. 'Now have another look.'

Chapman studied the photograph a second time. After a while he looked at Ridley over the tops of his spectacles. 'You think this was the man?'

'Let's just say, it's not impossible.'

He held the photograph a little closer. 'It does make quite a difference with the cap and the moustache.'

'Things like that can change a face completely for people who aren't trained observers and who don't know which points to look for. Ears are something which can't be changed. Would you say his ears—' Ridley indicated the photograph—'are similar to those of the man with the cup?'

'They could be.'

'And perhaps the chin's similar?'

'I think it is.'

'And the width of the face at cheekbone level?'

'That's certainly the same.'

'From the sound of things, then he might well . . .' Ridley let his voice die away.

'He might well be the same man. But I still can't be absolutely certain.'

'Never mind. You're saying the next best thing which is that if the man in the photo had a moustache and was wearing a baseball cap, he could very easily have been the man who tried to sell you the cup . . . Thanks very much, Mr Chapman, you've been of great assistance.'

Ridley led the way out of the shop, paused until the traffic eased, then crossed the road and walked briskly along the pavement.

'You were pushing hard, weren't you?' said the PC. 'Out to land Chummy, are you?'

The PC wasn't quite as thick as he'd first judged, thought Ridley. But that didn't really matter. Chapman was the kind of self-opinionated, fussy little man who, now that the seed had been well planted, would swear blind that there was a strong similarity between the two faces.

Because it had been a straight comparison and not a search for which Ridley had called, the fingerprint section were able to report on Tuesday afternoon. Some of the prints on the glass were the same as those on the mug; there were no prints on the bottle.

As Ridley replaced the receiver, he said aloud: 'I've got one of you, you bastards.'

CHAPTER 20

Rickmore was on his feet when he heard the car turn into the drive and he crossed to the window of the sitting-room and parted the curtains. Headlights swept round and then settled on the garage doors, just before being switched off.

'Can you see who it is?' asked Anne. She was knitting a sweater with a complex pattern and the various colours were, temporarily, in something of a cat's-cradle.

'No. Are you expecting someone?'

'Not that I know of.'

He left the sitting-room, switched on the hall and porch lights. He went into the porch and opened the outside door. The light drizzle had stopped, but the wind was damp, suggesting there was more rain to come; not a night for tramps or bald ducks, as his father would have said. He heard the squeal of the garden gate's hinges, then a few seconds later, Ridley came into view.

Ridley came to a stop. ''Evening.' There was no missing his cockiness. 'Got time for a bit of a chat, have you?'

'You'd better come in.' Once Ridley was in the hall, he offered to hang up the sergeant's short overcoat.

'That's very kind of you.' Now there was mockery as well as cockiness.

After hanging up the overcoat, Rickmore said: 'I'll just tell my wife what's happening and then we can go into the dining-room.' He went into the sitting-room and carefully closed the door behind him. 'It's the detective-sergeant. He wants a word. We can go into the dining-room . . .'

'No,' she said. He was trying to shield her from whatever trouble this visit was bringing and she was determined not to be shielded. 'Bring him in here—it's so much warmer.'

He hesitated, then finally nodded. He called Ridley into the room. Ridley said good-evening to Anne with exaggerated politeness. He sat on the settee, faced the fire, and remarked on how much heat it was giving out—he wished the fire in his house was half as good. It became obvious that he was savouring every minute of the run-in to whatever had brought him here.

Rickmore brought an end to the social chit-chat. He said, speaking tightly: 'You wanted a word about something?'

'That's right. About whether you feel like changing the evidence you gave at the station yesterday.'

'No, I don't.'

'You are quite certain?'

'I told you precisely what happened and there's nothing to change. And with regard to thinking I saw a dent in our car, my wife will confirm it all.'

'I'm sure she will. She'll confirm anything to help her brother-in-law escape conviction for running a man down and injuring him so badly that he later died, when he was too tight to know what he was doing.'

'What the devil do you mean?' Rickmore tried to sound indignant, rather than scared.

'I mean that we're not the simple fools you take us for. We know that originally you told us the truth, but now you're lying as hard as you can go.'

'You've no right to come into our house and talk like that,' said Anne fiercely.

'No right? No right when I'm faced by people who are supposed to be law-abiding and an example to the proles like me and I find 'em desperately trying to help one of their own kind escape the consequences of his drunken driving and cowardice?'

Anne spoke to Rickmore. 'You'd better telephone Mr Archer and ask him to drive over here right away.'

'Would that be Mr Archer, the solicitor?' asked Ridley. 'By all means telephone him and tell him to come here. That is, if you don't mind seeing your husband end up in prison.'

'What do you mean by that?'

'Exactly what I said.'

'He's done nothing.'

'Come off it, missus. He's lied his head off.'

'Sergeant,' said Rickmore angrily, 'I don't know what the hell you think you're at, but I do know you're not coming into my house and insulting my wife. Get out. And tomorrow I'll make an official complaint about your behaviour.'

'Sure. Maybe it'll make you feel good. Only perhaps I ought to tell you that complaints from someone about to be indicted for burglary don't cut much ice.'

'Indicted for burglary—are you crazy?'

'D'you know a man called Reginald Gilles? Ever been to his house?'

'And if I have?'

'It was burgled last Wednesday by someone who ought to have been wearing L-plates. Left a footprint in a flowerbed as clear as crystal, broke a pane of glass to force a window, nicked some cups and medals the old boy had won at running, but couldn't open a safe that only called for a bent hatpin. Then on Saturday he tried to sell one of the stolen cups to an antique shop in Lineport. The evidence says it was you who did that job.'

'That's utterly absurd.'

'Is it? Item. What size shoe d'you wear?'

'What's it matter what size?'

'Scared of answering?'

'Ten and a half,' snapped Anne.

Ridley smiled. 'Item. Chummy left a handkerchief with a laundry mark behind. That mark is yours.'

'It can't be . . .' began Rickmore.

'It is. Item. The intruder poured himself a drink to calm his nerves. Your fingerprints are on the glass.'

'They can't possibly have been mine.'

'Then the impossible's happened. Item. When you left the police station, a photograph of you was taken. After a moustache and a baseball cap were shaded in, the owner of the antique shop identified the person in the photo as the man who'd tried to sell him the stolen cup.'

'I haven't been in an antique shop in Lineport in the last couple of years.'

Anne said sharply. 'When was the burglary at Mr Gilles's house?'

'Last Wednesday.'

'I meant, at what time?'

'There's no saying. He went to bed around ten and got up at eight. So it was somewhere between those times.'

'On Wednesday, my husband was here all night.'

'So who's going to alibi him?'

'I am.'

'It's funny, but a wife's alibi never kind of rings very true.'

'He was here all night . . . Damnit, can't you see how ridiculous it is to claim my husband committed a burglary? People like him don't do that sort of thing.'

'If you were to ask me, I'd say that these days there's no knowing who'll do what. After all, there are people like him who drink too much, drive, knock someone over, and haven't the courage to stop and see how badly the victim's injured and if there's anything can be done for him.'

'That . . . that's different.'

'To whom? The victim?'

'You're trying to say Dennis has done something which is totally absurd. How can you begin to believe he'd commit a burglary in the house of someone we know?'

'Meaning he would in the house of someone you didn't know?'

'That's deliberately twisting what I said.' She forced herself to speak more calmly. 'Why would he ever do such a thing?'

'Ask him, not me.'

'You're determined not to understand . . .' She stopped, swung round to face her husband and stared at him for several seconds before she said: 'When was it that I woke up during the night and thought I heard someone downstairs?'

'God knows,' he muttered.

'Wasn't it . . . I know! It was the day I'd been to see Ruth and that was last Wednesday.' Her voice quickened. 'And it was on the Thursday that I couldn't find the handkerchief. You remember, I asked you about it.' She turned back to Ridley. 'What kind of handkerchief was it that was found in the house?'

'It was striped, in three colours; grey, chocolate, and light green.'

'That's the one that went missing! Then I did hear someone that night! And he stole the handkerchief and a glass with Dennis's fingerprints on it and left them at Reggie's house. He was trying deliberately to inculpate Dennis . . . You must see that that's what happened.'

'Must I?'

Rickmore said: 'You're obviously not surprised.'

Ridley did not answer.

'You know very well that I couldn't have carried out that burglary, whatever the evidence suggested. So why try and make out you believe I did?'

Ridley spoke contemptuously. 'You still can't read the score, can you? Not up in the art of self-survival; always had someone ready to come to the rescue . . . Your brother-in-law's a smart lawyer so it didn't take him any time at all to realize that if you persisted in standing by your original evidence, there was sufficient additional circumstantial evidence to nail him; that meant the end of his lifestyle. Equally, he could judge that if you could be persuaded to go back on your evidence, the circumstantial evidence on its own wouldn't be strong enough for him to be charged. So he did everything he could to persuade you to go back on what you'd told us. The trouble was, though, that you were so jealous of him, you wouldn't . . .'

'That's not true,' Anne cried sharply.

Ridley shrugged his shoulders. 'He reckoned your husband was and that's what counted.'

'It was a matter of principle. There are still people who have principles.'

'Sure. Just so long as they don't become inconvenient.'

'You don't know much about people, do you?'

'Mrs Rickmore, after you've been a copper for as long as I have, you know too much about people ever to believe in any of 'em again . . .' He turned to Rickmore. 'Since he wasn't getting anywhere asking, your brother-in-law set about saving himself in the only way left open to him—to destroy your value as a witness. That's why he found someone to set you up for a burglary.'

'He'd never have done such a thing,' said Anne.

'He'd have done anything to anybody to save his own skin.'

'Oh God, you've got a filthy mind!'

'Maybe. But I'll tell you one thing. I respect the law, not treat it with contempt.'

'My husband respects it just as much; maybe more.'

Ridley smiled. 'You could have fooled me, missus . . . Neither of you knew about the burglary before I told you, so Elham hasn't put the screws on you. Why go to all the trouble of fixing the burglary if not to use it? Obviously, because in the event he didn't need to. Why? Because after he'd set things rolling, the dead man was identified as a rapist and suddenly your principles weren't important enough. Like I said, people only hold principles until they become inconvenient.'

Rickmore bitterly acknowledged that in the present context, this was true.

'You decided to agree to go back on your evidence. So now there's no firm case against your brother-in-law, unless . . .'

'Unless what?'

'You decide to tell the truth after all.'

'I've told you the truth.'

'You told me a pack of bloody lies.'

'I swear it was the truth.'

Ridley said with pleasure: 'Still not understood? Not realized that when he set out to fix you for burglary, your brother-in-law did a good job; too good a job. If all the evidence is presented, you're going to go on trial and you're going to be found guilty.'

'That can't happen now,' said Anne.

'Why not?'

'You've admitted you don't believe Dennis had anything to do with it.'

'What I believe is immaterial; it's the evidence that counts. It always is.'

'But you know that he's innocent.'

'Strange how things work out, isn't it? You were ready to see someone guilty be found innocent, but now you're screaming because someone innocent may be found guilty.' He paused, then added: 'I hope you noticed I said "may be", not "is going to be".'

'What are you getting at now?' demanded Rickmore.

'Tell the truth about your brother-in-law and you won't be put on trial for burglary.'

'You're trying to blackmail me.'

'Blackmail, hell. I'm offering you a choice.'

'You're no better than the crooks you're meant to catch,' said Anne.

Ridley's anger finally overflowed. 'Me? All I want is to see justice done. But you lot—you want to bury justice. So who is it who's no bloody better than the villains?'

CHAPTER 21

Rickmore braked the Escort to a halt outside the garage of Popham House. Anne put her hand on his left arm. 'Don't lose your temper.'

'Do you know what I'd like to do . . .'

'Yes. But don't.'

'He doesn't give one solitary damn for anyone but himself. He'd see me jailed and our lives ruined, if that meant he could escape the consequences of his own drunkenness. He hasn't the guts to face . . .'

'I know all that, but I also know that if you lose your temper, as you can do when you're really worked up, you won't accomplish anything.'

A man who abhorred violence, no matter what the cause, he would have inflicted violence on Elham without a second's thought because, by his actions, Elham was threatening Anne.

She said quietly: 'If Terence knows the police have told us the facts, I'm sure he'll admit the truth. He can't have thought it would get to the point where you might actually be charged with burglary; all he was trying to do was destroy your potential value as a prosecution witness in the eyes of the police.'

'You'd have found an excuse for Judas Iscariot.' He climbed out of the car.

She joined him and linked her arm with his. 'Remember, count ten before you say anything.'

'I'll need a goddamn calculator.'

Penelope was in the kitchen and she greeted them with warmth, twice saying how nice it was to see them again so soon; but she could not hide her apprehension in the face of Rickmore's grimness.

'Is Terence back?' he asked.

'Not yet; he phoned to say he'd be catching the later train.' She looked up at the wall clock. 'But he shouldn't be long now. Let's go through and have a drink. And you will stay to supper, won't you?'

'No.'

'But you must; honestly, there's masses of food because I ordered a sirloin and the butcher must have thought we were entertaining an army. Terence so dislikes cold meat and if you don't eat with us, I don't know what I'll do with it all.'

'We can't stay.'

She nibbled her lower lip and looked at her sister, but merely gained confirmation that something was very, very wrong. 'I . . . Let's go through.'

They had been in the blue sitting-room less than ten minutes when they heard a car door slam. 'I'll go and tell him you're here.' Penelope hurried out.

A couple of minutes later, Elham, in black coat and striped trousers, entered the sitting-room, closely followed by Penelope. ''Evening, Anne; 'Evening, Dennis.' His manner was watchful, but not fearful, as was his wife's. 'Either of you ready for a refill while I get a drink for myself.'

'No, thanks,' answered Rickmore curtly.

'I'd like another vodka and tonic,' said Penelope hurriedly.

He took her glass and left. When he returned, and after handing her one glass, he moved to his favoured position in front of the fire.

'We had the detective-sergeant round at our place again,' said Rickmore.

'What did he want?'

'To tell me that you had done your damnedest to destroy

my value as a witness if I refused to change my original evidence; to tell me that you'd been a bit too clever before we learned the dead man was a rapist, and now the evidence against me is so strong that if I don't change my story back to what it was, I'll be on a charge of burglary and he'll personally guarantee that I'm found guilty.'

'God Almighty!'

'Don't bother to try to sound surprised and outraged . . .'

'You surely don't think that there's any truth in all that?'

'I'd say there's quite a bit.'

'You really believe I'd deliberately let you be falsely accused of a crime?'

'If it got you off a charge.'

'I promise you I had nothing to do with this. I know absolutely nothing about it . . . Did the detective-sergeant detail the evidence?'

'You don't remember what it was? The handkerchief, the glass with my prints on it, the attempt to sell the cup stolen from Reggie Gilles.'

'What cup was stolen from Reggie? What d'you mean by the handkerchief and the glass?'

'Forget the innocent act. Who else is going to bother to try to destroy my character? Who else stands to gain if it is destroyed? No one.'

'Tell me all the facts.'

'You bloody well know them better than I do.'

'I know nothing.'

He didn't want to believe Elham, yet the other's quiet sincerity, following a bewildered amazement that surely would have been difficult to simulate, began to undermine his certainty.

'What exactly did the detective say?'

Rickmore stared at him, still unwilling to admit his accusations might be unfounded, and it was Anne who answered.

Elham listened, saying nothing until she'd finished. 'You

definitely heard someone in the house that night?'

'No. If I'd been certain, I'd have woken Dennis. There was just this noise which wasn't repeated.'

'Did you miss a glass as well as a handkerchief?'

She shrugged her shoulders. 'I can't say how many glasses of each kind we should have; not to the nearest one. You know how it goes—some are smashed and get replaced, some don't—one just doesn't keep count of everyday drinking glasses.'

'Did the detective-sergeant indicate how strong an identification the owner of the antique shop made and how he made it?'

'As far as I can remember, he told us he'd got a photo of Dennis and when a cap and a moustache were shaded in, the owner identified the photo as being of the man who'd tried to sell him the cup.'

'Did he say anything to suggest that the owner was offered several photos of different people to choose from and he picked out this one?'

'I don't think so.' She looked at Rickmore and he shook his head.

Elham drained his glass, put it down on the table, began to pace the floor, passing between his wife and Anne. After a while, he came to a stop and faced Rickmore. 'I swear I did not have anything at all to do with this burglary—that was clearly designed to destroy your credibility as a witness.'

'Who else would have fixed it?'

'Precisely. When the only possible motive uniquely concerns myself . . . It could only have been one person.'

Elham entered chambers and stood in the doorway of the clerks' room. Arnold was on the phone, Betty was typing. ''Morning, Mr Elham,' she said.

''Morning. Tell Tom I want a word with him as soon as he's finished.'

She showed her surprise at so unnecessary an instruction
—Arnold always reported in the morning.

In his room, Elham crossed to the window and looked
down at the small square. He had no doubts, but until the
facts had been confirmed he could not begin to try to find
a way out of the seemingly hopeless position in which he
and Rickmore now found themselves. If things remained as
they were, he would go free, but Rickmore would be charged
with burglary and probably be found guilty. He could not
and would not let that happen. But the alternative was for
him to tell the truth about the accident and then he himself
would be on a criminal charge. He dare not let that
happen . . .

Arnold entered the room. 'Good morning, sir.'

Arnold was looking old, Elham thought, yet he was not
quite sixty. But then he'd probably never looked young. 'Sit
down.' He walked over to his desk.

Arnold moved one of the chairs and set it in front of the
desk.

Elham said: 'You fixed for someone to fake evidence
which would inculpate my brother-in-law on a charge of
burglary.'

There was a long silence.

'Didn't you?'

'I had to,' Arnold replied, pleading for understanding. 'I
had to try to make certain that if he went into court, the
jury wouldn't believe him.'

'Who planted the evidence?'

'A man called Dean. Two years ago, Mr Vernay defended
him and got him off, against the evidence. He was so pleased
that he said if either of us ever needed help, we had only to
ask.'

'You told him what to do?'

'Yes. I tried very hard to work out how best to arrange
things.'

'And succeeded a damned sight too well.'

'How d'you mean?'

'Mr Rickmore, when he learned the dead man was a rapist, decided to change his evidence . . .'

'To . . . to change it?'

'In my favour. But now the evidence you had planted is strong enough to have Mr Rickmore found guilty, despite the inherent unlikelihood of someone in his position turning to burglary.'

Arnold was uninterested in Rickmore's problems.

'So now either he tells the truth and I end up in court, or he doesn't and he ends up in court.'

'You?'

'Yes.'

'You can't . . .'

'I can't keep quiet and see him jailed.'

Arnold struggled to understand this sudden development, one he had entirely failed to foresee. He stared with anguish at Elham. 'I didn't . . . I didn't realize . . . I'll go to the police and tell them what I've done.'

'Then you'll have to explain about the car accident as well as the burglary, since your confession can only carry validity if your motive's fully explained.'

'But . . . but . . .'

'And do you think that anyone, in the light of all the facts as others will see them, will ever believe you acted entirely on your own initiative? The net result of your going to the police would just be a further charge of attempting to pervert the course of justice.'

'Then what am I to do?'

'God knows! But if you get any bright ideas, tell me what they are before you do anything . . . That's all.'

Arnold stared beseechingly at Elham, then stood and shuffled out of the room.

Elham returned to the window and once more stared

down at the square. A man, red bag in his hand, was just passing out of sight through the archway at the far end. Tewksbury-Smith, thought Elham, identifying him by the very characteristic way in which he walked with his head thrown back. A contemporary, whose career his own had closely parallelled, even to the fact that he was taking Silk at the same time . . . Or would have been, had the rapist not suddenly run out on to the road in a scene that was replayed again and again in his tortured mind . . . Again and again. Again and again. Had he discovered a way of escape?

CHAPTER 22

The rain, driven by a north-east wind, beat against the window of the sitting-room of Oak Tree Cottage. Intermittently, there was the teeth-twitching sound of an unpruned rose trail scratching at the glass.

They heard neither the rain nor the rose trail; only Elham as he explained the situation.

'That's how things stand,' he said finally. He took a handkerchief from his pocket and lightly wiped his mouth.

Rickmore was silent for a while, then he said: 'If your chief clerk confesses to the police what really happened, I'll be in the clear?'

'You would be, if he were believed.'

'Why shouldn't he be?'

'Because Dean, the man who carried out the burglary, will naturally deny everything and then Arnold's evidence will be uncorroborated. In those circumstances, he'll only be believed if his motive is obviously strong enough to make it likely he's telling the truth.'

'In other words, if he says he did it in order to incriminate me so that my evidence against you wouldn't be believed?'

'Yes.'

'Which makes it obvious that it was your car which ran down the rapist?'

'Yes.'

'Then what you're really saying is that one of us will be prosecuted?'

'On the face of things.' He paused, then said, very hurriedly: 'But so that there's no room for doubt, if one of us is to be prosecuted, I will make quite certain that it is not you.'

'I don't understand,' said Anne. 'One moment you say it has to be one or other of you, the next you say "if" it is.'

'A criminal case is usually concerned very much more with the evidence than the law, as opposed, for instance, to a complicated company case. The laws of evidence—which among other things lay down what is and what is not admissible—are very arcane and even to us lawyers not always certain. Added to this is the fact that the evidence often does not carry in the minds of the jurors the weight it should and would in an ordered and trained mind. That's why there'll often be a situation where the police are properly satisfied a man committed a crime, but the case never appears in court. Bitter experience has shown them that it's certain either some vital piece of evidence will be held to be inadmissible, or the jury, with their untrained, emotional, and frequently illogical minds, will incorrectly interpret the evidence in the accused's favour. Because of this, I think . . .' He stopped.

'You think what?'

'I think the value of the evidence against you can be undermined.'

'How?'

'By making certain it would be incorrectly interpreted in your favour.'

'That's impossible. When the detective listed it all, he almost had me believing I must have done it.'

'Difficult, not impossible.' He was plainly nervous and uncertain and there was a suggestion of humility in his manner. 'There is one way in which both of us can escape prosecution. But it would mean your taking a risk.'

'Both of us escape?'

'If it's certain the DPP would decide it would be stupid to bring a charge of burglary against you because no jury would ever find you guilty, the police won't be able to blackmail you into telling the truth about the night of the accident.'

'How much of a risk?' demanded Anne.

'Probably very little. Obviously, though, something can always go wrong.'

'What are you asking Dennis to do?'

Elham did not immediately answer her. He faced Rickmore and spoke quickly. 'I know we've never got on too well together. And so maybe you'd rather not risk anything. If so, I've told you, I'll tell the police the truth about the accident. But if you could do this . . .' He came to a stop. He was unwilling to plead any further, not because of pride, but because he did not want to seem to be using emotional pressure to persuade.

Anne looked at Rickmore and it was that look, more than anything Elham had said, which decided him. 'I'll give it a go.'

Rickmore had read many personal accounts of going into battle and he had often wondered how he would feel in the moments immediately before an action began. Now he thought he knew. Sick with fear.

He hid the bicycle in a clump of brambles and then listened for any sounds which might suggest that he had been spotted. He discovered that the night had a thousand tongues. A sound to the right convinced him all was over before it had begun; but the sound was repeated and he now identified it as some small animal, frantically scuttling away. Seconds later, a more distant sound made him freeze, but that turned out to be a bulling cow, declaring her passion. He shifted his weight and a twig snapped, sounding to his straining ears like a rifle shot . . .

He moved forward and almost tripped as a bramble trail caught his right foot. When he regained his balance, he could feel the sweat under his armpits. He'd been crazy to agree to this nightmare. He hadn't been under any obligation. Dammit, he didn't even like Elham. Elham had shown himself to be a coward and a traitor, ready to betray the law he served . . . Rickmore's right hand, which he'd been holding out in front of him, banged into the bole of a tree and he exclaimed aloud from the shock, not the very brief pain. Christ! he thought, a fool hits not the same tree that a wise man sees.

He briefly shone the torch ahead of him, the bowl carefully masked with tape to narrow the beam. Immediately to his right was the tree he'd just encountered, five feet further on was a hedge, beautifully cut and laid. So he'd reached the edge of the rough land and ahead was the field which led up to the garden of Heskthorne House.

Elham had said that the Moffats were on holiday in France. He hoped to God that was right. He'd only met Moffat once, but that had been sufficient to convince him that he was a man who'd pull both triggers of a twelve-bore before he asked what the intruder wanted.

He clambered over the hedge, snagging his trousers on one of the uprights around which the laid branches were woven. He moved forward into the field and there was a snort from his right and the sounds of several animals moving. Cows. He remembered the friend of Anne's whose herd of Ayrshires had suddenly and for no discernible reason attacked her, inflicting serious injuries. His mind had become a forcing ground for catastrophes.

The field was not large and he soon reached the tall yew hedge which surrounded the garden. A hundred yards to the right was a wooden gate, and looking over this he could see the black bulk of the house, just discernible against the clear, star-studded sky. There was a light on upstairs. Elham had said that there would be. The Moffats used time-switches in different parts of the house to give the impression of active habitation. But what if this light had not been activated by a time-switch, but by someone brought in to house-sit . . . ?

He pulled on a pair of gloves, opened the gate, and passed through. A grass verge ran the length of the kitchen garden and ended at a gravel path; just before the path, he carefully left a firm footprint in the rich loam. Then he crossed the path as carefully as he could, yet still making so much noise that he doubted whether an elephant could have made more.

To the right of the kitchen door was a window, some four feet above the ground. He picked up a stone and, praying that it was true that the kitchen lay outside the alarm system, threw it through the glass. The explosion of noise terrified him, but after it was over there was nothing to suggest it had alarmed anyone. He knocked away a couple of dangerous slivers of glass, then reached in and pushed the catch up so that the window could be opened inwards. He climbed over the sill. And as he stood in the kitchen, the unwelcome thought came to him of how ironic it was that he, a man who had always believed in the law, should now be committing burglary . . .

Elham had described the alarm system, explaining that Moffat had asked him what kind to install and he had suggested the same make and type as was in Popham House.

The kitchen was large and equipped with every conceivable piece of electrical equipment, including an extremely large refrigerator of American make. Immediately to the left of this was a built-in cupboard and in the cupboard was a wooden box which contained two switches, two pilot lights, one red, one green, and ten numbered buttons like those found on a simple pocket calculator. To de-activate the alarm system, which sounded not only in the house but also in the nearest police station, it was necessary to punch in a six-figure code before pushing one switch up and the other down. Get the code wrong and within minutes a police car would arrive . . . Moffat, a man with a very poor memory, had—so Elham swore—chosen the numbers of his birthday. Rickmore punched out one four one ten one seven. The green light went out, the red one came on. He pressed one switch up, the other down, reversing the positions in which they had been.

Mouth dry, heart thumping, he crossed to the far door and opened this. The alarm stayed silent. He stepped into the passage.

Moffat had been an administrator in the Colonial Service —which explained his aggressive manner—and when in West Africa he'd made a small but good collection of carved wooden masks which now hung on the walls of the sitting-room; Rickmore picked off the two smallest ones and put them on a chair. At the far end of the room, to the left of the fireplace, was a cupboard and on the shelves of this was a wide selection of bottles and glasses. He chose a bottle of Glenfiddich and put it on an unusually shaped table, carved out of a single piece of heavily grained wood. He brought from his coat pocket a glass which had been protected with bubbled plastic wrapping. He unwrapped the glass and placed it by the bottle, returned the wrapping to his pocket, poured just enough whisky into the glass to make it appear it had been used.

The library was traditional in style, with two alcoves. The safe was in one of the alcoves, concealed by panelling which matched that around the rest of the room. He left the concealing wooden door open. Finally, he dropped a handkerchief near the beautifully inlaid partner's desk.

After collecting up the two wooden masks, he returned to the kitchen. He crossed to the alarm control box and reversed the positions of the switches; the red light went out and the green one came on.

He went over to the door leading into the passageway he'd just come down, took a very deep breath, and opened the door. Immediately, the alarm sounded.

He left the house, assuring himself that more haste meant less speed, but nevertheless moving far more quickly than conditions—but not the thought of the approaching police car—warranted.

The gates of Popham House were shut, but not locked, and he opened the right-hand one and wheeled the bike through. Keeping within the cover of the garage—to obviate the very slight risk that one of the Cavajals was awake and looking out of a window—he returned the bike to the small lumber room at the back of the garage.

Elham, his face puffy from tension, met him in the kitchen. 'Well?' he demanded hoarsely.

'I've grown a wonderful crop of ulcers, but there was no alarm until the end.'

'Thank God!'

'Where's Anne?'

'I tried to persuade her to go to bed, but she wouldn't. She's fallen asleep on the settee.'

'Then I'll wake her up and inform her that she won't have to visit me in jail in the morning . . . But first, I could use a whisky in the biggest glass you've got.'

Elham's need was no less.

CHAPTER 23

DC Wrybot—his surname was a constant source of childish ribaldy in the CID general room—entered the DI's room. ''Morning, skipper.'

'If you insist,' muttered Ridley, who had had a heavy night with his wife and two other married couples.

'I thought you'd want to know that there was a break-in at Polhurst last night.'

'So why get excited?'

'The property belongs to Moffat, who they say is some sort of bigwig on the county council.'

Ridley swore. 'And I suppose now he's yelling blue murder and wants the whole bloody Force switched to his case?'

'Probably would if he knew about it, but he's on holiday in France somewhere. The lucky sod.'

'Was much nicked?'

'There's been no word through on that yet.'

'Find out.'

'But I am busy . . .'

'Do as you're told without bloody arguing.'

Pardon me for living, thought Wrybot, as he left.

County HQ rang to ask why hadn't they received the weekly T254 forms? Ridley replied that he'd posted them the previous evening, as he stared at them by the side of the blotter. After the call was over, he began to fill them in. He no longer wondered why MacMahon had always looked harassed. He'd been working for less than five minutes when the telephone rang again. He swore, but it kept on ringing.

'Midge here, skipper,' said Wrybot. 'I'm phoning from Heskthorne House. According to the daily, all that was nicked was two wooden masks that were hanging on the wall. Bloody ugly things if they were anything like the ones that are left. Anyway, that's all she can tell us about and it doesn't look as if we'll know any more until the owners get back. Chummy found the safe, with the family jewels inside —so the daily says—but he didn't do anything about it. And that's odd, really, since a sectional jemmy would have opened it up as easy as you like.'

A thought began to form in Ridley's mind, but then Wrybot spoke again and the thought failed to coalesce.

'He was either cool or bloody nervous. Helped himself to a whisky; Glenfiddich, no less!' Wrybot chuckled. 'Cool or nervous, he was careless. They found a hankie near the desk in the library and the daily swears it's nothing to do with her and wasn't there the last time she did that room.'

Ridley suddenly realized what that half-formed thought a moment ago had been signposting. 'Is there a laundry mark?'

'As a matter of fact, yeah, there is. I was just about to say . . .'

'Is it R one four four?'

'Jeez . . . How the hell d'you know that?'

'Because I'm bloody psychic, that's how. And I'll tell you something else. Somewhere outside, there's a nice clear footprint of Chummy.'

'If you know it all, skipper, why bother to send me out?'

'Because now you're going to search the place so hard that if a single grain of dust fell off Chummy, you'll find it. I'll send a couple of lads along to help.'

'All this for a job where only a couple of wooden masks have been nicked . . . Skipper, you wouldn't be thinking of standing for the council, would you?'

'Stop trying to be bloody smart . . . And get the bottle of whisky and the glass off to Dabs.'

'Will do . . . By the way, I was due to collect a couple of

witnesses' statements this morning from over Delsham way. What shall I do about them?'

'Forget 'em.'

'The pleasure's all mine.'

After he'd replaced the receiver, Ridley balled his fist and slammed it down on the desk in a display of impotent anger. This was one move he had not foreseen.

The fingerprint laboratory rang on Wednesday morning. The whisky bottle and glass had been checked for prints and comparison tests had been made. Several prints, from two different persons, were on the bottle; none of them had been made by the named person. The glass had been wiped clean at some recent time and there had been only one set of prints on it; these had been made by the named person.

Ridley turned off the road and into the yard of Oak Tree Cottage, where he parked. He and Wrybot climbed out.

'Neat little place,' said Wrybot, as they began walking. 'Give me half a chance and I'll be living in somewhere like this.' When there was no comment, he looked sideways at the detective-sergeant. Sour, he thought; like the girlfriend's quince jelly.

Ridley opened the gate and led the way round the brick path to the porch. He was about to ring the bell when Anne stepped into the porch and opened the outside door. 'I'd like a word with your husband,' he said curtly. 'I tried to ring him at the office, but they said he was ill.'

'That's right.'

'Not too ill, I imagine, to answer a few questions?'

'I can find out.' She showed them into the sitting-room, carefully reminding them both to duck their heads as they went in and to beware of the central beam once inside. She then offered them coffee, but Rickmore bad-temperedly refused.

'Then do sit down while I go and see how my husband's feeling now.' She left, closing the door behind herself.

Wrybot looked up at the beams. 'I really go for these, skipper.'

'Yeah?'

'It's a bit of history, like.'

'Never could stand the subject.'

Wrybot briefly wondered what was bugging the DS so hard, then let his mind wander. He was on holiday with his girlfriend, enjoying most of the pleasures that life had to offer, when footsteps overhead jerked his mind back to reality. Very soon afterwards, Anne returned with Rickmore who, Wrybot decided, did not look particularly ill.

'Sorry to be a bit of time,' said Rickmore, 'but I was lying down . . . My wife says you've refused coffee. Would you prefer a drink?'

'No, thanks,' replied Ridley, angered by their courtesy. 'We're investigating a burglary which took place on Monday. A house at Polhurst belonging to Sir Rupert Moffat was broken into. Do you know him?'

'We've met him and his wife once, but I think that's all.'

'Did you meet them at their house?'

'No, we've never been there. It was at a home belonging to mutual friends.'

'The intruder smashed a window to get in and then neutralized the alarm system. The method of entry was crude, but the alarm system is sophisticated and to de-activate it one has to punch in six figures on a control board. Obviously, the possible combinations are far too many for anyone to punch in the right one by chance. So the intruder had to know the correct code. This all says something, doesn't it?'

'I'm afraid I don't follow.'

'It says that the intruder didn't know much about house-breaking, but he did know a lot about the Moffats.'

'That sounds logical.'

'He found the safe, but didn't do anything about it. Yet any half-competent peterman with a sectional jemmy would have ripped it open inside five minutes. So he doesn't know much about safe-cracking either. Is this all beginning to sound rather familiar?'

'Should it?'

'He helped himself to a whisky and left the bottle and glass out, making it obvious. He dropped a handkerchief, which happened to have a laundry mark. He planted a footprint in the kitchen garden . . . Now has the penny dropped?'

'It sounds a bit like that other burglary.'

'Exactly similar. And just to make certain we weren't so dumb we didn't get the message, there were fingerprints on the glass.'

'Presumably that makes things easier for you?'

'The laundry mark was yours and the prints were yours.'

'Impossible.'

'Why won't you understand something? I'm not as thick as you'd bloody like me to be. I know that you broke into Heskthorne House, not to nick whatever was going, but to leave those clues.'

'When they appear to inculpate me? I'd have to be mad to do that.'

'Or trying to save both your brother-in-law's and your own skins.'

'How in the wide world do you bring him into it?'

'How d'you bloody think? . . . Understand something. I'm going to prove it was you. Not with the clues you wanted us to find, but with the ones you don't even know about. No one ever goes anywhere, or does anything, without leaving traces; I'll find 'em, if it takes me a bloody month of Sundays.'

'You hate my husband,' said Anne.

About to reply that he'd cause to, Ridley realized just in time that to do so would be both stupid and dangerous.

'You're twisting everything he says.'

'I've stated facts, nothing more.'

'The fact is,' said Rickmore, 'if a glass with my prints on it and a handkerchief with our laundry mark appeared in a house that's been burgled, someone is obviously trying to inculpate me.'

'That was true the first time, but not now. You've deliberately pointed the finger at yourself in the belief that it will never be accepted that anyone in his right senses would deliberately incriminate himself twice.'

'When was this burglary?'

'You know that just as well as me. You re-activated the alarm when you'd finished, to make certain that the police had a time. No doubt you're now going to offer an alibi?'

'I can't answer that until I know the time.'

'A quarter to one on Tuesday morning.' Ridley's voice became thick with sarcasm. 'Presumably you're now going to tell me that your wife will vouch for the fact that you were in this house at that time?'

'No, she won't do that.'

The answer completely surprised him. It was several seconds before he said: 'You don't have an alibi?'

'I do. But not one based on this house. That night, we had dinner at my brother-in-law's and stayed on very late.'

Ridley's confidence returned. 'You're hoping his evidence will carry a bit more weight than your wife's?'

'I imagine so, since his wife was there as well. That makes three people who can vouch that I'm telling the truth.'

'You're so goddamn naïve . . . They've all as much motive to lie as you have. They couldn't alibi Father Christmas.'

'Are you suggesting that not even the evidence of all three of them is sufficient?'

'I'm suggesting exactly that.'

'Then who would satisfy you? St Peter?'

'No need to bother him. Just give me someone who's even half-way independent.'

'How about Arnold?'

'Who?'

'Mr Elham's chief clerk. There was some problem that needed thrashing out, so Arnold came down and stayed at Popham House on Monday night. He and Mr Elham left us after dinner and went up to the study; they didn't come down until considerably later. Then, when we said we ought to go, my brother-in-law said he'd hardly had a chance to have a word with us and he persuaded us to stay on. I don't know what the time was when we left, except it was after one.'

Ridley knew a growing bitter frustration.

CHAPTER 24

A DC from the Metropolitan police telephoned Ridley on Friday. 'Reference your request to question Thomas Arnold. I'm just back from having a word with him. He states categorically that Rickmore and his wife were at Popham House all evening and didn't leave there until sometime after one on Tuesday morning.'

'The bastard's got to be lying.'

There was a short pause, then the DC said: 'He was pretty confident.'

'I don't care how confident, he was bloody lying.' Ridley forced himself to calm down. 'What's he like; how would he make out in a witness-box?'

'He's a funny old boy—all dust and antique. But I reckon if you matched him against a mule, you'd soon hear the mule shout uncle.'

Ridley swore.

*

Mrs MacMahon opened the front door of her house. She smiled. 'Hullo, Steve, nice to see you again. Come to have a word with Jim?'

'If he's up to it?'

'He's much better, especially since they say now that he did have a heart attack, but it was so minor that if he leads a sensible life he won't know any more about it. Of course, being him, he started talking about returning to work immediately, but I soon put a stop to that . . . But come on in instead of standing there and listening to me going on and on. The thing is, it's such a weight off my mind that half the time I feel as if I'd had a fix.' She laughed. 'Jim says I'm acting as giddy as when he first met me. Too much extra weight for anything like that, I told him.'

MacMahon was in the greenhouse in the back garden. 'I'm getting ready for Spring,' he said, pointing to a propagator. He studied Ridley. 'You're beginning to look like a man with responsibilities.'

'Frustrations.'

'The two go together, like corruption and politicians. And the best way of coping with 'em is to have a beer—and a fag, if the wife's not around to see me.'

They went into the kitchen, where MacMahon picked up two cans of beer, and then on through to the sitting-room. He handed Ridley a can. 'You don't mind managing without a glass, I hope? I'm doing the washing-up these days, so I keep it down as far as possible.' He sat, pulled the tab off the can, and drank. 'OK, so what's got you more frustrated than a eunuch in a harem?'

Ridley told him.

'You know something?' said MacMahon. 'You've largely got yourself to blame.'

'What the hell for?'

'For things being as they are now. Remember me saying softlee, softlee?'

'Not that again?'

'You pushed 'em too hard, too quickly. You squeezed 'em into a corner so that they had to do something dramatic if they were to do anything. If you'd moved slowly, maybe appearing a little soft as if you'd not understood what had been going on, they'd have assumed they were safe and their guards would have been down and then, like as not, you'd have been able to dig up something really incriminating that would have nailed Elham.'

Ridley said heatedly: 'You say I've made a balls-up. But it doesn't matter how smart they've been, I'll show'em I'm smarter. I'll get 'em.'

MacMahon looked quizzically at him, then stood and went over to the low bookshelf which was filled with book-club volumes. He brought out the first three volumes to reveal a pack of cigarettes. He offered this, then helped himself to one, replaced the pack and the books, and returned to his chair after accepting a light from Ridley. 'How?'

'How what?'

'How are you going to get them? How are you going to persuade a jury that any man in his right mind is going to lay a trail that points directly at himself?'

'By setting out the facts.'

MacMahon shook his head.

'Why not?'

'Can you prove Elham was driving the car which ran down Tamworth so long as Rickmore sticks to his present evidence?'

'No.'

'Then you're left with charging Rickmore. At his trial, evidence concerning Elham's hit-and-run is inadmissible. And if you can't show that that's the thread which binds together the hit-and-run case, the burglary at Gilles's place which appeared to have been committed by Rickmore but wasn't, and the burglary at Heskthorne House that was committed by him, you can't begin to offer a logical explanation of why Rickmore should deliberately incriminate himself.'

'It's bloody obvious.'

'To you and me, but not to any jury. And something else. You're faced with an alibi—four people prepared to swear that at the time of the burglary, Rickmore was in Popham House.'

'Four people all with a motive for seeing Rickmore gets off.'

'What are their motives?'

'Rickmore's wife is trying to protect him, Elham wants to save him in case he decides to tell the truth about the hit-and-run case, and Elham's wife is naturally backing up her husband.'

'And Arnold?' MacMahon tapped ash from the cigarette into the palm of his other hand. 'Who's not a relative by blood or marriage so that there's no obvious link to make him lie.'

'He works for Elham.'

'Not strong enough.'

'Well, it's obvious, isn't it? He helped rig the first burglary.'

'How do you go about proving that, which you must do to break the image of him as an independent witness?'

'By showing what . . .' He stopped.

'By showing what was his motive for helping Elham? But such evidence would be inadmissible in a trial of Rickmore for burglary.'

'All right, then,' said Ridley violently, 'add in the first burglary. Between them . . .'

'Put the two together and the proposition that Rickmore's twice left behind the same incriminating evidence becomes patently absurd . . . And, as a matter of interest, would you like to have it brought out in court that you've held back evidence?'

'I've done what?'

'Is it in the official records that the prints on the mug were Rickmore's and they matched the prints on the glasses found at the two burglaries?'

'I . . . Maybe I . . .'

'Maybe you've held that information back, hoping to use it to pressure Rickmore into telling the truth?'

There was a long silence. MacMahon drank some beer. As he put the can down, there was a sound from outside the room and he quickly held the cigarette ready to throw into the fireplace in an attempt to hide from his wife the fact that he had been smoking. But a moment later they heard her go up the stairs and he relaxed. 'There's something else you need to consider. How'd you feel in the witness-box, faced by a counsel determined and delighted to prove how inefficiently you've handled the case?'

'Come off it,' said Ridley angrily.

'Handled inefficiently because you've allowed yourself to be blinded by your dislike of the people involved.'

'What are you getting at?'

'Rickmore's wife spoke of hearing someone in their house on the Wednesday night, the suggestion being that an intruder stole the handkerchief and a glass bearing Rickmore's prints, to plant in Gilles's house. Did you have the other prints on the glass checked to see if they were Mrs Rickmore's?'

'No.'

'Did you check whether the glass matched others in the burgled house, or, alternatively, those in Oak Tree Cottage?'

'No.'

'Remember the bottle? There weren't any prints of Rickmore's on it. Why not? He wasn't wearing gloves when he handled the glass. Presumably, you wouldn't try to suggest that he wore gloves to pick up the bottle, but took them off to pick up the glass?'

'For Christ's sake, which side are you batting for?'

'Although you sound as if you'd have trouble understanding right now, yours. I don't want to see you ruin your career.'

'But you don't mind seeing them get off scot free?'

'They won't.'

'If they never appear in court, they goddamn will.'

MacMahon shook his head. He drank and emptied the can, drew on the cigarette and then leaned over to stub it out in the ashtray that Ridley was using. 'They're not villains, they're just ordinary people who got caught up in a situation where cowardice, stupidity, fear and a mistaken sense of loyalty, drove them to breaking the law. They're people whose entire lives would be shattered by being found guilty of a crime. So from now on they'll be living in fear that one day some extra piece of evidence will come to light that will be enough to shoot one or both of them into court. And on top of that, it's an odd thing, but in my experience people who commit crimes almost always suffer some kind of a loss, never mind what the state does to them. I sometimes think it must be an outside force which makes certain all of us pay a penalty for our misdeeds.'

To Ridley's bitter anger, there was now added contempt for such Holy-Joe philosophy.

It was February 18th. In the main bedroom of Popham House, Penelope drew her dress up over her shoulders, hung it on a hanger, put it in one of the built-in cupboards. Elham, already in bed, watched her and experienced a growing desire. She took off her lace-edged petticoat and dropped this into the Ali-Baba basket by the side of her dressing-table; she never wore underwear more than once. She reached up behind her back and unclipped her brassière, removed it, put it in the hamper. She had pert breasts, with prominent nipples and generous areolæ. He imagined his fingers caressing her nipples and his mouth dried. She slid off her pants and put those in the basket, bent down to pick up the lid which she put in place. Obviously aware of the intensity with which he was regarding her, she walked over to her bed, unzipped the bag in the shape of an elephant, and brought out her frothy and very expensive nightdress.

'Leave that and come over here,' he said thickly.

'No. It's been a heavy day and I'm tired.' She slipped on the nightdress and climbed into bed.

By her actions and the way in which she had spoken, he understood something which should have been clear to him before. Until the accident, he had always been proud of her, not least because she aroused envy in other men, but he had condescendingly assumed his superiority; this superiority had made him the dominant partner. She had accepted her subservience. But after the accident, he had shown himself to be weak and she had proved herself to be strong. His dominion had been destroyed, just as she had ceased to be subservient. And because she had grown strong at his expense, she was now going to deny him her body as well as her passion in revenge for the past.

He stared up at the ceiling and in his mind saw Lucy, naked, passionate, and he knew an impotent desire so strong that it was pain.

Anne said: 'Do I dare risk offering you a penny for them?'

Rickmore jerked his mind back to the present and looked across the sitting-room at her.

'Or are your thoughts too interesting to be traded for sordid money?'

He smiled.

'You'd rather not tell me?'

'I don't remember what I was thinking.'

'You're a very poor liar. Your ears give you away because they wiggle.'

'Rubbish!'

'Was she blonde or brunette?'

'A redhead, with a body to make the Venus de Milo go on a crash diet.'

'No hands? What a pity. Cuts out so much of the fun . . . In fact, it wasn't a woman, was it? You were looking sad, not lustful. What's the trouble?' Her tone was no longer light and bantering; now it was soft and comforting. 'Were you mourning your lost principles?'

He looked at her with uneasy surprise.

She stood, crossed to his chair, kissed him. 'It's not a total disaster, you know. One good result is, it makes you more at one with the rest of us.'

' "Damn your principles! Stick to your party." ?'

'Perhaps . . . Come on, love, let's move and go to bed.' She kissed him again.

He stood and reached out for the fire-guard to put in front of the fire which had burned low. He wondered how long it would be before he could stick to his party without any regrets.